DOMESDAY BOOK

Cornwall

History from the Sources

DOMESDAY BOOK

A Survey of the Counties of England

LIBER DE WINTONIA

Compiled by direction of

KING WILLIAM I

Winchester
1086

DOMESDAY BOOK

general editor

JOHN MORRIS

10

Cornwall

edited by
Caroline and Frank Thorn

from a draft translation prepared by
Oliver Padel

PHILLIMORE
Chichester
1979

1979
Published by
PHILLIMORE & CO. LTD.,
London and Chichester

Head Office: Shopwyke Hall,
Chichester, Sussex, England

ISBN 0 85033 155 2 (case)
ISBN 0 85033 156 0 (limp)

Printed in Great Britain by
Titus Wilson & Son Ltd.,
Kendal

CORNWALL

History from the Sources
General Editor: John Morris

The series aims to publish history
written directly from the sources
for all interested readers, both
specialists and others. The first
priority is to publish important
texts which should be widely
available, but are not.

DOMESDAY BOOK

The contents, with the folio on which each county begins, are:

Domesday Book is termed *Liber de Wintonia* (The Book of Winchester) in column 332c

INTRODUCTION

The Domesday Survey

In 1066 Duke William of Normandy conquered England. He was crowned King, and most of the lands of the English nobility were soon granted to his followers. Domesday Book was compiled 20 years later. The Saxon Chronicle records that in 1085

> at Gloucester at midwinter ... the King had deep speech with his counsellors ... and sent men all over England to each shire ... to find out ... what or how much each landholder held ... in land and livestock, and what it was worth ... The returns were brought to him.[1]

William was thorough. One of his Counsellors reports that he also sent a second set of Commissioners 'to shires they did not know, where they were themselves unknown, to check their predecessors' survey, and report culprits to the King.'[2]

The information was collected at Winchester, corrected, abridged, chiefly by omission of livestock and the 1066 population, and fair-copied by one writer into a single volume. Norfolk, Suffolk and Essex were copied, by several writers, into a second volume, unabridged, which states that 'the Survey was made in 1086'. The surveys of Durham and Northumberland, and of several towns, including London, were not transcribed, and most of Cumberland and Westmorland, not yet in England, was not surveyed. The whole undertaking was completed at speed, in less than 12 months, though the fair-copying of the main volume may have taken a little longer. Both volumes are now preserved at the Public Record Office. Some versions of regional returns also survive. One of them, from Ely Abbey,[3] copies out the Commissioners' brief. They were to ask

> The name of the place. Who held it, before 1066, and now?
> How many *hides*?[4] How many ploughs, both those in lordship and the men's?
> How many villagers, cottagers and slaves, how many free men and Freemen?[5]
> How much woodland, meadow and pasture? How many mills and fishponds?
> How much has been added or taken away? What the total value was and is?
> How much each free man or Freeman had or has? All threefold, before 1066,
>   when King William gave it, and now; and if more can be had than at present?

The Ely volume also describes the procedure. The Commissioners took evidence on oath 'from the Sheriff; from all the barons and their Frenchmen; and from the whole Hundred, the priests, the reeves and six villagers from each village'. It also names four Frenchmen and four Englishmen from each Hundred, who were sworn to verify the detail.

The King wanted to know what he had, and who held it. The Commissioners therefore listed lands in dispute, for Domesday Book was not only a tax-assessment. To the King's grandson, Bishop Henry of Winchester, its purpose was that every 'man should know his right and not usurp another's'; and because it was the final authoritative register of rightful possession 'the natives called it Domesday Book, by analogy

---

[1] Before he left England for the last time, late in 1086.   [2] Robert Losinga, Bishop of Hereford 1079-1095 (see *E.H.R.* 22, 1907, 74).   [3] *Inquisitio Eliensis*, first paragraph.   [4] A land unit, reckoned as 120 acres.   [5] *Quot Sochemani.*

from the Day of Judgement'; that was why it was carefully arranged by Counties, and by landholders within Counties, 'numbered consecutively ... for easy reference'.[6]

Domesday Book describes Old English society under new management, in minute statistical detail. Foreign lords had taken over, but little else had yet changed. The chief landholders and those who held from them are named, and the rest of the population was counted. Most of them lived in villages, whose houses might be clustered together, or dispersed among their fields. Villages were grouped in administrative districts called Hundreds, which formed regions within Shires, or Counties, which survive today with minor boundary changes; the recent deformation of some ancient county identities is here disregarded, as are various short-lived modern changes. The local assemblies, though overshadowed by lords great and small, gave men a voice, which the Commissioners heeded. Very many holdings were described by the Norman term *manerium* (manor), greatly varied in size and structure, from tiny farmsteads to vast holdings; and many lords exercised their own jurisdiction and other rights, termed *soca*, whose meaning still eludes exact definition.

The Survey was unmatched in Europe for many centuries, the product of a sophisticated and experienced English administration, fully exploited by the Conqueror's commanding energy. But its unique assemblage of facts and figures has been hard to study, because the text has not been easily available, and abounds in technicalities. Investigation has therefore been chiefly confined to specialists; many questions cannot be tackled adequately without a cheap text and uniform translation available to a wider range of students, including local historians.

Previous Editions

The text has been printed once, in 1783, in an edition by Abraham Farley, probably of 1250 copies, at Government expense, said to have been £38,000; its preparation took 16 years. It was set in a specially designed type, here reproduced photographically, which was destroyed by fire in 1808. In 1811 and 1816 the Records Commissioners added an introduction, indices, and associated texts, edited by Sir Henry Ellis; and in 1861-1863 the Ordnance Survey issued zincograph facsimiles of the whole. Texts of individual counties have appeared since 1673, separate translations in the Victoria County Histories and elsewhere.

This Edition

Farley's text is used, because of its excellence, and because any worthy alternative would prove astronomically expensive. His text has been checked against the facsimile, and discrepancies observed have been verified against the manuscript, by the kindness of Miss Daphne Gifford of the Public Record Office. Farley's few errors are indicated in the notes.

[6] *Dialogus de Scaccario* 1,16.

The editor is responsible for the translation and lay-out. It aims at what the compiler would have written if his language had been modern English; though no translation can be exact, for even a simple word like 'free' nowadays means freedom from different restrictions. Bishop Henry emphasized that his grandfather preferred 'ordinary words'; the nearest ordinary modern English is therefore chosen whenever possible. Words that are now obsolete, or have changed their meaning, are avoided, but measurements have to be transliterated, since their extent is often unknown or arguable, and varied regionally. The terse inventory form of the original has been retained, as have the ambiguities of the Latin.

Modern English commands two main devices unknown to 11th century Latin, standardised punctuation and paragraphs; in the Latin, *ibi* ('there are') often does duty for a modern full stop, *et* ('and') for a comma or semi-colon. The entries normally answer the Commissioners' questions, arranged in five main groups, (i) the place and its holder, its hides, ploughs and lordship; (ii) people; (iii) resources; (iv) value; and (v) additional notes. The groups are usually given as separate paragraphs.

King William numbered chapters 'for easy reference', and sections within chapters are commonly marked, usually by initial capitals, often edged in red. They are here numbered. Maps, indices and an explanation of technical terms are also given. Later, it is hoped to publish analytical and explanatory volumes, and associated texts.

The editor is deeply indebted to the advice of many scholars, too numerous to name, and especially to the Public Record Office, and to the publisher's patience. The draft translations are the work of a team; they have been co-ordinated and corrected by the editor, and each has been checked by several people. It is therefore hoped that mistakes may be fewer than in versions published by single fallible individuals. But it would be Utopian to hope that the translation is altogether free from error; the editor would like to be informed of mistakes observed.

The maps are the work of Jim Hardy and Frank Thorn.

The preparation of this volume has been greatly assisted by a generous grant from the Leverhulme Trust Fund.

Conventions

*	refers to a note to the Latin text
[ ]	enclose words omitted in the MS.
( )	enclose editorial explanations.

EXTRACTS TO SHOW COMPARISON BETWEEN
EXON. AND EXCHEQUER DB ENTRIES

CORNWALL DB 1,6   *For the Latin see the main text.*

BLISLAND. 4 h. but it paid tax for 2 h. Land for 30 ploughs; in lordship 1 h;
2 ploughs; 12 slaves.
    40 villagers and 20 smallholders with 17 ploughs.
    Meadow, 1 acre; pasture, 3 leagues long and 1½ leagues wide; woodland,
       1 league long and ½ league wide.
It pays £6 by weight.
    In PENDAVEY 1 h. has been taken away from this manor. Land for 6 ploughs.
Boia the priest holds it from the Count of Mortain. Formerly 20s; value now 10s.

Exon 101 b 1 - 2

01. b.   Rex hĩ. 1. manſionẽ quẹ uocat Gluſtona. q̃ tenuit herald⁹ comes.

ea die q̃ rex E. f u. 7. m.   In ea ſt̃. IIII. hidẹ. 7 reddidert̃ Gildũ p II. hiđ.

has IIII. poſsĩ arare xxx. carr̃. De his hĩ Rex. 1. hiđa 7 II. carr̃ indnĩo. 7 uilla

                          xl.
ni hñt III. hiđ. 7 x. 7 VII. carr̃.   Ibi hĩ R. uillanos. 7 xx. borđ. 7 XII. ſeruos.

7 III. uaccas. 7. lxx. oues. 7. I. leugã nemoris in long̃. 7 dim̃ ĩ lat̃. 7. I. agrũ pti.

7. III. leugas paſcuẹ ĩ long̃. 7. I. leugã 7 dim̃ ĩ latitud̃. 7 reddit p annũ VI. liħ ad

               de hac manſione ablata eſt. 1. manſio q̃ uocat pendauid. q̃ ptinebat ad pſcript̃a
pondus.   manſionẽ ea die q̃ rex. E. f. u. 7. m.   In ea eſt. 1. hiđ trẽ q̃ poſsĩ arare VI. carr̃.
                    de comite.
   m ten& eã boia ſacerdos de bomine. 7 ual& x. ſot 7 q̃do comes accep̃ ualebat. xx. ſot.

The King has a manor called BLISLAND, which Earl Harold held in 1066*.
4 hides there; they paid tax for 2 hides. 30 ploughs can plough these 4. Of them
the King has 1 hide and 2 ploughs in lordship, and the villagers have 3 hides and
17 ploughs. The King has 40 villagers, 20 smallholders, 12 slaves, 3 cows, 70 sheep,
1 league of woodland in length and ½ in width, 1 acre of meadow, 3 leagues of
pasture in length and 1½ leagues in width. It pays £6 a year by weight.
From this manor has been taken away a manor called PENDAVEY, which belonged
to the above manor in 1066*. 1 hide of land there, which 6 ploughs can plough.
Boia the priest of Bodmin holds it now from the Count. Value 10s; when the
Count received it**, value 20s.

Exon 507 a 5 (*Terrae Occupatae*)

   Rex. hĩ. 1. manſ quẹ uocat. Gluſtona quã teñ harald⁹ comes. de hac

ablata. c̃. 1. manſio. quẹ uocat. Pendauid. quẹ ibi ptinebat die qua rex

E. f. u. 7 m. hanc tenet. Boia. cleric⁹. de bodmine. de com̃ moritonienſi.

7 uali p anñ. x. ſot. 7 qñ. Comes accep̃ uat xx. ſot.

The King has a manor called BLISLAND, which Earl Harold held. From it has been
taken away 1 manor called PENDAVEY, which belonged there in 1066*. Boia the
clerk of Bodmin holds it from the Count of Mortain. Value 10s a year; when the
Count received it**, value 20s.

* *ea die qua rex Edward fuit vivus et mortuus* ('on the day on which King Edward was alive and
dead'); it is always translated in this edition as 'in 1066' and is equivalent to DB *TRE*, 'before 1066'.

**   *quando Comes accepit* is equivalent to DB *olim*, 'formerly'.

THE EXETER DOMESDAY FOR CORNWALL

For the South Western counties there exists another set of returns, the Exeter Book (*Liber Exoniensis*). This contains the returns, differently arranged and worded, for Somerset, Devon and Cornwall, with part of Dorset and one Wiltshire holding. Comparison with the Exchequer version shows that some information is clearly missing in Exon, such as the rest of Wiltshire, a great part of Dorset and some entries for Devon. Arrangement is by fiefs, and within these by counties, though the counties do not always follow each other in the same order each time. Within each county places are often grouped in Hundreds, although without the Hundred name given, and frequently the Hundreds occur in the same order under different holders. This provides primary evidence for the identification of places and in part supplies the lack of Hundred headings in the text of Exchequer DB here. Information is often duplicated, as for example in Cornwall where the same 11 hides are listed under the King's manor of Winnianton (99–100) and among the Count of Mortain's holdings (224–227). After the fiefs in Exon there are details for Devon, Cornwall and Somerset of 'Appropriated Lands' (*Terrae Occupatae*), folios 495–525. These contain condensed entries of certain manors, which had had land taken from, or added to, them, or which had been held as two or more manors before 1066 by one or more holders, or which had not paid their customary dues, or which were unusual in some other way. The information given almost always repeats what is in the main Exeter Domesday, but occasionally new information is given. In this edition the whole of the corresponding entry in the *Terrae Occupatae* is only given when it differs from, or adds information to, the DB entry; the reference to it, however, is always given. Exon also includes the returns of the tax levied in 1084 for all five counties, which it is hoped will be published in a separate volume. The Exon folios dealing with Cornwall are 63b; 72a–73a; 99a–102b; 111b–112a; 180b–181b; 199a–208b; 224a–265a; 334b; 397b; 507a–508b; 528b. A convenient contents table of the whole of Exon is printed in V. H. Galbraith, *Domesday Book*, Oxford 1974, pp. 184–88.

The MS is preserved in the library of Exeter Cathedral and was printed in 1816 by Sir Henry Ellis in the third volume of the Record Commission's edition of DB, from a transcript made by Ralph Barnes, Chapter Clerk. No facsimile, such as the Ordnance Survey made for Exchequer DB, exists for Exon. The MS consists of 532 folios of parchment, measuring about 6½ by 9¾ inches (16½ by 25 cms). Each folio contains a single column on each side of about 20 lines. These folios fall into a series of quires, or gatherings, varying in number between one and twenty folios. Generally a new quire was started for each major landholder, and a new side for most tenants. This led to many blanks, which were increased by spaces sometimes left for information not to hand. There is no indication of the original sequence of quires, and the present order and system of reference dates from the last rebinding in 1816. The MS is the work of about a dozen scribes and the hand changes often between entries and even within them.

The text cannot here be economically reproduced; nine tenths of it repeats the DB survey, with discrepancies of a fraction of one per cent in many tens of thousands of figures. Ellis' edition has here been used in the main, though the MS has been checked where Exon and DB differ and in a number of other places. The principal corresponding Exon reference is given beside each entry in the translation, with other references in the Exon notes; the last number refers to the order of the entry on each side, as indicated in the MS generally by gallows marks. All discrepancies and all additional information are given, either in small type in the translation, or in the Exon notes, signalled in the translation by E, or by L (for details of lordship omitted in DB). A specimen entry, with the DB equivalent, showing the differences in formulae, is given opposite. The substance, though not the working, of the whole of the Exeter Domesday returns is therefore here reproduced.

For a detailed description and evaluation of Exon, see R. Welldon Finn, *The Liber Exoniensis*, London 1964; N. R. Ker, *Medieval Manuscripts in British Libraries*, vol. ii, pp. 800–807; Sir Henry Ellis, *DB3*, Introduction, pp. ix ff.

The county editors would like to thank Mrs. A. M. Erskine of Exeter Cathedral Library for her help in making available the Exon MS.

In Cornwall the translation uses the abbreviations: h = hide; v = virgate; f = furlong; and, in the tabulated notes, lg = league and a = acre.

HIC ANNOTANTVR TENENTES TERRAS IN CORNVALIA,

.I.REX WILLELMVS.   .V.Comes Moritonienfis.

.II.Eps de Execeftre.   .VI.Judhail de Totenais,

.III Eccla de Taueftoch.   .VII,Gofcelmus,

.IIII.Ecclæ aliquoʒ Scoʒ.

TERRA REGIS.

REX tenet *WINETONE*. Ibi fuer T.R.E.xv.hidæ.

Tra.ē.lx.car. De ea.ē in dnio.i.hida.7 ibi.ii.car.7 uilli

hñt.iii.hid.7 xxiiii.car. Ibi sf.xxiiii.uilti.7 xli.colibt.

7 xxxiii.bord.7 xiiii.ferui.Ibi.vi.ac pti.Paftura.iiii.leu

long.7 ii.leu lat.Silua.i.leu lg.7 dim leu lat.

Redd.xii.lib ad pond 7 arfura.

De his.xv.hid ten comes moriton.xi.hid.Has teneb

xvii.taini.T.R.E.q non poterant a Manerio fepari.

De hac tra hf ipfe comes in dnio uñ maner 7 uocat Renti.

Ibi.ē.una virgata træ.Tra.ii.car.Valet.xv.fot.

De comite ten Vluuard uñ Maner *RENTI*.Ibi.ē.i.hida.

Tra.ē.xii.car.Ibi hf Vluuard.i.car.7 viii.colibtos.

7 iiii.feruos.Paftura dimid leu lg.7 tntd laf.Vaf.x.fot,

CORNWALL

LIST OF LANDHOLDERS IN CORNWALL

1 King William
2 The Bishop of Exeter
3 Tavistock Church
4 The Churches of various Saints

5 The Count of Mortain
6 Iudhael of Totnes
7 Gotshelm

[1] LAND OF THE KING

The King holds

1 WINNIANTON. Before 1066, 15 h. Land for 60 ploughs.
In lordship 1 h; 2 ploughs. The villagers have 3 h. and 24 ploughs.
24 villagers, 41 freedmen, 33 smallholders, 14 slaves.
Meadow, 6 acres; pasture, 4 leagues long and 2 leagues wide; woodland, 1 league long and ½ league wide.
It pays £12 weighed and assayed.
14 unbroken mares; 3 cattle; 128 sheep.
Of these 15 h. the Count of Mortain holds 11 h. 17 thanes who could not be separated from the manor held them before 1066.
Of this land the Count has a manor called RINSEY himself, in lordship. 1 v. of land. Land for 2 ploughs. Value 15s.
Wulfward holds a manor, RINSEY, from the Count. 1 h.
Land for 12 ploughs. Wulfward has 1 plough,
8 freedmen, 4 slaves.
Pasture, ½ league long and as wide. 1 cow; 30 sheep.
Value 10s; when the Count received it, 40s.

99 a 1

E E E E. L

Chenret ten̅ de comite *SCHEWIT*. Ibi . e̅ una uirg̅ træ.

Blechu ten̅ *TRENANT*. Ibi, e̅ dimid̅ hida.

Goduin ten̅ *GARVEROT*. Ibi. e̅ tcia pars uni̅ uirg̅ træ,

Brixi ten̅ *TRENBRAS*. Ibi. e̅ tcia pars uni̅ uirg̅ træ.

Wihumar ten̅ *KICOI*. Ibi . e̅ una hida.

Hamelin ten̅ *CARIAHOIL*. Ibi. e̅ dimid̅ hida,

Ricard ten̅ *LVSART*. Ibi. e̅ . I . hida.

Brictric ten̅ *SCANCT MAWAN*. Ibi . e̅ . I . hida.

Andreas ten̅ *BOTEN*. Ibi. e̅ una v̅ træ. .

Turſtin ten̅ *TRELLEWARET*. Ibi . e̅ . I . hida.

Turſtin ten̅ *HELIGIN*. Ibi. e̅ una v̅ træ 7 tcia pars uni̅ virg̅,

Brictric ten̅ *BODEWORWEI*. Ibi una virg̅ træ.

Turſtin ten̅ *TROVTHEL*. Ibi, e̅ dimid̅ hida.

Aluuin ten̅ *TREVRNIVET*. Ibi . e̅ una ac̅ træ.

Dodo ten̅ *TRETLAND*. Ibi st̅ . IIII . ac̅ træ.

Leuenot ten̅ *TRETDEWORD*. Ibi. e̅ una hida,

Aluuard ten̅ *TREWODE*. Ibi. e̅ una hida,

Grifin ten̅ *ROSCARNAN*. Ibi . e̅ una virg̅ træ,

Turſtin ten̅ *TRAGOL*. Ibi st̅ . II . ac̅ træ

Vluuard ten̅ *TRAVIDER*. Ibi. e̅ una virg̅ træ,

Int̅ tot̅. e̅ tra. LXVIII . car̅. Olim. xx, lib̅ 7 x . ſolid̅,

Modo ualent . VI . lib̅ 7 XIIII . ſolid̅,

Rex ten̅ *HENLISTONE* . Ibi st̅ . VI . hidæ 7 dimidia . Ex
quib₃ . II . tant̅ hidæ geldb̅ T.R.E. Tra. e̅ . XL . car̅. De ea
e̅ in dn̅io. I . hida. 7 ibi. III . car̅. 7 XXIII . ſerui. 7 XXX . uilli,
7 XL . ceruiſarij . 7 XX . bord̅ cu̅ . XVII . car̅. Ibi . IIII . ac̅ p̅ti,
Paſtura . V . leu̅ lg̅. 7 III . leu̅ lat̅. Silua . I . leu̅ lg̅. 7 dimid̅
leu̅ lat̅. Redd̅ . VIII . lib̅ ad pondus 7 arſura̅.

Kenred holds SKEWES from the Count. 1 v. of land. E 99 a 2

Bletcu holds TRENANCE. ½ h. 10 sheep.

Godwin holds GARAH? The third part of 1 v. of land. 99 b 1
7 cattle; 1 cob; 10 sheep.

Brictsi holds TREMBRAZE. The third part of 1 v. of land.

Wihomarch holds TREGOOSE. 1 h. L

Hamelin holds 'CRAWLE'. ½ h. 1 cow. L

Richard holds LIZARD. 1 h. 4 wild mares; 3 cattle; 20 pigs; 60 sheep. L

Brictric holds MAWGAN(-in-Meneage). 1 h. L

Andrew holds BODEN. 1 v. of land. 2 cattle; 20 sheep. L

Thurstan holds TRELOWARREN. 1 h.
4 wild mares; 2 cobs; 4 cattle; 6 pigs; 30 sheep. L

Thurstan holds HALLIGGYE. 1 v. of land and the third part of 1v. 100 a 1

Brictric holds BOJORROW. 1 v. of land. 1 cow; 15 sheep. L

Thurstan holds TRUTHALL. ½ h. 1 cow; 30 sheep; 10 goats. L

Alwin holds TREWARNEVAS. 1 acre of land.

Doda holds TRELAN. 4 acres of land. 1 cow; 15 sheep. L

Leofnoth holds TREDOWER. 1 h.

Alfward holds TREWORDER? 1 h.

Griffin holds ROSCARNON. 1v. of land. L

Thurstan holds TREAL. 2 acres of land.

Wulfward holds TREVEDOR?. 1 v. of land. 100 b1

In total, land for 68 ploughs.

Formerly £20 10s; value now £6 14s.

2 HELSTON. 6½ h, of which only 2 h. paid tax before 1066.

Land for 40 ploughs; in lordship 1 h; 3 ploughs; 23 slaves. 100 b 2

30 villagers, 40 ale-men and 20 smallholders with 17 ploughs & 5½ h.

Meadow, 4 acres; pasture, 5 leagues long and 3 leagues wide;
woodland, 1 league long and ½ league wide. E

It pays £8 weighed and assayed.
2 cobs; 14 unbroken mares; 8 cattle; 200 sheep.

Rex ten *BEWINTONE* . Ibi s̄t . III . hidæ . fed ꝑ una hida
geldb̄ T.R.E. T̄ra . ē : xx . car̄ . De ea . ē in dn̄io dim̄ hida .

7 ibi s̄t . II . car̄ . 7 IX . ſerui . 7 XVI . uitti 7 XL . bord̄ cū . XVI . car̄ ,
Ibi . II . ac̄ p̄ti . Paſtura . III . leū l̄g . 7 una leū l̄g . Silua
dimid̄ leū l̄g . 7 III . q̄ʒ lat̄ . Redd̄ . c . ſolid̄ ad pond̄

ꝟ 7 arſuram .

Rex ten *LANEHOC* . Ibi s̄t . v . hidæ . ſed ꝑ . II . hid̄ geldb̄ .
T̄ra . ē . xxII . car̄ . De ea . ē in dn̄io . I . hida . 7 ibi . II . car̄ . 7 VIII .
ſerui . 7 LIX . uitti 7 xxVI . bord̄ cū . xx . car̄ . Ibi . I . ac̄ p̄ti .
7 XL . ac̄ paſturæ . Silua . I . leū l̄g . 7 III , q̄ʒ lat̄ .
Redd̄ . vI . lib̄ ad pond̄ 7 arſurā ,
De hoc m̄ ablata s̄t . II . Maner̄ Podeſtot 7 Sanguinas ,
Ibi . ē . I . hida 7 dimid̄ , T̄ra . ē , xII . car̄ . Jouuin̄ ten de comite
moriton̄ . Olim . LX . ſolid̄ , Modo ual̄ . XL . ſolid̄ .
Rex ten *CHILCHETONE* . T . R . E . geldb̄ ꝑ . vII , hid̄ . T̄ra . ē . xL .
car̄ . De ea . ē in dn̄io . I . hida . 7 ibi . IX . car̄ . 7 xx . ſerui . 7 xxVI .
uitti 7 xxIII . bord̄ cū . xxVI . car̄ . Ibi . xxx . ac̄ p̄ti , Paſtura
, v . q̄ʒ l̄g . 7 IIII . q̄ʒ lat̄ . Silua . I . leū l̄g . 7 una q̄ʒ lat̄ .
Redd̄ . xvIII . lib̄ ad pondus
Rex ten *GLYSTONE* . Ibi s̄t . IIII . hidæ . ſed geld̄ ꝑ . II . hid̄ .
T̄ra . ē . xxx . car̄ . De ea . ē in dn̄io . I . hida . 7 ibi . II . car̄ . 7 xII .
ſerui . 7 XL . uitti 7 xx . bord̄ cū . xvII . car̄ . Ibi . I . ac̄ p̄ti . Paſtura
III . leū l̄g . 7 una leū 7 dim̄ lat̄ . Silua . I . leū l̄g . 7 dim̄ leū lat̄ .
Redd̄ . vI . lib̄ ad pondus .
De hoc m̄ ablata . ē una hida in *PENDAVID* . T̄ra . ē . vI . car̄ .
Boie pbr̄ ten de comite moriton̄ , Oli . xx . ſol̄ . m̄ ual̄ . x . ſol̄ .
Rex ten *PAINDRAN* . Ibi . ē . I . hida . ſed geld̄ ꝑ dimid̄
hida . T̄ra . ē . vI . car̄ . De ea . ē in dn̄io . I . virḡ træ . 7 ibi . I .
car̄ . 7 III . ſerui . 7 xIII . bord̄ cū . I . car̄ . Ibi . cc . ac̄ paſturæ .
Silua . I . leū l̄g . 7 dim̄ leū lat̄ . Redd̄ . III . lib̄ ad pondus .

3 TOWAN. 3 h, but it paid tax for 1 h. before 1066. Land for 20
ploughs; in lordship ½ h; 2 ploughs; 9 slaves.
    16 villagers and 40 smallholders with 16 ploughs & 2½ h.   100
    Meadow, 2 acres; pasture, 3 leagues long and 1 league [wide] ;   b 3
        woodland, ½ league long and 3 f. wide.
It pays 100s weighed and assayed.
  1 cob; 5 unbroken mares; 17 cattle; 200 sheep.

4 ST. KEW. 5 h, but it paid tax for 2 h. Land for 22 ploughs;   120 b
in lordship 1 h; 2 ploughs; 8 slaves.   101
    59 villagers and 26 smallholders with 20 ploughs & 4 h.   a 1
    Meadow, 1 acre; pasture, 40 acres; woodland, 1 league long
        and 3 f. wide.
It pays £6 weighed and assayed. 9 cattle; 120 sheep.
    Two manors, POUNDSTOCK and ST. GENNYS, have been taken from   E
this manor. 1½ h. Land for 12 ploughs. Iovin holds them from the   101
Count of Mortain. Formerly 60s; value now 40s.   a 2

5 KILKHAMPTON. Before 1066 it paid tax for 7 h. Land for 40 ploughs;
in lordship 1 h; 9 ploughs; 20 slaves.   101
    26 villagers and 23 smallholders with 26 ploughs & 6 h.   a 3
    Meadow, 30 acres; pasture, 5 f. long and 4 f. wide;
        woodland, 1 league long and 1 f. wide.
It pays £18 by weight. 50 cattle; 600 sheep; 20 pigs; 40 goats.

6 BLISLAND. 4 h, but it paid tax for 2 h. Land for 30 ploughs;
in lordship 1 h; 2 ploughs; 12 slaves.   101
    40 villagers and 20 smallholders with 17 ploughs & 3 h.   b 1
    Meadow, 1 acre; pasture, 3 leagues long and 1½ leagues wide;
        woodland, 1 league long and ½ league wide.
It pays £6 by weight. 3 cows; 70 sheep.
    In PENDAVEY 1 h. has been taken from this manor. Land for 6   101
ploughs. Boia the priest holds it from the Count of Mortain.   b 2
Formerly 20s; value now 10s.   E

7 PENDRIM. 1 h, but it paid tax for ½ h. Land for 6 ploughs;
in lordship 1 v. of land; 1 plough; 3 slaves.   101
    13 smallholders with 1 plough.   b 3
    Pasture, 200 acres; woodland 1 league long and ½ league wide.
It pays £3 by weight.

De hoc M̄ st̄ ablatæ .iii. træ Pennadeluuan 7 Botconoan,

7 Botchatuuo. Ibi st̄ .ii. hidæ 7 dimid̄. Tra. ē. x. car̄,

Canonici S̄ Stefani de Lancauetone ten̄ de comite morit̄

Olim. xl. solid̄. Modo ual̄. xx. solid̄.

Rex ten̄ CARNETON. Ibi st̄. v. hidæ. sed geld̄ p. iii. hid̄.

Tra. ē. xxx. car̄. De ea. ē in dn̄io dimid̄ hida. 7 ibi. iii. car̄.

7 xx. serui. 7 xliii. uitti 7 xvii. bord̄ cū. xvii. car̄, Ibi, ii, ac̄

pti. Paſtura. i. leū lḡ. 7 tntd̄ lat̄, Redd̄. vii. lib ad pond̄.

Rex ten̄ CLISMESTONE. Ibi st̄. v. hidæ, ſed p. ii. hid̄ 7 dim̄

geld̄ T.R.E. Tra. ē, xxiiii, car̄. De ea. ē in dn̄io. i. hida.

7 ibi. iii. car̄. 7 ix. ſerui. 7 xxx, uitti 7 xxiiii. bord̄ cū. xvii. car̄.

Ibi. iii. ac̄ pti. Paſtura. iiii. leū lḡ. 7 tntd̄ lat̄. Silua. iii.

leū lḡ. 7 una leū lat̄. Redd̄. vi. lib ad pondus,

Rex ten̄ CALWETONE. Ibi st̄. iiii. hidæ. ſed p, ii. hid̄ geld̄.

Tra. ē. xxx. car̄. De ea. ē in dn̄io. i. hida. 7 ibi. iii. car̄.

7 xi. ſerui. 7 xxiiii, uitti 7 xliii. bord̄ cū. xv. car̄.

Ibi paſtura. iii. leū lḡ. 7 dim̄ leū lat̄. Silua dimid̄ leū lḡ,

7 ii. q̴ lat̄, Redd̄. vi. lib ad pond̄.

Rex ten̄ RITWORE. T.R.E. geld̄ p una hida. Tra. ē. xxx.

car̄. De ea. ē in dn̄io una v̄ træ. 7 ibi. iii. car̄. 7 viii. ſerui.

7 xiii. uitti 7 xv. bord̄ cū. x. car̄. Ibi. ii. ac̄ pti, Paſtura. i. leū

lḡ. 7 dim̄ leū lat̄. Silua dimid̄ leū lḡ. 7 ii. q̴ lat̄.

Redd̄. iiii. lib ad pondus,

Rex ten̄ PENNEHEL. Ibi st̄, ii. hidæ 7 dim̄. ſed p una hida

geld̄. Tra. ē. xxx. car̄. De ea. ē in dn̄io dimid̄ hida. 7 ibi, ii,

car̄. 7 x. ſerui. 7 xxiiii. uitti 7 xvi. bord̄ cū. xx. car̄,

Ibi. xi. ac̄ pti. 7 xxx. ac̄ paſturæ. 7 xiii, ac̄ ſiluæ.

Redd̄. c. solid̄ ad pondus.

Three lands, BONYALVA, BUCKLAWREN, BODIGGA, have been taken from this manor. 2½ h. Land for 10 ploughs. The Canons of St. Stephen's of Launceston hold them from the Count of Mortain.
Formerly 40s; value now 20s.

8 CARADON? 5 h, but it paid tax for 3 h.
    Land for 30 ploughs; in lordship ½ h; 3 ploughs; 20 slaves.   102 a 1
      43 villagers and 17 smallholders with 17 ploughs & 4½ h.
    Meadow, 2 acres; pasture, 1 league long and as wide.
    It pays £7 by weight. 6 cattle; 200 sheep less 20.

9 CLIMSOM. 5 h, but before 1066 it paid tax for 2½ h.
    Land for 24 ploughs; in lordship 1 h; 3 ploughs; 9 slaves.   102 a 2
      30 villagers and 24 smallholders with 17 ploughs & 4 h.
    Meadow, 3 acres; pasture, 4 leagues long and as wide; woodland, 3 leagues long and 1 league wide.
    It pays £6 by weight. 7 cattle; 200 sheep less 13.

10 CALLINGTON. 4 h, but it paid tax for 2 h. Land for 30 ploughs.
    In lordship 1 h; 3 ploughs; 11 slaves.   102 a 3
      24 villagers and 14 smallholders with 15 ploughs & 3 h.
    Pasture, 3 leagues long and ½ league wide; woodland, ½ league long and 2 f. wide.
    It pays £6 by weight. 7 cattle; 200 sheep less 20.

11 ROSEWORTHY. Before 1066 it paid tax for 1 h. Land for 30 ploughs;
    in lordship 1 v. of land; 3 ploughs; 8 slaves.   102 b 1
      13 villagers and 15 smallholders with 10 ploughs & 3 v.
    Meadow, 2 acres; pasture, 1 league long and ½ league wide; woodland, ½ league long and 2 f. wide.
    It pays £4 by weight. 2 cobs; 6 cattle; 150 sheep.

12 PENHEALE. 2½ h, but it paid tax for 1 h. Land for 30 ploughs;
    in lordship ½ h; 2 ploughs; 10 slaves.   102 b 2 E
      24 villagers and 16 smallholders with 20 ploughs & 1½ h.
    Meadow, 11 acres; pasture, 30 acres; woodland, 13 acres.
    It pays 100s by weight. 7 cattle; 100 sheep.

HAS PRÆSCRIPTAS.XII.TRAS TENVIT HERALDVS T.R.E.

INFRASCRIPTAS VERO Brictric teneɓ.7 Poſt Mathild regina,

REX ten *CONARDITONE*. Ibi ſt.VII.hidæ,ſed geldɓ

p̄.III.hiɗ.Tra.ē.XL.car̄.De ea.ē in dn̄io,I.hida,7 ibi.VI.car̄.

120 c

7 XXX.ſerui.7 XXX.uilłi 7 XX.borɗ cū.XXV.car̄.Ibi moliñ redɗ

XXX.denar.7 una ač p̄ti.Paſtura.II.leū lḡ.7 una leū lať.

Redɗ.XII.liɓ ad numerū.

REX ten *GVDIFORD*.Ibi.ē.I.hida 7 III.uirg træ.7 geldɓ p̄ una

uirg T.R.E.Tra.ē.XVI.car̄.De ea.ē in dn̄io una v̄ træ.7 ibi.I.car̄.

cū.I.ſeruo.7 VII.uilłi 7 VI.borɗ cū.IX.car̄.Redɗ.III.liɓ.

De hoc m̄ habeɓ S̄ Petroc T.R.E.p̄ c̄ſuetuɗ.XXX.den.aut.I.bouē.

REX ten *BENNARTONE*.Ibi ſt.VIII.hidæ.ſed p̄.IIII.hiɗ geldɓ

T.R.E.Tra.ē.LX.car̄.De ea.ē in dn̄io dimiɗ hida.7 ibi.III.car̄.

7 X.ſerui.7 XXXII.uilłi 7 XXV.borɗ cū.XV.car̄.Ibi.II.ač p̄ti.

Paſtura.II.leū lḡ.7 tn̄tɗ lať.Silua.I.leū lḡ.7 dim̄ leū lať.

Redɗ.X.liɓ.

REX ten *MELLEDHAM*.Ibi.ē.I.hida.7 geldɓ p̄ dim̄ hida.

Tra.ē.VIII.car̄.De ea.ē in dn̄io dimiɗ hida.7 ibi.II.car̄.7 III.

ſerui.7 IIII.uilłi 7 VII.borɗ cū.III.car̄.Ibi paſtura.I.leū lḡ.

7 dimiɗ leū lať.Redɗ.IIII.liɓ.

De tris Brictric ten Aiulf uñ Maner *CAREWRGE*.T.R.E.

geldɓ p̄ una v̄ træ.Tra.ē.II.car̄.Ibi.ē.I.car cū.III.borɗ.

Oli 7 m̄ uał.VII.ſoł 7 VI.deñ.Redɗ S̄ petroco p̄ c̄ſuetuɗ.VIII.deñ.

De tris Brictric ten Walter de Clauile.I.virg træ.Tra.ē

II.car.Olim.X.ſoliɗ.Modo uał.V.ſoliɗ.

.II. TERRA EP̄I DE EXECESTRE.

EP̄S EXONIENSIS tenet *TREWEL*.T.R.E.geldɓ p̄.I.hida

7 dimiɗ.Tra.ē.XX.car̄.In dn̄io ſt.II.car̄.7 IIII.ſerui.7 XXX.

uilłi 7 IIII.borɗ cū.XII.car̄.Ibi paſtura.II.leū lḡ.7 II.leū lať.

7 LX.ač ſiluæ.Olim 7 modo uał.IIII.liɓ.

13 Before 1066 Earl Harold held the twelve lands listed above.
Brictric, and afterwards Queen Matilda, held those listed below.

The King holds

14 'CONNERTON'. 7 h, but it paid tax for 3 h. Land for 40 ploughs;
in lordship 1 h; 6 ploughs; 30 slaves.   120 c
   30 villagers and 20 smallholders with 25 ploughs & 6 h.
   A mill which pays 30d; meadow, 1 acre; pasture, 2 leagues   111
     long and 1 league wide.   b 1
It pays £12 at face value.
  3 cobs; 40 wild mares; 13 cattle; 300 sheep; 5 goats.

15 COSWARTH. 1 h. 3 v. of land; before 1066 it paid tax for 1 v.
Land for 16 ploughs; in lordship 1 v. of land; 1 plough, with 1 slave. 111
   7 villagers and 6 smallholders with 9 ploughs & 1 h. 2 v.   b 2
It pays £3. 4 cattle; 45 sheep.
   Before 1066 St. Petroc's had 30d or 1 ox by custom   111
from this manor.   b 3
                                 E

16 BINNERTON. 8 h, but before 1066 it paid tax for 4 h.
Land for 60 ploughs; in lordship ½ h; 3 ploughs; 10 slaves.   111
   32 villagers and 25 smallholders with 15 ploughs & 7½ h.   b 4
   Meadow, 2 acres; pasture, 2 leagues long and as wide;
     woodland, 1 league long and ½ league wide.
It pays £10. 45 unbroken mares; 13 cattle; 5 pigs; 60 sheep.

17 TREVALGA. 1 h; it paid tax for ½ h.
Land for 8 ploughs; in lordship ½ h; 2 ploughs; 3 slaves.   112
   4 villagers and 7 smallholders with 3 ploughs & ½ h.   a 3
   Pasture, 1 league long and ½ league wide.
It pays £4. 5 cattle; 100 sheep; 5 goats.

18 Of Brictric's lands, Aiulf holds a manor, CARWORGIE. Before 1066 it
paid tax for 1 v. of land. Land for 2 ploughs; 1 plough there, with   112
   3 smallholders.   a 1
Value formerly and now 7s 6d. It pays 8d to St. Petroc's by custom. E

19 Of Brictric's lands, Walter of Claville holds 1 v. of land.   112
Land for 2 ploughs. Formerly 10s; value now 5s.   a 2

2   LAND OF THE BISHOP OF EXETER

1 The Bishop of Exeter holds TRELIEVER. Before 1066 it paid tax for 1½ h.
Land for 20 ploughs; in lordship 2 ploughs; 4 slaves; ½ h.   199
   30 villagers and 4 smallholders with 12 ploughs & 1 h.   a 1
   Pasture, 2 leagues long and 2 leagues wide; woodland, 60 acres.
Value formerly and now £4. 5 wild mares; 2 cows; 30 sheep.

Idē eps teñ *MATELE*.T.R.E.geldb̄ .p.i.hida.ſed tā ibi.ē
una hida 7 dim̄.Tra.ē.xv.car̄.In dñio.ē.i.car̄.7 iii.ſerui.
7 xv.uilti 7 iiii.bord̄ cū.viii.car̄.Ibi.xl.ac̄ paſturæ.7 lx.ac̄
ſiluæ minutæ.Olim 7 modo ual.xl.ſolid̄.

Forū huj Manerij h̄t com̄ moriton.qd̄ eps habet T.R.E.

Idē eps teñ *KEGEL*.T.R.E.geldb̄ .p.ii.hid̄.ſed tā st̄ ibi
xii.hidæ.Tra.ē.lx.car̄.In dñio st̄.ii.car̄.7 vi.ſerui.7 xviii.
uilti 7 xii.bord̄ cū.xvi.car̄.Ibi paſtura dim̄ leū lḡ.7 tñtd̄
lat̄.Silua.i.leū lḡ.7 dim̄ lat̄.Oli.c.ſolid̄.M̄ ual.viii.lib̄.

Idē eps teñ *PAVTONE*.T.R.E.geldb̄ .p.viii.hid̄.ſed tā
ibi st̄.xliiii.hidæ.Tra.ē.lx.car̄.In dñio st̄.iii.car̄.7 vi.ſer
ui.7 xl.uilti 7 xl.bord̄ cū.xl.car̄.Ibi paſtura.vi.leū lḡ.
7 ii.leū lat̄.Silua.ii.leū lḡ.7 una lat̄.Oli.x.lib̄.Modo ual

Id̄ eps teñ *BERNERH*.T.R.E.7 geldb̄ .p.i.hida.✠xxiiii.lib̄.
Tra.ē.xii.car̄.In dñio st̄.ii.car̄.7 vi.ſerui.7 viii.uilti 7 xii.
bord̄ cū.vi.car̄.Ibi.lx.ac̄ paſturæ.7 x.ac̄ ſiluæ.

Olim 7 modo ual.xl.ſolid̄.

Idē eps teñ Maner̄ qd̄ uocat̄ æccta S̄ Germani.Ibi|xxiiii.
hidæ.Ex his.xii.hidæ st̄ canonicoȝ q̄ nunq̄ geldauer̄.7 aliæ
xii.hide st̄ epi.7 geldb̄ .p.ii.hid T.R.Æ.In hac parte epi
Tra.ē.xx.car̄.In dñio st̄.ii.car̄.7 iiii.ſerui.7 xxx.uilti 7 xii.
bord̄ cū.xvi.car̄.Ibi paſtura.iiii.leū lḡ.7 ii.leū lat̄.Silua
.ii.leū lḡ.7 una leū lat̄.Oli.c.ſot.Modo ual.viii.lib̄.

In parte canonicoȝ Tra.ē.xl.car̄.In dñio st̄.ii.car̄.7 ii.
ſerui.7 xxiiii.uilti 7 xx.bord̄ cū.xxiiii.car̄.Ibi paſtura.ii.
leū lat̄.7 una leū lat̄.Silua.iiii.leū lḡ.7 ii.leū lat̄.

Valet.c.ſolid̄ canonicis.

The Bishop also holds

2 METHLEIGH. Before 1066 it paid tax for 1 h; but 1½ h. there,
however. Land for 15 ploughs; in lordship 1 plough; 3 slaves; ½ h.
    15 villagers and 4 smallholders with 8 ploughs & 1 h.   199
    Pasture, 40 acres; underwood, 60 acres.   a 2
Value formerly and now 40s. 3 cows; 20 sheep.
    The Count of Mortain has the fair of this manor; the Bishop   E
had it before 1066.

3 TREGAIRE. Before 1066 it paid tax for 2 h; but 12 h. there, however.
Land for 60 ploughs; in lordship 2 ploughs, 6 slaves; ½ h.
    18 villagers and 12 smallholders with 16 ploughs & 11½ h.   E
    Pasture ½ league long and as wide; woodland 1 league long   199
      and ½ wide.   a 3
Formerly 100s; value now £8. 2 cows; 40 sheep.

4 PAWTON. Before 1066 it paid tax for 8 h; but 44 h. there, however.   199
Land for 60 ploughs; in lordship 3 ploughs; 6 slaves; 1 h.   b 1
    40 villagers and 40 smallholders with 40 ploughs & 43 h.
    Pasture, 6 leagues long and 2 leagues wide; woodland, 2 leagues
      long and 1 wide.
Formerly £10; value now £24. 5 cattle; 50 sheep.

5 BURNIERE. Before 1066 it paid tax for 1 h. Land for 12 ploughs;   E
in lordship 2 ploughs; 6 slaves; ½ h.   199
    8 villagers and 12 smallholders with 6 ploughs & 1 h.   b 2
    Pasture, 60 acres; woodland, 10 acres.
Value formerly and now 40s. 4 cattle; 6 pigs; 150 sheep.
    Richard son of Thorold holds from the Bishop.

6 The manor called ST. GERMAN'S Church. 24 h; of these, 12 h. are   199
the Canons', and have never paid tax; the other 12 h. are the   b 3
Bishop's, and paid tax for 2 h. before 1066. In the Bishop's part,
land for 20 ploughs; in lordship 2 ploughs; 4 slaves; 1 h.
    30 villagers and 12 smallholders with 16 ploughs & 11 h.
    Pasture, 4 leagues long and 2 leagues wide; woodland, 2 leagues
      long and 1 league wide.
Formerly 100s; value now £8. 30 sheep.
    In the Canons' part, land for 40 ploughs; in lordship 2 ploughs;
2 slaves; 1 h.
    24 villagers and 20 smallholders with 24 ploughs & 11 h.
    Pasture, 2 leagues long and 1 league wide; woodland, 4 leagues
      long and 2 leagues wide.
Value 100s, to the Canons. 60 sheep.

In hoc Manerio.ē mercatū in die dñico . ſed adnichilū redi
gituꞃ ꝑ mercato͡ꝯmitis moriton̛ qd ibi.ē ꝓximū.

Idē eꝑs ten̛ *LANHERWEV*.T.R.E.geldb̛ ꝑ.ı.hida.ſed tam̛
ſt ibi.ııı.hidæ.Tra.ē.x.caꝛ.In dñio.ē.ı.caꝛ.7 ıııı.ſerui.
7 vııı.uitti 7 vı.borđ cū.ııı.caꝛ.Ibi paſtura.ıı.leū lḡ.7 una
leū laꝛ.Olim.c.ſoliđ.Modo uat.ʟ.ſoliđ.Fulcard ten̛

Ricarđ ten de eꝑo *THINTEN*.T.R.E.geldb̛ ꝑ dim̛ hida.
Ibi tam̛.ē.ı.hida.Tra.ē.vı.caꝛ.In dñio.ē caꝛ 7 dimiđ.
cū.ı.ſeruo.7 v.uitti.7 ıı.borđ cū.ııı.caꝛ.7 ı.aꝯ ſiluæ.
Olim 7 modo uat.xxv.ſoliđ.

Iꝑſe eꝑs ten̛ *LANGVITETONE*.T.R.E.geldb̛ ꝑ.ııı.hiđ.
Ibi tam̛ ſt.xı.hidæ.Tra.ē.xʟ.caꝛ.In dñio ſt.ıı.caꝛ.
7 vıı.ſerui.7 xxvıı.uitti 7 xx.borđ cū xxıx.caꝛ.
Ibi.vııı.aꝯ ꝑti.7 c.aꝯ paſture.7 x.aꝯ ſiluæ minutæ.
Olī.vııı.lib̛.Modo uat.xvıı.lib̛.

Rolland ten de eꝑo *LANDICLE*.T.R.E.geldb̛ ꝑ.ı.hida.
Ibi tam̛.ē.ı.hida 7 dimiđ.Tra.ē.xıı.caꝛ.In dñio.ē.ı.caꝛ.
7 ııı.ſerui.7 xııı.uitti 7 ıııı.borđ cū.ııı.caꝛ.Ibi.ıı.aꝯ ꝑti.
7 paſtura.ıı.leū lḡ.7 una leū laꝛ.Olī 7 modo uat.ııı.lib̛.

Godefriđ ten de eꝑo *SANWINVEC*.T.R.E.geldb̛ ꝑ.ı.hida.
Tra.ē.vı.caꝛ.In dñio.ē.ı.caꝛ.7 ıı.ſerui.7 v.uitti 7 vı.borđ
cū.ıı.caꝛ.Ibi paſtura dim̛ leū lḡ.7 tntđ laꝛ.Silua dimiđ
leū lḡ.7 una q̄ꝛ̣ laꝛ.Olim.xʟ.ſot.Modo uat.xx.ſoliđ.

De æccta S Germani ablata.ē.ı.hida træ.q̄ reddeb̛ ꝑ c̄ſue
tudin̛ unā cupā ceruiſæ 7 xxx.denaꝛ T.R.E.eiđ æcctæ.
De eađ æccta.ē ablata.ı.aꝯ træ.7 ē tra.ı.caꝛ.
De eađ æccta.ē ablata.ı.virg træ. ꟊ lin de comite morit̛.
H̄ erant T.R.E.in dñio ejđ æcctæ.Modo ten̛ Rainalđ 7 Hame
Ōꝰ ʜᴀs ᴛʀᴀs tenuit Leuric eꝑs T.R.E.

In this manor there is a market on Sunday, but it is reduced
to nothing by the Count of Mortain's market which is nearby,
in a castle of his, on the same day.

E

7 LANHERNE. Before 1066, it paid tax for 1 h; but 3 h. there, however.
Land for 10 ploughs; in lordship 1 plough; 4 slaves; 1 v.
    8 villagers and 6 smallholders with 3 ploughs & 2 h. 3 v.
    Pasture, 2 leagues long and 1 league wide.
  Formerly 100s; value now 50s.
  Fulchard holds from the Bishop.

120 d

200
a 1

8 Richard holds TINTEN from the Bishop. Before 1066 it paid
tax for ½ h; 1 h. there, however. Land for 6 ploughs;
in lordship 1½ ploughs, with 1 slave; 1 v.
    5 villagers and 2 smallholders with 3 ploughs & 3 v.
    Woodland, 1 acre.
Value formerly and now 25s. 3 cattle; 20 sheep.

200
b 1

9 The Bishop himself holds LAWHITTON. Before 1066 it paid
tax for 4 h; 11 h. there, however. Land for 40 ploughs;
in lordship 2 ploughs; 7 slaves; 1 h.
    27 villagers and 20 smallholders with 29 ploughs & 10 h.
    Meadow, 8 acres; pasture, 100 acres; underwood, 10 acres.
Formerly £8; value now £17. 1 cob; 2 cows; 40 sheep.

200
b 2

10 Roland holds GULVAL from the Bishop. Before 1066 it paid
tax for 1 h; 1½ h. there, however. Land for 12 ploughs;
in lordship 1 plough; 3 slaves; 1 v.
    13 villagers and 4 smallholders with 3 ploughs & 1 h. 3 v.
    Meadow, 2 acres; pasture, 2 leagues long and 1 league wide.
Value formerly and now £3. 1 cob; 3 cows; 30 sheep.

E
200
b 3

11 Godfrey holds ST. WINNOW from the Bishop. Before 1066 it paid
tax for 1 h. Land for 6 ploughs; in lordship 1 plough; 2 slaves; 1 v.
    5 villagers and 6 smallholders with 2 ploughs & 3 v.
    Pasture, ½ league long and as wide; woodland, ½ league
      long and 1 f. wide.
Formerly 40s; value now 20s. 30 sheep.

201
a 1

12 From ST. GERMAN'S Church 1 h. of land has been taken away; it
paid 1 barrel of ale and 30d to this Church by custom before 1066.

201
a 2-4

13 From this Church 1 acre of land has been taken away. Land for 1 plough.

14 From this Church 1 v. of land has been taken away.
They were in the lordship of this Church before 1066. Now Reginald
and Hamelin hold them from the Count of Mortain.

E

15 Bishop Leofric held all these lands before 1066.

ECCLA S̃ MICHAELIS ten̄ *KEIWAL*. Brifmar teneɓ T.R.E.
Ibi ſt̄. II. hidæ q̃ nunq̃ geldaueʳ. Tra. ē. VIII. caʳ. Ibi. ē. I. caʳ
cū. I. uiɫɫo 7 II. borɗ. 7 x. ac̄ pafturæ. Vaɫ. xx. ſoliɗ.
De his. II. hiɗ abſtulit comes moritō. I. hidā. Vaɫ. xx. ſoɫ.

CANONICI S̃ STEFANI ten̄ *LANSCAVETONE*. Ibi ſt̄. IIII.
hide træ. q̃ nunq̃ geldaueʳ. Tra. ē. xx. caʳ. Ibi ſt̄. III. caʳ.
7 III. leū pafturæ. 7 LX. ac̄ ſiluæ. Oɫi. VIII. liɓ. Modo uaɫ. II. liɓ.
De hoc c̃ abſtulit comes moritō uñ mercat̄ qɗ ibi T.R.E.
jaceɓ. 7 uaɫ. xx. ſoliɗ.

ECCLA S̃ PETROC ten̄ *BODMINE*. Ibi. ē una hida træ
quæ nunq̃ geldau. Tra. ē. IIII. caʳ. Ibi. v. uiɫɫi hñt. II.
caʳ. cū. VI. borɗ. Ibi. xxx. ac̄ pafturæ. 7 VI. ac̄ ſiluæ mi
nutæ. Ibi ht̄ S̃ Petroc. LXVIII. dom. 7 uñ mercatū.
Totū ualet. xx. v. ſoliɗ.

Ipſa æccɫa ten̄ *LANWENEHOC*. q̃ nunq̃ geldau. Ibi. ē una
hida. Tra. IIII. caʳ. Ibi. VIII. uiɫɫi cū. IIII. borɗ hñt. II.
caʳ. Ibi. xxIMI. ac̄ pafturæ. Tot̄ uaɫ. x. ſoliɗ.

Ipſa æccɫa ten̄ *RIELTONE*. q̃ erat q̇eta ab om̃i ſerutio
T.R.E. Ibi ſt̄. VII. hidæ. Tra. xxx. caʳ. In dñio. ē. I. caʳ.
7 II. ſerui. 7 xxx. uiɫɫi 7 xv. borɗ cū. XI. caʳ. Ibi. LX. ac̄
ſiluæ. 7 ccc. ac̄ pafturæ. Vaɫ. IIII. liɓ.

BERNER ten̄ de S̃ Petroc *LANGHEHOC*. Caduualant teneɓ
de Sc̄o T.R.E. nec ab eo poterat ſepari. Ibi. ē. I. hida. Tra
IIII. caʳ. Ibi. ē. I. caʳ 7 II. ſerui. 7 VI. borɗ. 7 paftura. I. leū lg̃
ᵱ 7 tñtɗ lat̄. Valet. x. ſoliɗ.

† Chapters 4 and 3 are entered in the wrong order, corrected by transposition signs.

4   LAND OF ST. MICHAEL'S

1 St. Michael's Church holds TRUTHWALL. Brictmer held it
before 1066. 2 h, which never paid tax. Land for 8 ploughs;
1 plough there, with
  1 villager and 2 smallholders.
  Pasture, 10 acres.
Value 20s. 4 cattle; 60 sheep.
  Of these 2 h, the Count of Mortain took away 1 h. Value 20s.   E

    208
    b 1

2 The Canons of St. Stephen's hold (St. Stephens by) LAUNCESTON. 4 h. 206 E
of land, which never paid tax. Land for 20 ploughs; 3 ploughs there. b 1
  Pasture, 3 leagues; woodland, 60 acres.   L / E
Formerly £8; value now £4. 5 cattle; 50 sheep.
  The Count of Mortain took away a market from this manor, which
lay there before 1066; value 20s. He put it in his castle.

3 St. Petroc's Church holds BODMIN. 1 h. of land which never paid tax.
Land for 4 ploughs.
  5 villagers have 2 ploughs, with 6 smallholders.
  Pasture, 30 acres; underwood, 6 acres.
  St. Petroc's has 68 houses and a market.
Total value 25s.

    202
    a 1

4 The Church holds PADSTOW itself; it never paid tax. 1 h.   E
Land for 4 ploughs.   202
  8 villagers with 4 smallholders have 2 ploughs.   a 2
  Pasture, 24 acres.
Total value 10s.

5 The Church holds RIALTON itself; it was exempt from
all service before 1066. 7 h. Land for 30 ploughs;
in lordship 1 plough; 2 slaves; 2 h.
  30 villagers and 15 smallholders with 11 ploughs & 5 h.
  Woodland, 60 acres; pasture, 300 acres.
Value £4. 20 sheep.

    202
    a 3

6 Berner holds NANCEKUKE from St. Petroc's. Cadwallon held from
St. (Petroc's) before 1066; he could not be separated from it.
1 h. Land for 4 ploughs; 1 plough there; 2 slaves.
  6 smallholders.
  Pasture, 1 league long and as wide.
Value 10s. 6 cattle; 80 sheep.

    202
    b 1
    L

Comes moriton̄ ten̄ de S Petroco *TIWARTHEL*. Algar teneb̄
T.R.E.7 n̄ poterat a sc̄o ſepari. Ibi ſt̄. VII. hidæ. Tra. xx. car̄.
In dn̄io ſt̄. IIII. car̄ 7 x. ſerui. 7 xv. uilli 7 xvi. bord̄. cū. x. car̄.
Ibi. XII. ac̄ ſiluæ. 7 paſtura. v. leū lḡ. 7 una leū lat̄.
Redd̄. XIIII. lib̄. xx. denar min.

Idē com̄ ten̄ de S Petroco *ELHIL*. Vn̄ tain teneb̄ T.R.E. 7 non
poterat a Sc̄o ſepari. Ibi. ē. I. hida. Tra. III. car̄. q̄ ibi ſt̄ cū.
uno ſeruo 7 II. uilłis 7 vi. bord̄. Ibi. I. ac̄ p̄ti. 7 xx. ac̄ paſturæ.
Olim. XL. ſolid̄. Modo ual̄. xx. ſolid̄.

Idē com̄ ten̄ de S Petroc *CALESTOCH*. Vn̄ tain teneb̄ T.R.E.
7 n̄ poterat a Sc̄o ſepari. Ibi. ē. I. hida. Tra. IIII. car̄.
Ibi ſt̄. XII. ſerui. 7 x. ac̄ ſiluæ. Oli. xx. ſol̄. M ual̄. III. ſolid̄.

Idē com̄ ten̄ de S Petroc *CARGAV*. Vn̄ tain teneb̄ T.R.E.
nec poterat a S ſepari. Ibi ſt̄. II. hidæ. Tra. xv. car̄. In dn̄io
ſt̄. III. car̄. 7 xvi. ſerui. 7 xii. uilłi 7 xxii. bord̄ cū. vi. car̄.
Ibi molin̄ redd̄. xxx. den̄. 7 IIII. ac̄ ſiluæ. Paſtura. II. leū lḡ.
7 una leū lat̄. Oli. x. lib̄. Modo ual̄. III. lib̄.

Idē com̄ ten̄ de S Petroc *TRELLOI*. Godric teneb̄ T.R.E. nec
poterat a sc̄o ſepari. Ibi. ē. I. hida. Tra. IIII. car̄. Ibi ſt̄. II. car̄.
7 v. ſerui. 7 VIII. bord̄. 7 xv. ac̄ paſturæ. Oli. XL. ſol̄. m̄ ual̄

Idē com̄ ten̄ de S Petroc *HEGLOSENVDER*   ᵮ xx, ſolid̄.
Godric teneb̄ T.R.E. Ibi eſt una hida quæ nūq̄ geld̄.
Tra. vi. car̄. Ibi ſt̄. II. car 7 III. ſerui. 7 II. uilłi 7 VIII. bord̄.
7 xx, ac̄ paſturæ. Oli 7 modo ual̄. xx. ſolid̄.

Idē com̄ ten̄ de S Petroc *BOTCINNII*. Eluui teneb̄ T.R.E.
7 n̄ poterat a S ſepari. Ibi. ē. I. hida. Tra. vi. car̄. Ibi. ē. I.
car̄. cū. r̄. ſeruo. 7 III. uilłi 7 III. bord̄ 7 xxx. ac̄ paſturæ.
Oli. xx. ſolid̄. Modo ual̄. xv. ſolid̄.

7 The Count of Mortain holds 'TYWARNHAYLE' from St. Petroc's. Algar   121 a
  held it before 1066; he could not be separated from St. (Petroc's).   E
  7 h. Land for 20 ploughs; in lordship 4 ploughs; 10 slaves; ½ h.   202
    15 villagers and 16 smallholders with 10 ploughs & 6½ h.   b 2
  Woodland, 12 acres; pasture, 5 leagues long and 1 league wide.
  It pays £14 less 20d. 20 unbroken mares; 10 cattle; 250 sheep.

The Count also holds from St. Petroc's
8 'HALWYN'. A thane held it before 1066; he could not be separated
  from St. (Petroc's). 1 h. Land for 3 ploughs, which are there,
  with 1 slave and   L 202
    2 villagers and 6 smallholders.   b 3
  Meadow, 1 acre; pasture, 20 acres.
  Formerly 40s; value now 20s. 1 cow; 75 sheep.

9 CALLESTICK. A thane held it before 1066; he could not be separated
  from St. (Petroc's). 1 h. Land for 4 ploughs. 12 slaves.
    Woodland, 10 acres.   202
  Formerly 20s; value now 3s. 2 cattle; 30 sheep.   b 4

10 CARGOLL. A thane held it before 1066; he could not be separated
  from St. (Petroc's). 2 h. Land for 15 ploughs;
  in lordship 3 ploughs; 16 slaves; ½ h.   203
    12 villagers and 22 smallholders with 6 ploughs.   a 1
  A mill which pays 30d; woodland, 4 acres; pasture, 2
    leagues long and 1 league wide.
  Formerly £10; value now £3. 12 mares; 7 cattle; 7 pigs; 60 sheep; 12 goats.

11 TRELOY. Godric held it before 1066; he could not be separated
  from St. (Petroc's). 1 h. Land for 4 ploughs; 2 ploughs
  there; 5 slaves.   L 203
    8 smallholders.   a 2
  Pasture, 15 acres.
  Formerly 40s; value now 20s. 7 cattle; 80 sheep; 20 goats.

12 ST. ENODER. Godric held it before 1066. 1 h, which never   E
  paid tax. Land for 6 ploughs; 2 ploughs there; 3 slaves.   203
    2 villagers and 8 smallholders.   a 3
  Pasture, 20 acres.
  Value formerly and now 20s. 3 cattle; 20 sheep; 10 goats.   E

13 BOSSINEY. Alfwy held it before 1066; he could not be separated   E
  from St. (Petroc's). 1 h. Land for 6 ploughs; 1 plough
  there, with 1 slave.   L 203
    3 villagers and 3 smallholders.   b 4
  Pasture, 30 acres.
  Formerly 20s; value now 15s. 6 cattle; 40 sheep.

Idē cõm̃ tenͭ de S̃ Petroc *TREMAIL*. Eiulf teneͭ T.R.E.

7 n̄ poterat a S̃ ſepari. Ibi ſt̃. iii. virg̃ træ. Tra. ē. v. car̃.

Ibi ſt̃. iii. car̃. 7 ii. ſerui. 7 ii. uiłłi 7 vi. borđ. 7 c. ac̃ paſturæ.

Oł.ͭ xxx. ſoł. Modo uał. xx. ſoliđ.

Idē cõm̃ tenͭ *POLRODE*. Vn̄ tain̄ teneͭ T.R.E. 7 n̄ poterat

a S̃ ſepari. Ibi. ē dimiđ hida. Tra. iii. car̃. Ibi ſt̃. ii. car̃ cū. i.

ſeruo. 7 iiii. uiłłi 7 iii. borđ. 7 iii. ac̃ ſiluæ. 7 xvii. ac̃ paſturæ.

Oł.ͭ xx. ſoliđ. modo uał. xv. ſoliđ.

Ricarđ tenͭ de S̃ Petroco *TVRGOIL*. Godric teneͭ de S̃ T.R.E.

nec poterat ab eo ſepari. Ibi. ē. i. hida. Tra. vi. car̃. Ibi ſt̃. iiii.

car̃. 7 iiii. ſerui. 7 iiii. uiłłi 7 iiii. borđ. 7 lx. ac̃ paſturæ. 7 iii. ac̃

ſiluæ minutæ. Olim 7 modo uał. xx. ſoliđ.

Machus tenͭ de S̃ Petroco *FOSNEWIT*. Ipſe teneͭ T.R.E.

nec poterat a S̃ ſepari. Ibi. ē. i. hida. Tra. viii. car̃. Ibi ſt̃. iiii.

car̃. cū. i. ſeruo. 7 viii. uiłłi 7 viii. borđ. 7 xxx. ac̃ paſturæ.

Redđ. x. ſoliđ.

Ipſe S̃c̃s Petro tenͭ *ELIL*. Ibi ſt̃. ii. hidæ. Tra. viii. car̃.

Ibi ſt̃. iiii. car̃. 7 iiii. ſerui. 7 viii. uiłłi 7 viii. borđ. Paſtura

una leū łg̃. 7 dimiđ leū łat̃. Vał. xx. ſoliđ.

Ipſe S̃c̃s Petroç tenͭ *WIDIE*. Ibi. ē una hida. Tra. ē. viii. car̃.

Ibi ſt̃. iiii. car̃ 7 ii. ſerui. 7 viii. uiłłi 7 xv. borđ. 7 xii. ac̃ ſiluæ.

Paſtura. i. leū łg̃. 7 tntđ łat̃. Oł.ͭ xxv. ſoł qđo cõm̃ accepit.

modo uał. xv. ſoliđ.

Ipſe S̃ Petroç tenͭ *TRETDENO*. Ibi ſt̃. ii. hidæ. Tra. viii. car̃.

Ibi ſt̃. iii. car̃ 7 dĩm̃. 7 ii. ſerui. 7 vii. uiłłi 7 viii. borđ. 7 c. ac̃

paſturæ. Qđo cõm̃ accep̄. xxv. ſoł. Modo uał. xv. ſoliđ.

14 TREMAIL. Aiulf held it before 1066; he could not be separated from St. (Petroc's). 3 v. of land. Land for 5 ploughs; 3 ploughs there; 2 slaves.
    2 villagers and 6 smallholders.
    Pasture, 100 acres.
Formerly 30s; value now 20s. 15 cattle; 100 sheep.

L 204
a 1

15 The Count also holds POLROAD. A thane held it before 1066; he could not be separated from St. (Petroc's). ½ h.
Land for 3 ploughs; 2 ploughs there, with 1 slave.
    4 villagers and 3 smallholders.
    Woodland, 3 acres; pasture, 17 acres.
Formerly 20s; value now 15s. 3 cattle; 20 sheep; 4 goats.

204
a 2
E

16 Richard holds TREGOLE from St. Petroc's. Godric held it from St. (Petroc's) before 1066; he could not be separated from it. 1 h.
Land for 6 ploughs; 4 ploughs there; 3 slaves.
    4 villagers and 4 smallholders.
    Pasture, 60 acres; underwood, 3 acres.
Value formerly and now 20s. 5 cattle; 50 sheep.

204
E b 1
L

17 Maccus holds FURSNEWTH from St. Petroc's. He held it himself before 1066; he could not be separated from St. (Petroc's). 1 h.
Land for 8 ploughs; 4 ploughs there, with 1 slave.
    8 villagers and 8 smallholders.
    Pasture, 30 acres.
It pays 10s.

204
b 2
L

18 St. Petroc's holds ELLENGLAZE itself. 2 h. Land for 8 ploughs; 4 ploughs there; 4 slaves.
    8 villagers and 8 smallholders.
    Pasture, 1 league long and ½ league wide.
Value 20s. 20 sheep.

E
203
b 1
L

19 St. Petroc's holds WITHIEL itself. 1 h. Land for 8 ploughs; 4 ploughs there; 2 slaves.
    8 villagers and 15 smallholders.
    Woodland, 12 acres; pasture, 1 league long and as wide.
Formerly 25s, when the Count received it; value now 15s. 24 sheep.

L 203
b 2

20 St. Petroc's holds TREKNOW itself. 2 h. Land for 8 ploughs; 3½ ploughs there; 2 slaves.
    7 villagers and 8 smallholders.
    Pasture, 100 acres.
When the Count received it, 25s; value now 15s.

L 203
b 3

Herald abſtulit S̃ Petro injuſte . I . hidā træ . p quá . W . rex
p̃cepit judicam̃tū teneri . 7 S̃cm p juſticiā reſaiſiri.

De æcła S̃ Petroc ablata . ē CVDIFORD . q̃ reddeb̃ T . R . E.
ipſi æccłæ p c̃ſuetuđ . I . bouē 7 VII . oues . Rex tenet.

Hæ INFRASCRIPTÆ TRÆ SVꝶ ABLATÆ S̃ PETROÇO. Com moriton ten.

In TREGON . ē una v træ . q̃ reddeb̃ . XV . denar de c̃ſuetuđ.

In KEFORNOC dimiđ hida træ . reddeb̃ . XII . oues 7 XV . denar.

In KENHAL una virg træ . reddeb̃ . VI . oues 7 VIII . denar.

In TALCARN dimiđ hida træ . reddeb̃ uñ bouē.   ꝸ oues.

In KEMHOR dimiđ hida træ . reddeb̃ uñ bouē 7 XV . denar 7 XII.

In NANCHERT una virg tre . reddeb̃ . XV . denar.

In KINNONEC una virg træ . reddeb̃ XV . den 7 V . oues.

Om̃s Sup̃ius deſcriptas tras teneb̃ T . R . E . S̃cs Petrocus.

Huj|terræ nunq̃ reddideꝛ geldū niſi ipſi æccłæ.

CANONICI S̃CI ACHEBRANNI ten LANNACHEBRAN . 7 teneb̃
T . R . E . Ibi ſt . XI . ac træ . Tra . ē . VII . car̃ . Ibi . ē . I . car̃ . 7 XX.
ac paſturæ . Q̃do com̃ accep̃ ualeb̃ . XL . ſoł . m̃ uał . V . ſoliđ.

CANONICI S̃ PROBI ten LANBREBOIS . Rex Eduuard teneb̃
in uita ſua . Ibi . ē . I . hida 7 una virg træ . 7 nunq̃ geldauit.
Tra . ē . VIII . car̃ . Ibi ſt . IIII . car̃ 7 dimiđ . 7 V . ſerui . 7 III . uiłłi
7 VIII . borđ . 7 XX . ac paſturæ . Valet . XL . ſoliđ.

21 Earl Harold wrongfully took away from St. Petroc's 1 h. of land, for which King William commanded that a judicial enquiry be held, and that it be restored to St. (Petroc's) by judgement.

204
b 3
E

22 COSWARTH has been taken away from St. Petroc's Church; before 1066 it paid this Church 1 ox and 7 sheep by custom. The King holds it. Brictric held it in 1066.

205
a 1

The lands listed below have been taken from St. Petroc's; the Count of Mortain holds them, and his men from him.

121 b
E

    In TREGONA 1 v. of land, which paid 15d in customary dues.

204
b 5

    In TREVORNICK ½ h. of land paid 12 sheep and 15d.

205
a 2

    In 'TRENHALE' 1 v. of land paid 6 sheep and 8d.

205
a 3

    In TOLCARNE ½ h. of land paid 1 ox.

205
a 4

    In TREMORE ½ h. of land paid 1 ox, 15d and 12 sheep.

205
a 5

    In LANCARFFE 1 v. of land paid 15d.

205
a 6

    In TRENINNICK 1 v. of land paid 15d and 5 sheep.

205
a 7

Before 1066 St. Petroc's held all the lands listed above. This Saint's lands never paid tax, save to this Church.

23 The Canons of St. Achebran's hold ST. KEVERNE, and held it before 1066. 11 acres of land. Land for 7 ploughs; 1 plough there. Pasture, 20 acres. 8 cattle; 30 sheep.

205
b 1

When the Count received it, value 40s; value now 5s.

24 The Canons of St. Probus hold PROBUS. During his life, King Edward held it. 1 h. and 1 v. of land. It never paid tax. Land for 8 ploughs; 4½ ploughs there; 5 slaves.

206
a 1

    3 villagers and 8 smallholders.
    Pasture, 20 acres. 20 cattle; 160 sheep.
Value 40s.

Canonici S Carentoch ten *Langoroch*,7 teneb T.R.E.
Ibi st.iii.hidæ.ii.acs min.|Tra.x.car,Ibi.ē.i.car 7 dim
7 iii.uilli.Valet.v.sol.Qdo comes tra saisiuit.ualeb.xl.sol.
Canonici S Pierani ten *Lanpiran*.q liba fuit T.R,E.sep.
Ibi st.iii.hidæ.Tra.ē.viii.car.Ibi st.ii.car.7 ii.serui,7 iiii.
uilli 7 viii.bord,7 x.ac pasturæ.Valet.xii.solid.
Qdo comes accepit.ualeb,xl.solid.
De hoc Maner ablatæ st.ii,træ.q reddeb canonicis T.R.E.firma
iiii.septimanaru,7 decano.xx.solid p csuetudine.
Haru una ten Berner de comite moriton,7 de alia hida qua
ten odo de S Pierano.abstulit com tota pecunia.
Canonici S Berrione ten *Eglosberrie*,q fuit liba
T.R,E.Ibi.ē.i.hida.Tra.viii.car,Ibi.ē dim car 7 vi.uilli
7 vi.bord.7 xx.ac pasturæ,Val.x,solid,Qdo comes tram
accep.ualeb.xl.solid,
Clerici S Neoti ten *Neotestov*.7 tneb T,R.E.Ibi st,ii,hidæ.
q nunq geldauer.Ibi st.iiii.bord.Val.v.solid.
Tota hanc tra pter una acra træ qua pbri hnt abstulit
comes ab æccla.Odo ten de eo.7 ual.v.sol.pus ualeb.xx.sol.
Scs Constantin ht dimid hid træ q fuit qeta ab omi ser
uitio T.R.E.sed postq com tra accep.reddid geldu injuste
sic tra uillano.Tra.ē.iiii.car.Val.x,solid,Qdo com
tra accep.ualeb.xl.solid.

25 The Canons of St. Carantoc's hold CRANTOCK, and held it
before 1066. 3 h. less 2 acres. It never paid tax. Land for 10
ploughs; 1½ ploughs there.   206
    3 villagers. 15 cattle; 6 pigs; 110 sheep.   a 2
Value 5s; value when the Count took possession of the land, 40s.   E

26 The Canons of St. Piran's hold 'PERRANZABULOE'; before 1066 it was
always free. 3 h. Land for 8 ploughs; 2 ploughs there; 2 slaves.   206
    4 villagers and 8 smallholders.   b 2
    Pasture, 10 acres. 8 cattle; 30 sheep.   L
Value 12s; value when the Count received it, 40s.
    Two lands have been taken from this manor which before 1066
paid four weeks' revenue to the Canons and 20s. to the Dean by
custom. Berner holds one of them from the Count of Mortain;
the Count has taken away all the stock from the other hide, which
Odo holds from St. Piran's.

27 The Canons of St. Buryan's hold ST. BURYAN; it was free before
1066. 1 h. Land for 8 ploughs; ½ plough there.   207
    6 villagers and 6 smallholders.   a 2
    Pasture, 20 acres. 12 cattle; 12 sheep.
Value 10s; when the Count received the land, value 40s.

28 The clergy of St. Neot's hold ST. NEOT, and held it before 1066. 2 h.
they never paid tax.   207
    4 smallholders.   a 3
Value 5s. 1 ox; 20 sheep; 10 goats.
    The Count has taken all this land away from the Church, except
for 1 acre of land, which the priests have. Odo holds it from him.
Value 5s; previously 20s.

29 ST. CONSTANTINE'S has ½ h. of land, which was exempt from all
service before 1066, but since the Count received the land, it   207
had paid tax wrongfully, like villagers' land. Land for 4 ploughs. a 1
Value 10s; when the Count received the land, value 40s.

.III ECCĹA de TAVESTOCH teñ *SAVIOCH*.7 Ermenhald de ea.
T.R.E.geldb̃ ᵱ una hida.Tra.ē.ıx.caȓ.Iŋ dñio sƭ,ıı,caȓ.
7 ıııı.ſerui.7 vı.uilli 7 xvıı.borđ cū.ııı.caȓ.Ibi.xxx.aǒ
paſturæ.7 ʟx.aǒ filuæ.Olim 7 m̃ ual.ʟx.folıđ.

Idē Ermenhald teñ de ipſa æccla *ANTONE*,T.R.E.geldb̃
ᵱ dimiđ hida.Tra.ē.vı.caȓ.In dñio sƭ.ıı.caȓ.7 ıııı.ſerui.
7 xıı.uilli 7 xv.borđ cū,v,caȓ.Ibi,x.aǒ paſturæ
7 xxx.aǒ filuæ minutæ.Olim 7 modo ual,c,folıđ.
Abb̃ de hortune calūniat̃ hanc trã.

Idē.Er.teñ de ipſa æccla *RAME*.Ibi,ē,ı.hida.7 gelđ
ᵱ dım hida.Tra,ē.vıı.caȓ,In dñio.ē.ı.caȓ.7 ıııı.ſerui.
7 ıııı.uilli 7 xv.borđ çū,ııı,caȓ.Ibi.xxx.aǒ paſturæ.7 x.
aǒ filuæ minutæ,Olim 7 modo ual,xʟ.folıđ.

121 c

Idē Erm teñ de ipſa æccla *TREGRENON*.T.R.E.geldb̃ ᵱ dım
hida.Tra.ē.ıııı.caȓ.Ibi sƭ.ııı.caȓ.7 ıı.ſerui.7 ıx.uilli.7 una
aǒ pƭi.7 ıı.aǒ paſturæ.Olim 7 modo ual.xx.folıđ.

Idē Erm teñ de ipſa æccla *PENNEHALGAR*.Ibi.ē una virg
træ.7 gelđb̃ ᵱ dimiđ virg.Tra.ē.ıı.caȓ.Ibi.ē.ı.caȓ.7 vı.
uilli.7 x.aǒ filuæ.7 x.aǒ paſturæ.Olim 7 modo ual.x.fol.

Idē teñ de ipſa æccla *TALGAR*.T.R.E.geldb̃ ᵱ dimiđ v træ.
Tra.ē.ı.caȓ.Ibi sƭ.ıı.borđ.7 una aǒ paſturæ.Oli 7 m̃ ual
De ipſa æccla teñ comes moriton injuſtæ.ıııı. ſ v.folıđ.
maneria.*BOIETONE*.*ELENT*.*ƘEBICHEN*.*ƘEWANT*.
Abb̃ calūniat̃   qa de æccla ablata ſunt.

3   LAND OF TAVISTOCK CHURCH

1 The Church of Tavistock holds SHEVIOCK, and Ermenhald from it. Before 1066 it paid tax for 1 h. Land for 9 ploughs; in lordship 2 ploughs; 4 slaves; 1 v.
    6 villagers and 17 smallholders with 3 ploughs & the rest of the land. Pasture, 30 acres; woodland, 60 acres.
Value formerly and now 60s. 3 cattle; 80 sheep; 12 goats.

E
180
b 2

Ermenhald also holds from this Church
2 ANTONY. Before 1066 it paid tax for ½ h. Land for 6 ploughs; in lordship 2 ploughs; 4 slaves; a third of the land.
    12 villagers and 15 smallholders with 5 ploughs & the rest of the land. Pasture, 10 acres; underwood, 30 acres.
Value formerly and now, 100s. 7 cattle; 80 sheep.
The Abbot of Horton claims this land.

180
b 3

3 RAME. 1 h. It paid tax for ½ h. Land for 7 ploughs; in lordship, 1 plough; 4 slaves; 1 v.
    4 villagers and 15 smallholders with 3 ploughs & the rest of the land. Pasture, 30 acres; underwood, 10 acres.
Value formerly and now 40s. 8 cattle; 100 sheep; 18 goats.

181
a 1

4 TREGRENNA. Before 1066 it paid tax for ½ h. Land for 4 ploughs; 3 ploughs there; 2 slaves.
    9 villagers.
Meadow, 1 acre; pasture, 2 acres.
Value formerly and now 20s. 3 cattle; 12 pigs; 108 sheep.

121 c
L 181
a 2

5 PENHARGET. 1 v. of land; it paid for ½ v. Land for 2 ploughs; 1 plough there.
    6 villagers.
Woodland, 10 acres; pasture, 10 acres.
Value formerly and now 10s. 3 cows; 2 pigs; 30 sheep; 6 goats.

L 181
a 3

6 He also holds TOLCARNE from this Church. Before 1066 it paid tax for ½ v. of land. Land for 1 plough.
    2 smallholders; they have 2 oxen.
Pasture, 1 acre.
Value formerly and now 5s.

181
b 1

7 The Count of Mortain holds four manors wrongfully from this Church, BOYTON, ILLAND?, TREBEIGH and TREWANTA. The Abbot claims them because they have been taken away from the Church.

E
181
b 2
E

CTERRA COMITIS MORITONIENSIS.

COMES MORITONIENS ten de rege *FAWINTONE*.

Merlefuain teneb T.R.E.7 geldb ꝑ.1.hida.Ibi tam sꝽ
II.hidæ.Tra.xxx.car.In dnio sꝽ.vi.car.7 xx.ferui.7 xxx.
uitti.7 xx.borđ cū.xv.car.Ibi.cc.ac filuæ.7 paftura.vii.leū
lḡ.7 iiii.leū laꝽ.Oli.viii.lib.M uaꝽ.xvi.lib.7 xviii.foꝽ.7 iiii

Ipfe com ten *LISCARRET*.Merlefuain teneb T.R.E.   Ꝼden.
7 geldb ꝑ.ii.hiđ.Ibi tam sꝽ.xii.hidæ.Tra.e̅.lx.car.In dnio
sꝽ.iii.car.7 xx.ferui.7 xxxv.uitti.7 xxxvii.borđ.cū.xiii.car.
Ibi mercatū redđ.iiii.foliđ.7 molin redđ.xii.foliđ.7 cccc.ac
filuæ.Paftura.iiii.leū lḡ.7 ii.leū laꝽ.

Olim.viii.lib.Modo uaꝽ.xxvi.lib.xx.denar min.

Ipfe com ten *STRATONE*.Ostn eps 7 Alured marefcal teneb
T.R.E.7 geldb ꝑ.i.hida.Ibi sꝽ.ii.hide tam.Tra.e̅.xxx.car.
In dnio sꝽ.iiii.car.7 xx.ferui.7 xxx.uitti 7 xx.borđ.cū.xv.
car.Ibi.x.falinæ redđ.x.foliđ.7 xx.ac filuæ.7 cc.ac pa
fturæ.Oli.xxx.lib.Modo uaꝽ.xxxvi.lib.xx.den min.

Ipfe com ten *HENLISTON*.Algar teneb T.R.E.7 geldb pro
una hida. Ibi tam' sꝽ.ii.hide. Tra.e̅.xv.car.In dnio sꝽ.iiii.car.7 xviii.ferui.
7 xx.uitti 7 xv.borđ cū.viii.car.Ibi.x.ac filuæ.7 Paftura
.iii.leū lḡ.7 ii.leū laꝽ.Olim 7 modo redđ.xvi.lib.xx.den min.

Ipfe com ten *TEGLASTON*.Herald teneb T.R.E.7 geldb pro
.ii.hiđ.Ibi tam sꝽ.vi.hidæ.Tra.e̅.xx.car.In dnio sꝽ.ii.car.
7 xv.ferui.7 xxiiii.uitti 7 xx.borđ cū.xii.car.Ibi.ccc.
ac pafturæ.Olim.xii.mark argenti.Modo uaꝽ.xvi.lib

Ipfe Com ten *TIBESTEV*.Radulf ftalre   Ꝼxx.den min.
teneb T.R.E.7 geldb ꝑ.i.hida.Ibi tam sꝽ.iii.hidæ.Tra.xxx.
car.In dnio sꝽ.iii.car.7 xiiii.ferui.7 xxvii.uitti 7 xx.borđ
cū.x.car.Ibi.xl.ac filuæ.Paftura.iii.leū lḡ.7 i.leū laꝽ.
Olim.xii.lib.Modo uaꝽ.xv.lib.7 xviii.foliđ.7 iiii.denar.

5,1   LAND OF THE COUNT OF MORTAIN

1 **The Count of Mortain** holds FAWTON from the King; Merleswein
held it before 1066, and paid tax for 1 h; 2 h. there, however.
Land for 30 ploughs; in lordship 6 ploughs; 20 slaves; 1 h.   228
   30 villagers and 20 smallholders with 15 ploughs & 1 h.   a 1
   Woodland, 200 acres; pasture, 7 leagues long and 4 leagues wide.
Formerly £8; value now £16 18s 4d.
   33 unbroken mares; 23 cattle; 7 pigs; 300 sheep less 13; 15 goats.

The Count himself holds

2 LISKEARD. Merleswein held it before 1066, and paid tax for 2 h;
12 h. there, however. Land for 60 ploughs; in lordship, 3 ploughs;
20 slaves; 1 h.   228
   35 villagers and 37 smallholders with 13 ploughs & 11 h.   a 2
   A market which pays 4s; a mill which pays 12s; woodland,   E
     400 acres; pasture, 4 leagues long and 2 leagues wide.
Formerly £8; value now £26 less 20d. 8 unbroken mares; 10 cattle; 250 sheep.

3 STRATTON. Bishop Osbern and Alfred the Marshal held it before 1066,
and paid tax for 1 h; 2 h. there, however. Land for 30 ploughs;
in lordship 4 ploughs; 20 slaves; 1 h.
   30 villagers and 20 smallholders with 15 ploughs & 1 h.   237
   10 salt-houses which pay 10s; woodland, 20 acres;   a 1
     pasture, 200 acres.
Formerly £30; value now £36 less 20d. 30 cattle; 300 sheep.

4 HELSTONE. Algar held it before 1066, and paid tax for 1 h; 2 h. there,
however. Land for 15 ploughs; in lordship 4 ploughs; 18 slaves; 1 h.   237
   20 villagers and 15 smallholders with 8 ploughs & 1 h.   a 2
   Woodland, 10 acres; pasture, 3 leagues long and 2 leagues wide.
Formerly and now it pays £16 less 20d.
   18 unbroken mares; 10 cattle; 150 sheep; 5 pigs; 12 goats.

5 TREGLASTA. Earl Harold held it before 1066, and paid tax for 2 h;
6 h.there, however. Land for 20 ploughs; in lordship 2 ploughs;   237
15 slaves; 1 h.   a 3
   24 villagers and 20 smallholders with 12 ploughs & 5 h.
   Pasture, 300 acres. 4 unbroken mares; 4 cattle; 50 sheep.
Formerly 12 silver marks; value now £16 less 20d.

6 'TYBESTA'. Ralph the Constable held it before 1066, and paid tax for
1 h; 3 h. there, however. Land for 30 ploughs; in lordship   247
3 ploughs; 14 slaves; 1 h.   a 1
   27 villagers and 20 smallholders with 10 ploughs & 2 h.
   Woodland, 40 acres; pasture, 3 leagues long and 1 league wide.
Formerly £12; value now £15 18s 4d. 14 cattle; 4 pigs; 160 sheep.

Ipfe Com̄ ten̄ *TRENWIT*. Sitric abb̄ teneb̄ T.R.E. 7 geldb̄
p̄. II. hid̄. Ibi tam̄ st̄. VI. hidæ. Tra. XL. car̄. In dn̄io st̄. V. car̄.
7 XVI. ferui. 7 xxx. uilli 7 xxx. bord̄ cū. XII. car̄. Ibi. XL. ac̄
filuæ. 7 mille ac̄ pafturæ. Olim. XII. mark argenti. Modo
reddit. xxv. lib̄ 7 xVIII. folid̄. 7 IIII. denarios.

121 d

Ipfe com̄ ten̄ *BERNEL*. Brifmar teneb̄ T.R.E. 7 geldb̄ p̄ un̄a
hida. Ibi tam̄ eft. I. hida 7 dimid̄. Tra. ē. xx. car̄. In dn̄io
st̄. III. car̄. 7 x. ferui. 7 XII. uilli 7 xVIII. bord̄ cū. xx. car̄.
Ibi. XL. ac̄ filuæ. Paftura. IIII. leū lḡ. 7 II. leū lat̄.
Oli. XII. mark argenti. m̄ ual XII. lib̄. 7 xVIII. fol. 7 IIII. den.
Ipfe com̄ ten̄ *MOIREIS*. Ordulf teneb̄ T.R.E. 7 geldb̄ pro
una hida. Ibi tam̄ st̄. II. hidæ. Tra. ē. x. car̄. In dn̄io st̄
. II. car̄. 7 III. ferui. 7 v. uilli 7 x. bord̄ cū. v. car̄. Ibi. c. ac̄ pā
fturæ. 7 cc. ac̄ filuæ. Olim. c. folid̄. Modo ual. IX. lib̄.
7 xVIII. folid̄. 7 IIII. denar̄.
Ipfe com̄ ten̄ *TREWITGHI*. Merlefuain teneb̄ T.R.E.
7 geldb̄ p̄ una hida. Ibi tam̄ st̄. II. hidæ. Tra. ē. xVI. car̄.
In dn̄io st̄. v. car̄. 7 VII. ferui. 7 xv. uilli 7 xVII. bord̄ cū. vīII.
car̄. Ibi. LX. ac̄ filuæ. 7 ccc. ac̄ pafturæ.
Olim. c. folid̄. Modo ual. vIII. lib̄.
Ipfe com̄ ten̄ *ALWARETONE*. Aluuard teneb̄ T.R.E.
7 geldb̄ p̄. II. hid̄. Ibi tam̄ st̄. III. hidæ. Tra. LX. car̄. In dn̄io
st̄. III. car̄. 7 xI. ferui. 7 xxxv. uilli 7 xxv. bord̄ cū. XII. car̄.
Ibi. III. ac̄ p̄ti. Paftura. II. leū lḡ. 7 una leū lat̄.
Olim. vIII. lib̄. Modo redd. xx. lib̄.
Ipfe com̄ ten̄ *TEDINTONE*. Ordulf teneb̄ T.R.E. 7 geldb̄
p̄. II. hid̄. Ibi tam̄ st̄. III. hidæ. Tra. ē. L. car̄. In dn̄io st̄
v. car̄. 7 xIII. ferui. 7 xxv. uilli 7 xxx. bord̄ cū. XII. car̄.
Ibi. II. ac̄ p̄ti. Paftura. III. leū lḡ. 7 una leū lat̄. Silua
una leū lḡ. 7 tn̄td lat̄. Olim. vIII. lib̄. Modo ual. xx. lib̄.

7   TRENOWTH. Abbot Sihtric held it before 1066 and paid tax for 2 h;
6 h. there, however. Land for 40 ploughs; in lordship 5 ploughs;   249
16 slaves; 1 h.   a 1
>30 villagers and 30 smallholders with 12 ploughs & the rest of the land.
>Woodland, 40 acres; pasture, 1000 acres.
Formerly 12 silver marks; now it pays £25 18s 4d.
21 unbroken mares; 12 cattle; 200 sheep.   E

8   BRANNEL. Brictmer held it before 1066 and paid tax for 1 h; 1½ h. 121 d
there, however. Land for 20 ploughs; in lordship 3 ploughs;
10 slaves; ½ h.
>12 villagers and 18 smallholders with [6] ploughs & 1 h.   249
>Woodland, 40 acres; pasture, 4 leagues long and 2 leagues wide.   a 2
Formerly 12 silver marks; value now £12 18s 4d.
20 unbroken mares; 2 cattle; 150 sheep.

9   MORESK. Ordwulf held it before 1066, and paid tax for 1 h; 2 h. there,
however. Land for 10 ploughs; in lordship 2 ploughs; 3 slaves; ½ h.   249
>5 villagers and 10 smallholders with 5 ploughs & the rest of the land.   a 3
>Pasture, 100 acres. woodland, 200 acres.
Formerly 100s; value now £9 18s 4d. 10 cattle; 100 sheep; 7 goats.

10   TREWIRGIE. Merleswein held it before 1066, and paid tax for 1 h;
2 h. there, however. Land for 16 ploughs; in lordship 5 ploughs;   249
7 slaves; ½ h.   b 1
>15 villagers and 17 smallholders with 8 ploughs & the rest of the land.
>Woodland, 60 acres; pasture, 300 acres.
Formerly 100s; value now £8. 4 wild mares; 10 cattle; 200 sheep less 20.

11   'ALVERTON'. Alfward held it before 1066, and paid tax for 2 h;   255
3 h. there, however. Land for 60 ploughs; in lordship 3 ploughs;   a 1
11 slaves; ½ h.
>35 villagers and 25 smallholders with 12 ploughs & 2½ h.
>Meadow, 3 acres; pasture, 2 leagues long and 1 league wide.
Formerly £8; it now pays £20.
1 cob; 17 unbroken mares; 9 cattle; 4 pigs; 100 sheep.

12   TEHIDY. Ordwulf held it before 1066 and paid tax for 2 h; 3 h.
there, however. Land for 50 ploughs; in lordship 5 ploughs;
13 slaves; ½ h.   255
>25 villagers and 30 smallholders with 12 ploughs & 2½ h.   a 2
>Meadow, 2 acres; pasture, 3 leagues long and 1 league wide;
>   woodland, 1 league long and as wide.
Formerly £8; value now £20.
15 unbroken mares; 10 cattle; 140 sheep.

Ipse com̃ teñ *Risleston*. Brismar teneb̃ T.R.E.7 geldb̃ ꝑ una hida. Tra. ẽ. xv. car̃. In dñio sτ̃. ii. car̃.7 xii. serui. 7 xv. uitti 7 xxiiii. bord cũ. viii. car̃. Ibi. lx. ac̃ siluæ. 7 ccc. ac̃ pasturæ. Olim. xxx. lib̃. Modo ual. xv. lib̃. 7 una mark argti.7 v. solid.

Ipse com̃ teñ *Landiner*. Eddida teneb̃ T.R.E.7 geldb̃ pro uno ferling træ. Ibi. ẽ tam̃ una uirg træ. Tra. ii. car. Ibi sτ̃. vi. bord 7 v. ac̃ ṗti.7 xl. ac̃ pasturæ. Olim. x. solid. Modo ual. xxx. denar.

Ipse com̃ teñ *hela*. Ailm teneb̃ T.R.E.7 geldb̃ ꝑ dimid ferling. Ibi. ẽ tam̃ uñ ferling træ. Tra. i. car̃. Ibi sτ̃. ii. bord 7 una ac̃ ṗti.7 xxx. ac̃ pasturæ. Oli. xxx. deñ. M̊ ual. xii.

Ipse com̃ teñ *Treiswantel*. Sistric teneb̃ T.R.E. ⁊ deñ. 7 geldb̃ ꝑ uno ferling. Ibi. ẽ tam̃ una virg træ. Tra. ẽ. ii. car. Ibi sτ̃. v. bord 7 xxx. ac̃ pasturæ. Oli. x. sol. M̊ ual. xxx. deñ.

Ipse com teñ *heli*. Sistric teneb̃ T.R.E.7 geldb̃ ꝑ uno fer ling træ. Ibi. ẽ tam̃ dimid hida træ. Tra. ii. car̃. Ibi sτ̃. ii. uitti.7 ii. bord 7 xxx. ac̃ pasturæ. Oli. xv. sol. Modo ual. v. sol.

Ipse com̃ teñ *Peret*. Wadhel teneb̃ T.R.E.7 geldb̃ ꝑ uno ferling træ. Ibi. ẽ tamen una virg træ. Tra. ẽ. ii. car. Ibi sτ̃. ii. uitti 7 ii. bord 7 v. ac̃ pasturæ. Oli. vii. sol. Modo ual. ii. sol.

Ipse com̃ teñ *Trewille*. Alestan teneb̃ T.R.E.7 geldb̃ pro uno ferling træ. Ibi tam̃. ẽ dimid hida.7 uñ bord.7 v. ac̃ siluæ.7 lx. ac̃ pasturæ. Oli. x. solid. Modo ual. iii. sol.

Ipse com̃ teñ *Trebihan*. Osulf teneb̃ T.R.E.7 geldb̃ ꝑ uno ferling. Ibi tam̃ dim hida. Tra. ẽ. ii. car̃. Ibi sτ̃. iii. bord 7 cc. ac̃ pasturæ. Olim. xx. solid. Modo ual. v. solid.

13   RILLATON. Brictmer held it before 1066, and paid tax for 1 h.
Land for 15 ploughs; in lordship 2 ploughs; 12 slaves; ½ h.
   15 villagers and 24 smallholders with 8 ploughs & ½ h.
   Woodland, 60 acres; pasture, 300 acres.   264
Formerly £30; value now £15, 1 mark of silver and 5s.   a 1
   15 unbroken mares; [...] cattle; 60 sheep.

14   LANDINNER. Edith held it before 1066, and paid tax for 1 f. of   E
land; 1 v. of land there, however. Land for 2 ploughs.
   6 smallholders.   261
   Meadow, 5 acres; pasture, 40 acres.   b 1
Formerly 10s; value now 30d.

15   HELA. Aelmer held it before 1066 and paid tax for ½ f; 1 f.
of land there, however. Land for 1 plough.   261
   2 smallholders.   b 4
   Meadow, 1 acre; pasture, 30 acres.
Formerly 30d; value now 12d.

16   TREWANTA? Sihtric held it before 1066, and paid tax for 1 f; 1 v.   E
of land there, however. Land for 2 ploughs.
   5 smallholders.   261
   Pasture, 30 acres.   b 5
Formerly 10s; value now 30d.   2 cattle.

17   ILLAND? Sihtric held it before 1066, and paid tax for 1 f. of land;
½ h. of land there, however. Land for 2 ploughs.
   2 villagers and 2 smallholders.   262
   Pasture, 30 acres.   a 1
Formerly 15s; value now 5s.

18   PATRIEDA. Waddell held it before 1066, and paid tax for 1 f. of
land; 1 v. of land there, however. Land for 2 ploughs.   262
   2 villagers and 2 smallholders.   a 2
   Pasture, 5 acres.
Formerly 7s; value now 2s.

19   TREVELL? Alstan held it before 1066, and paid tax for 1 f. of
land; ½ h. there, however.
   1 smallholder.   262
   Woodland, 5 acres; pasture, 60 acres.   a 3
Formerly 10s; value now 3s.

20   TREBEIGH. Oswulf held it before 1066, and paid tax for 1 f; ½ h.
there, however. Land for 2 ploughs.
   3 smallholders.   262
   Pasture, 200 acres.   a 4
Formerly 20s; value now 5s.

Ipſe cõm tenͬ *HESLAND* . Aleſtan teneƀ T.R.E. 7 geldƀ ꝓ. 11.

ferlings træ. Tra . ē . 11 . carͬ . Ibi sͭ . 111 . borđ . 7 xxx . aͨ paſturæ.

Olim . xx . ſoliđ . Modo uaꝉ . 11 . ſoliđ.

Ipſe cõm tenͬ *DVNHEVET* . T.R.E . geldƀ ꝓ una v̄ træ . Ibi

tãm eſt . 1 . hida, Tra . ē . x . carͬ . In dñio . ē . 1 . carͬ . 7 111 . ſerui.

7 un uiꝉꝉs 7 x111 . borđ cū . 1111 . carͬ . Ibi . 11 . molini redđ . xL.

ſoliđ . 7 xL . aͨ paſturæ . Olͥ . xx . liƀ, Modo uaꝉ . 1111 . liƀ.

Ibi . ē caſtrū comitis.

122 a

Rainald tenͬ de comite *ƘEWELLE* . Briſmar teneƀ T.R.E. cū ma

nerio qđ uocatͭ *GARGALLE* . 7 geldƀ ꝓ una v̄ træ . Tra . ē . v . carͬ.

In dñio . ē . 1 . carͬ . 7 1111 . ſerui . 7 v1 . uiꝉꝉi 7 v1 . borđ cū . 111 . carͬ.

Ibi ſilua . 111 . leū lͧg . 7 una leū laͭt . Olͥ . Lx . ſoꝉ . ᷃m uaꝉ . xxv . ſoꝉ.

Idē tenͬ de co . *ƘEWELLOGEN* . Aluuin teneƀ T.R.E . 7 geldƀ

ꝓ . 111 . ferlings træ . Ibi tãm . ē dim hida . Tra . ē . v1 . carͬ.

In dñio . ē . 1 . carͬ . 7 v111 . ſerui . 7 1111 . uiꝉꝉi 7 1111 . borđ cū . 11 . carͬ.

Ibi . xL . aͨ paſturæ . 7 Lx . aͨ ſiluæ . Olim 7 modo uaꝉ . Lx . ſoꝉ.

Idē tenͬ de . co . *LANHER* . Edmer teneƀ T.R.E . 7 geldƀ ꝓ uno

ferling . Ibi . ē tãm una v̄ træ . Tra . 1 . carͬ . ᷎q ibi . ē cū . 11 . borđ

7 v1 . ſeruis . Ibi . x . aͨ paſturæ . 7 xxx . aͨ ſiluæ . Olͥ 7 ᷃m uaꝉ . v111 . ſoꝉ.

Idē tenͬ *LANGVER* . Grim teneƀ T.R.E . 7 geldƀ ꝓ uno ferling

Ibi tãm eſt una v̄ træ . Tra . 1 . carͬ . Ibi sͭ . 11 . borđ 7 x . aͨ ſiluæ.

Olͥ . 1111 . ſoꝉ . Modo uaꝉ . 11 . ſoliđ.

Idē tenͬ *BRODEHOG* . Aluric teneƀ T.R.E . 7 geldƀ ꝓ una v̄ træ.

Ibi tãm . ē dim hida . Tra . 1111 . carͬ . Ibi sͭ . 11 . carͬ 7 11 . ſerui . 7 111.

uiꝉꝉi 7 1111 . borđ . 7 c . aͨ paſturæ . 7 xx . aͨ ſiluæ.

Olim . x11 . ſoliđ . Modo uaꝉ . x . ſoliđ.

21 HENNETT? Alstan held it before 1066, and paid tax for 2 f. of land. Land for 2 ploughs.
   3 smallholders.
   Pasture, 30 acres.
Formerly 20s; value now 2s.

262
a 5

22 LAUNCESTON. Before 1066 it paid tax for 1 v. of land; 1 h. there, however. Land for 10 ploughs; in lordship 1 plough; 3 slaves;
   1 villager and 13 smallholders with 4 ploughs.
   2 mills which pay 40s; pasture, 40 acres.
Formerly £20; value now £4. 5 cattle; 50 sheep.
The Count's castle is there.

264
b 1

5,2

1 **Reginald** holds TREWIDLAND? from the Count. Brictmer held it before 1066 together with the manor called TREGARLAND?, and paid tax for 1 v. of land. Land for 5 ploughs; in lordship 1 plough; 4 slaves; 1 v.
   6 villagers and 6 smallholders with 3 ploughs, & the rest of the land.
   Woodland, 3 leagues long and 1 league wide.
Formerly 60s; value now 25s.

E
122 a

235
b 1

He also holds

2 TRELAWNE from the Count. Alwin held it before 1066 and paid tax for 3 f. of land; ½ h. there, however. Land for 6 ploughs; in lordship 1 plough, 8 slaves; 1 f.
   4 villagers and 4 smallholders with 2 ploughs, & the rest of the land.
   Pasture, 40 acres; woodland, 60 acres.
Value formerly and now 60s. 6 cattle; 5 pigs; 40 sheep; 12 goats.

235
b 2

E

3 MUCHLARNICK from the Count. Edmer held it before 1066 and paid tax for 1 f; 1v. of land there, however. Land for 1 plough, which is there, with
   2 smallholders and 6 slaves.
   Pasture, 10 acres; woodland, 30 acres.
Value formerly and now 8s. 20 sheep; 10 goats.

L

235
b 3

4 LEWARNE. Grim held it before 1066 and paid tax for 1f. 1v. of land there, however. Land for 1 plough.
   2 smallholders.
   Woodland, 10 acres.
Formerly 4s; value now 2s.

236
a 1

5 BRADDOCK. Aelfric held it before 1066 and paid tax for 1 v. of land; ½ h. there, however. Land for 4 ploughs; 2 ploughs there; 2 slaves.
   3 villagers and 4 smallholders.
   Pasture, 100 acres; woodland, 20 acres.
Formerly 12s; value now 10s. 30 sheep; 10 goats.

236
L a 2

Idē ten RASWALE . Alueua teneƀ T.R.E.7 geldƀ ꝑ una v̅
træ.Ibi tam̄.ē dimiđ hida.Tra.iii.car̄.Ibi sƚ.ii.car̄.7 iii.
ſerui.7 ii.uiƚƚi 7 ii.borđ 7 xxx.ac̄ paſturæ.Olí.x.ſoƚ.M̊ uaƚ.vii.ſoƚ.

Idē ten CHILORGORET. Vƣred teneƀ T.R.E.7 geldƀ ꝑ dimidio
ferling.Ibi.ē un̊ ager træ.Tra.i.car̄.Ibi.ē un̊ ſeruus.7 x.ac̄
ſiluæ.Olim 7 modo uaƚ.iii.ſoliđ.

Idē ten TELBRIG.Aluric teneƀ T.R.E.7 geldƀ ꝑ dimiđ ferling
Ibi.ē un̊ ager træ.Tra.i.car̄.Ibi.ē.i.borđ.7 xxx.ac̄ paſturæ.
Olim ualeƀ.xv.denar̄.

Idē ten LANTIEN.Alric teneƀ T.R.E.7 geldƀ ꝑ uno ferling.
Tra.ē.ii.car̄.|Ibi sƚ.iii.borđ 7 iii.ac̄ ſiluæ.Olí.x.ſoƚ.M̊ uaƚ.ii.ſoƚ.
_{Ibi tamen.i.v̄ terre.}

Idē ten LANLARON.Sbern teneƀ T.R.E.7 geldƀ ꝑ uno ferling,
Tra.ē.iii.car.Ibi.ē.i.car̄.7 ii.ſerui.7 iiii.borđ.7 lx.ac̄ paſturæ.
_{'Ibi tam'.ēſt.i.v̄ fre.}
7 v.ac̄ ſiluæ.Olim.x.ſoliđ.Modo uaƚ.v.ſoliđ.

Idē ten de Co.TREMETONE.Briſmar teneƀ T.R.E.7 geldƀ ꝑ.ii.
hiđ 7 dimiđ.|Tra.ē.xxiiii.car.In dn̄io sƚ.iii.car̄.7 l.ſerui.7 xx.
_{Ibi tam'.v.hide.}
uiƚƚi 7 xxx.borđ cū.vii.car̄.Ibi.xl.ac̄ paſturæ.7 xx.ac̄ ſiluæ.
Olim.x.liƀ.Modo uaƚ.viii.liƀ.

Ibi habet comes unū caſtrū.7 mercatū redđ.iii.ſoliđ.

Idem ten de co.CALESTOCH.Aſgar teneƀ T.R.E.7 geldƀ
ꝑ una hida.Tra.ē.xii.car̄.In dn̄io sƚ.ii.car̄.7 xii.ſerui.
_{Ibi tam'.ii.hide 7 dimiđ.}
7 xxx.uiƚƚi 7 xxx.borđ cū.vi.car̄.Ibi.c.ac̄ ſiluæ.Paſtura
iii.leū lḡ.7 una leū laƚ.Olí.vi.liƀ.Modo uaƚ.iii.liƀ.

6 **RAPHAEL.** Aelfeva held it before 1066 and paid tax for 1 v. of land;
½ h. there, however. Land for 3 ploughs; 2 ploughs there; 3 slaves.
    2 villagers and 2 smallholders.   236
    Pasture, 30 acres.   L a 3
Formerly 10s; value now 7s. 3 cattle; 5 pigs; 40 sheep.

7 **KILLIGORRICK.** Uhtred held it before 1066 and paid tax for ½ f.
1 acre of land there. Land for 1 plough.   236
    1 slave.   L b 1
    Woodland, 10 acres.
Value formerly and now 3s. 3 pigs; 10 sheep; 10 goats.

8 **ELLBRIDGE.** Aelfric held it before 1066, and paid tax for ½ f. 1 acre
of land there. Land for 1 plough.
    1 smallholder.   245
    Pasture, 30 acres.   b 1
Value formerly 15d.

9 (Castle by) **LANTYAN.** Alric held it before 1066 and paid tax for 1 f.
1 v. of land there, however. Land for 2 ploughs.   L
    3 smallholders.   251
    Woodland, 3 acres.   b 4
Formerly 10s; value now 2s.

10 **LANHADRON.** Osbern held it before 1066 and paid tax for 1 f.
1 v. of land there, however. Land for 3 ploughs; 1 plough there;
    2 slaves; 4 smallholders.   L 252
    Pasture, 60 acres; woodland, 5 acres.   a 1
Formerly 10s; value now 5s. 20 sheep.

11 **TREMATON** from the Count. Brictmer held it before 1066 and paid
tax for 2½ h; 5 h.there, however. Land for 24 ploughs; in lordship
3 ploughs; 50 slaves; 2 h.   256
    20 villagers and 30 smallholders with 7 ploughs & 3 h. a 1
    Pasture, 40 acres; woodland, 20 acres.
Formerly £10; value now £8. 15 sheep; 25 goats.
    The Count has a castle there, and a market which pays 3s.   E

12 **CALSTOCK** from the Count. Asgar held it before 1066 and paid tax
for 1 h; 2½ h. there, however. Land for 12 ploughs; in lordship   E
2 ploughs, 12 slaves; 1 v.   256
    30 villagers and 30 smallholders with 6 ploughs & 2 h. 1 v. a 2
    Woodland, 100 acres; pasture, 3 leagues long and 1 league wide.
Formerly £6; value now £3. 3 pigs.

Idē teñ *PENNHALGAR*.Elmer teneƀ T.R.E.7 geldƀ pro
una virg træ.Ibi tam̄.ē una hida.Tra.ē.xvi.caŕ.In dñio
eſt.ı.caŕ.7 ıııı.ſerui.7 xı.uilti 7 xxx.borđ cū.vıı.caŕ. ſoliđ.
Ibi.xxx.ađ paſturæ.7 ıııı.ađ ſiluæ.Olı.ıx.ſoł.Modo uał.xxx.
Idē teñ de cọ.*MACRETONE*.Eduuard teneƀ T.R.E.7 geldƀ
ꝑ una v̄ træ.Ibi tam̄.ē una hida.Tra.ē.vııı.caŕ.Ibi ſt.ııı.
caŕ.7 ıııı.ſerui.7 vı.uilti 7 vııı.borđ.7 ıx.ađ paſturæ.
Olim.xxx.ſoliđ.Modo uał.xx.ſoliđ.
Idē teñ *KEHINOCH*.Algar teneƀ T.R.E.7 geldƀ ꝑ una ađ træ.
Ibi tam̄.ē.ı.uirg træ.Tra.ē.ı.caŕ.q̄ ibi.ē cū.ı.ſeruo.7 ıı.
uilti 7 ıı.borđ.Olim 7 m̄ uał.x.ſoliđ.
Idē Rainald teñ *ARGENTEL*.Briſmar teneƀ T.R.E.7 geldƀ
ꝑ una v̄ træ.Tra.ē.ııı.caŕ.Ibi ſt.ıı.caŕ.7 ııı.uilti 7 vı.borđ.
Olim.xx.ſoliđ.Modo uał.xv.ſoliđ.
Idē teñ de com̄ *HALTONE*.Herald teneƀ T.R.E.7 geldƀ ꝑ una
virg træ.Ibi tam̄.ē una hida.Tra.ē.x.caŕ.Ibi ſt.ıııı.caŕ
7 vıı.ſerui.7 x.uilti 7 x.borđ.7 xı.ađ paſturæ.7 xıı.ađ ſiluæ.
Olim.xı.ſoliđ.Modo uał.xxx.ſoliđ.
Idē teñ *PILETONE*.Merleſuain teneƀ T.R.E.7 geldƀ ꝑ una
uirg træ.Ibi tam̄.ē dim hida.Tra.ē.vı.caŕ.Ibi ſt.ııı.caŕ.
7 ııı.ſerui.7 vıı.uilti 7 vıı.borđ.7 c.ađ paſturæ.7 xı.ađ ſiluæ

122 b Olı.xxx.ſoł.M uał.xx.ſoliđ.

Idē Rainald teñ *KEMOR*.Briſmar teneƀ T.R.E.7 geldƀ
ꝑ uno ferling.Ibi tam̄.ē una v̄ træ.Tra.ē.ıı.caŕ.Ibi.ē.ı.caŕ.
cū.ı.uilto 7 ııı.borđ.7 x.ađ ſiluæ.7 x.ađ paſturæ.
★ Olim 7 modo uał.x.ſoliđ.
Iđ teñ *LANGVER*.Grim teneƀ T.R.E.7 geldƀ ꝑ uno ferling.
Ibi tam̄.ē una v̄ træ.Tra.ı.caŕ.Ibi ſt.ıı.borđ cū.ı.ſeruo.7 x.ađ
ſiluæ.Valet.ıı.ſoliđ.

13 PENHAWGER. Aelmer held it before 1066 and paid tax for 1 v. of land; 1 h. there, however. Land for 16 ploughs; in lordship 1 plough; 4 slaves; 1 v.
    11 villagers and 30 smallholders with 7 ploughs. & 3 v.
    Pasture, 30 acres; woodland, 4 acres.   256
Formerly 60s; value now 30s.   a 3

14 MAKER from the Count. Edward held it before 1066 and paid tax for 1 v. of land; 1 h. there, however. Land for 8 ploughs; 3 ploughs L there; 4 slaves;
    6 villagers and 8 smallholders.   256
    Pasture, 60 acres.   b 1
Formerly 30s; value now 20s.

15 TREDINNICK? Algar held it before 1066 and paid tax for 1 acre of land; 1 v. of land there, however. Land for 1 plough, which is there, with 1 slave;   L
    2 villagers and 2 smallholders.   256
Value formerly and now 10s. 2 cows; 20 sheep.   b 2

16 Reginald also holds **TREGANTLE.** Brictmer held it before 1066, and paid tax for 1 v. of land. Land for 3 ploughs; 2 ploughs there. 256
    3 villagers and 6 smallholders.   b 3
Formerly 20s; value now 15s. 40 sheep.   L

17 He also holds **HALTON** from the Count. Earl Harold held it before 1066, and paid tax for 1 v. of land; 1 h. there, however. Land for 10 ploughs; 4 ploughs there. 7 slaves.   257
    10 villagers and 10 smallholders.   a 1
    Pasture, 40 acres; woodland, 12 acres.   L
Formerly 40s; value now 30s. 2 cattle; 6 pigs; 40 sheep; 10 goats; 1 cob.

18 He also holds **PILLATON.** Merleswein held it before 1066 and paid tax L for 1 v. of land; ½ h. there, however. Land for 6 ploughs; 3 ploughs E there; 3 slaves.
    7 villagers and 7 smallholders.   257
    Pasture, 100 acres; woodland, 40 acres.   a 2
Formerly 30s; value now 20s. 2 cattle; 30 sheep; 10 goats.

19 Reginald also holds **TREMOAN?** Brictmer held it before 1066, and 122 b paid tax for 1 f; 1 v. of land there, however, Land for 2 ploughs; L 1 plough there, with E
    1 villager and 3 smallholders.   257
    Woodland, 10 acres; pasture, 10 acres.   a 3
Value formerly and now 5s.   2 cattle; 4 pigs; 30 sheep.

  He also holds
20 LEWARNE. Grim held it before 1066 and paid tax for
    1 f; 1 v. of land there, however. Land for 1 plough.   257
    2 smallholders with 1 slave.   b1
    Woodland, 10 acres.
Value 2s.

Id̄ ten̄ *KEHAVOC* . Brismar teneb̄ T.R.E.⁊ geldb̄ ꝑ uno ferling.
Ibi tam̄ . ē una v̄ træ.Tra.ii.car̄.Ibi.ē.i.car̄ ⁊ ii.borđ.⁊ v.ac̄ pa
sturæ.Olı̄ ⁊ m̄ uat.v̄.soliđ.

Id̄ ten̄ *PÆNBAV* . Aluric teneb̄ T.R.E.⁊ geldb̄ ꝑ uno agro træ.
Tra.ē.iii.car̄.q̄ ibi st̄.⁊ iiii.serui.⁊ vi.uiłłi ⁊ vi.borđ.⁊ iii.ac̄ p̄ti.
⁊ vi.ac̄ siluæ.⁊ xxx.ac̄ pasturæ.Olim ⁊ modo uat.xxx.soliđ.

Id̄ ten̄ *KEVERIM*.Leueron teneb̄ T.R.E.⁊ geldb̄ ꝑ uno ferling.
Ibi tam̄.ē.i.v̄ træ,Tra.iii.car̄.Ibi st̄.ii.car̄ ⁊ dimiđ.cū.i.seruo.
⁊ v.uiłłi ⁊ v.borđ.⁊ x.ac̄ siluæ.⁊ lx.ac̄ pasturæ.Vat.x.sot.

Id̄ ten̄ *NIWETON*. Aluric teneb̄ T.R.E.⁊ geldb̄ ꝑ una v̄ træ.
Ibi tam̄.ē dim̄ hida.Tra.vi.car̄.Ibi st̄.ii.car̄.⁊ iii.serui.
⁊ iii.uiłłi ⁊ xii.borđ.⁊ xii.ac̄ pasturæ.Olı̄.xxx.sot.M̄ uat.xx,sot.

Idē ten̄ *PEDELEFORD*.Chinestan teneb̄ T.R.E.⁊ geldb̄ pro
una virḡ træ.Tra.ē.vi.car̄.Ibi st̄.ii.car̄.cū.i.seruo,⁊ iii.uiłłi
⁊ iii.borđ.⁊ c.ac̄ pasturæ.⁊ v.ac̄ siluæ.Olı̄.xx.sot.M̄ uat.xv.sot.

Id̄ ten̄ *BICHETONE*.Chinestan teneb̄ T.R.E.⁊ geldb̄ ꝑ uno ferling
Ibi tam̄.ē una v̄ træ.Tra.ii.car̄.Ibi st̄.ii.serui.⁊ iiii.borđ
⁊ x.ac̄ pasturæ.⁊ xv.ac̄ siluæ.Olı̄.v.soliđ.Modo uat.iii.soliđ.

Id̄ ten̄ *AISSETONE*.Aluric teneb̄ T.R.E.⁊ geldb̄ ꝑ una v̄ træ.
Ibi tam̄.ē dim̄ hida.Tra.ē.ii.car̄.Ibi st̄.iiii.borđ cū dimiđ car̄.
⁊ una ac̄ pasturæ.Silua.vi.q̄ᷧ lḡ.⁊ iii.q̄ᷧ lat̄.Vat.x.soliđ.

21 TREHAWKE. Brictmer held it before 1066 and paid tax for 1 f;   E
1 v. of land there, however. Land for 2 ploughs; 1 plough there.   257
    2 smallholders.   b 2
    Pasture, 5 acres.
Value formerly and now 5s. 5 cattle; 3 pigs; 60 sheep.

22 PENPOLL. Aelfric held it before 1066 and paid tax for 1 acre of land.
Land for 3 ploughs, which are there; 4 slaves.   1 acre of land there.   L
    6 villagers and 6 smallholders.   257
    Meadow, 3 acres; woodland, 6 acres; pasture, 30 acres.   b 3
Value formerly and now 30s. 5 cattle; 15 pigs; 60 sheep; 1 cob.

23 TREFRIZE? Leofrun held it before 1066 and paid tax for 1 f; 1 v.
of land there, however. Land for 3 ploughs; 2½ ploughs there, with   L
1 slave.   257
    5 villagers and 5 smallholders.   b 4
    Woodland, 10 acres; pasture, 60 acres.
Value 10s.

24 NEWTON (Ferrers). Aelfric held it before 1066 and paid tax for 1 v.
of land; ½ h. there, however. Land for 6 ploughs; 2 ploughs there;   L
3 slaves.   258
    3 villagers and 12 smallholders.   a 1
    Pasture, 12 acres.
Formerly 30s; value now 20s. 5 cattle; 40 sheep; 10 goats.

25 APPLEDORE. Cynestan held it before 1066 and paid tax for 1 v. of
land. Land for 6 ploughs; 2 ploughs there, with 1 slave.   L
    3 villagers and 3 smallholders.   258
    Pasture, 100 acres; woodland, 5 acres.   a 2
Formerly 20s; value now 15s. 20 sheep; 5 pigs; 4 goats.

26 BICTON. Cynestan held it before 1066 and paid tax for 1 f; 1 v. of   E
land there, however. Land for 2 ploughs; 2 slaves.   L
    4 smallholders.   258
    Pasture, 10 acres; woodland, 15 acres.   a 3
Formerly 5s; value now 3s.

27 ASHTON. Aelfric held it before 1066 and paid tax for 1 v. of
land; ½ h. there, however. Land for 2 ploughs.   L
    4 smallholders with ½ plough.   E 258
    Pasture, 1 acre; woodland, 6 f. long and 3 f. wide.   b 1
Value 10s. 3 cattle; 2 pigs.

Id ten *NIWETONE*. Aluric teneƀ T.R.E. 7 geldƀ ꝑ una v́ t́ræ.
Ibi tam̄.ē una hida. T́rą. VIII. car̄. Ibi sƚ. x. uiƚƚi 7 xx. borđ.
cū. I. car̄. 7 III. ſerui. 7 dimiđ leūu paſturæ. Silua. II. leū l͠g. 7 una
q́rent lat́. Olim. xL. ſoƚ. Modo uaƚ. xxx. ſolid.

Id ten *LANDER*. Saulf teneƀ T.R.E. 7 geldƀ ꝑ uno ferling. Ibi
tam̄.ē una v́ t́ræ. T́ra. I. car̄. q̄ ibi.ē cū. I. ſeruo 7 I. uiƚƚo 7 III. borđ.
Ibi. VIII. ac̄ p̄ti. 7 xxx. ac̄ paſturæ. Olim 7 modo uaƚ. v. ſolid.

Id ten *RICHAN*. Wallo teneƀ T.R.E. 7 geldƀ ꝑ uno ferling.
Ibi.ē tam̄ una v́ t́ræ. T́ra.ē. II. car̄. Ibi sƚ. II. ſerui. 7 II. borđ.
7 x. ac̄ paſturæ. Olim. x. ſoƚ. Modo uaƚ. III. ſolid.

Id ten *LANGENEWIT*. Briƈtric teneƀ T.R.E. 7 geldƀ ꝑ uno
ferling. Ibi tam̄.ē una v́ t́ræ. T́ra.ē. II. car̄. Ibi sƚ. VIII. borđ
7 III. ſerui. 7 x. ac̄ ſiluæ. 7 v. ac̄ paſturæ. Olī. x. ſoƚ. M̄ uaƚ. v. ſolid.

Id ten *KEWILLEN*. Alric teneƀ T.R.E. 7 geldƀ ꝑ dimiđ
ferling. Ibi tam̄.ē un̄ ferling t́ræ. T́ra.ē. I. car̄. Ibi sƚ. II.
ſerui. Olim 7 modo uaƚ. II. ſolid.

Id ten *CAER*. Briſmar teneƀ T.R.E. 7 geldƀ ꝑ uno ferling. Ibi
tam̄.ē una v́ t́ræ. T́ra. II. car̄. Ibi sƚ. III. ſerui. 7 v. ac̄ paſturæ.
7 XII. ac̄ ſiluæ. Olim. xxv. ſolid. Modo uaƚ. v. ſolid.

Ricarđ ten de comite *CVDAWOID*. Aluuįn teneƀ T.R.E. 7 geldƀ
ꝑ. I. hida. T́ra.ē. XII. car̄. In dn̄io sƚ. IIII. car̄. 7 XII. ſerui. 7 xv.
uiƚƚi 7 xx. borđ. cū. v. car̄. Ibi. Lx. ac̄ ſiluæ. Paſturą. v. leū
l͠g. 7 II. leū lat́. Olim. c. ſolid. Modo uaƚ. xL. ſolid.

Ricarđ teń *POLESCAT*. Alnod teneƀ T.R.E. 7 geldƀ ꝑ uno
ferling. Ibi tam̄ sƚ. II. ferlings t́ræ. T́ra.ē. I. car̄. Ibi sƚ. III.
borđ. 7 xL. ac̄ paſturæ. Olim 7 modo uaƚ. xxx. denaŕ.

28 NEWTON (Ferrers). Aelfric held it before 1066 and paid tax for 1v. E
of land; 1 h. there, however. Land for 8 ploughs. 258
    10 villagers and 20 smallholders with 1 plough; 3 slaves. b 2
    Pasture, ½ league; woodland, 2 leagues long and 1 f. wide.
Formerly 40s; value now 30s.

29 LANDREYNE? Saewulf held it before 1066, and paid tax for 1 f;
however, 1 v. of land there. Land for 1 plough, which is there, L
with 1 slave and 261
    1 villager and 3 smallholders. b 2
    Meadow, 8 acres; pasture, 30 acres.
Value formerly and now 5s.

30 TRECAN. Wallo held it before 1066, and paid tax for 1 f; 1 v. of
land there, however. Land for 2 ploughs. 2 slaves. 229
    2 smallholders. a 4
    Pasture, 10 acres. E
Formerly 10s; value now 3s.

31 LANGUNNETT. Brictric held it before 1066, and paid tax for 1 f;
1 v. of land there, however. Land for 2 ploughs. 229
    8 smallholders and 3 slaves. b 1
    Woodland, 10 acres; pasture, 5 acres.
Formerly 10s; value now 5s.

32 TREVELYAN. Alric held it before 1066, and paid tax for ½ f.
1 f. of land there, however. Land for 1 plough. 2 slaves. 229
Value formerly and now 2s. E b 2

33 GEAR. Brictmer held it before 1066, and paid tax for 1 f; 1 v. of
land there, however. Land for 2 ploughs. 3 slaves. 225
    Pasture, 5 acres; woodland, 12 acres. b 1
Formerly 25s; value now 5s.

5,3

1 **Richard** holds COSAWES from the Count. Alwin held it before 1066, E
and paid tax for 1 h. Land for 12 ploughs. In lordship 4 ploughs;
12 slaves; 1v. 224
    15 villagers and 20 smallholders with 5 ploughs   & 3v. b 3
    Woodland, 60 acres; pasture, 5 leagues long and 2 leagues wide.
Formerly 100s; value now 40s. 20 unbroken mares; 17 cattle; 13 pigs; 240 wethers.

2 Richard holds POLSCOE. Alnoth held it before 1066, and paid tax for
1 f. 2 f. of land there, however. Land for 1 plough. 228
    3 smallholders. a 3
    Pasture, 40 acres.
Value formerly and now 30d.

Id ten THERSENT. Aluuin teneb T.R.E.7 geldb p.1.hida
Ibi tam st.11.hidæ.Tra.e.x11.car. In dnio st.11.car.7 v1.
ferui.7 v.uitti 7 x1.bord cu.v.car.Ibi paftura,111,leu lg.
7 11.leu lat.Silua.1.leu lg.7 dimid leu lat.
Olim.xxx.folid.Modo uat,xx,folid.
Id ten BVCHENT,Briftuald teneb T.R.E,7 geldb p uno
ferling.Ibi tam.e una v træ,Tra,e,11,car.Ibi.e dimid car.
7 1111.bord.7 xx.ac pafturæ.7 xx,ac filuæ.
Olim 7 modo uat,111,folid.

122 c

Ide Ricard ten de com CROFTEDEDOR.Colo teneb T.R.E.
7 geldb p dim hida.Ibi tam.e hida 7 dimid.Tra.e.x.
car.Ibi st.1111.car.7 11.ferui.7 v1.uitti 7 v11.bord.7 xx.
ac pafturæ.7 x11.ac filuæ.Oli.xl.fot.m uat.xxv.folid.
Ide ten LAVREDOCH.Aluric teneb T.R.E.7 geldb p 111.v træ.
Ibi tam.e una hida.Tra.v111.car.Ibi st.111.car.7 1111.ferui.
7 1111.uitti 7 x.bord.7 xxx.ac pafturæ.7 xl.ac filuæ.
Olim.xxx.folid.Modo uat.xxv.folid.
Ide ten LANSALHVS.Almar teneb T.R.E.7 geldb p una v
træ.Ibi tam.e.1.hida.Tra.v.car.Ibi st.11.car 7 111.ferui.
7 11.uitti 7 11.bord.7 xxx.ac pafturæ.Oli 7 modo uat.x.folid.
Ricard ten de comite TIWARDRAI.Colo teneb T.R.E.7 geldb
p una hida.Ibi tam st.11.hidæ.Tra.x11.car.In dnio st.1111.
car.7 v11.ferui.7 v111.uitti 7 xv111.bord cu.111.car.Ibi.v1.ac filuæ.
7 c.ac pafturæ.Olim.1111.lib.modo uat.xl.folid.

3 He also holds TREZANCE. Alwin held it before 1066, and paid tax
for 1 h. 2 h. there, however. Land for 12 ploughs. In lordship
2 ploughs; 6 slaves; 1 v.
    5 villagers and 11 smallholders with 5 ploughs & 3 v.   228
    Pasture, 3 leagues long and 2 leagues wide; woodland, 1 league   b 1
      long and ½ league wide.
Formerly 30s; value now 20s. 3 cattle; 1 wild mare; 35 sheep; 8 goats.

4 He also holds BOSENT. Brictwold held it before 1066, and paid
tax for 1 f. 1 v. of land there, however. Land for 2 ploughs; ½   L
plough there.
    4 smallholders.   228
    Pasture, 20 acres; woodland, 20 acres.   b 2
Value formerly and now 3s. 16 sheep.

5 Richard also holds CARTUTHER from the Count. Cola held it   122 c
before 1066, and paid tax for ½ h. 1½ h. there, however.
Land for 10 ploughs; 4 ploughs there; 2 slaves.   L
    6 villagers and 7 smallholders.   228
    Pasture, 20 acres; woodland, 12 acres.   b 3
Formerly 40s; value now 25s. 2 cattle; 60 sheep.

6 He also holds LANREATH. Aelfric held it before 1066, and paid
tax for 3 v. of land; 1 h. there, however. Land for 8 ploughs;   E
3 ploughs there; 4 slaves.   L
    4 villagers and 10 smallholders.   229
    Pasture, 30 acres; woodland, 40 acres.   a 1
Formerly 30s; value now 25s. 3 cattle; 60 sheep.

7 He also holds LANSALLOS. Aelmer held it before 1066, and paid
tax for 1 v. of land; 1 h. there, however. Land for 5 ploughs;
2 ploughs there; 3 slaves.   L
    2 villagers and 2 smallholders.   229
    Pasture, 30 acres.   a 2
Value formerly and now 10s. 3 cattle; 3 pigs; 34 sheep; 5 goats.

8 Richard holds TYWARDREATH from the Count. Cola held it before
1066, and paid tax for 1 h; 2 h. there, however. Land for 12
ploughs; in lordship 4 ploughs; 7 slaves; 1 v.   247
    8 villagers and 18 smallholders with 3 ploughs & the rest of the land.   a 2
    Woodland, 6 acres; pasture, 100 acres.
Formerly £4; value now 40s. 11 cattle; 12 pigs; 200 sheep.

Id ten *BODEWITGHI*. Aluric teneƀ T.R.E.7 geldƀ ꝓ dim hida. Ibi tam.ē.I.hida. Tra.VII.car.7 tot ibi st.7 IX.serui.7 X.uitti 7 XXII.bord.7 una leū pasturæ. Olī.XL.solid. Modo ual.XXX.sol.

Idē ten *BODEWORGOIN*. Aluuin teneƀ T.R.E.7 geldƀ ꝓ.III. virg træ. Ibi tam.ē.I.hida. Tra.X.car. Ibi st.III.car.7 IIII. serui.7 IIII.uitti 7 XII.bord.7 IIII.ac̄ siluæ.7 CC.ac̄ pasturæ. Olim.LX.sol. Modo ual.XXX.solid.

Idē ten *TICOITH*. Godric teneƀ T.R.E.7 geldƀ ꝓ una virg træ. Tra.ē.V.car. Ibi st.III.car.7 V.serui.7 IIII.uitti 7 VIII.bord. 7 VIII.ac̄ siluæ.7 XL.ac̄ pasturæ. Olī.XXX.sol. M̊ ual.XX.solid.

Idē ten *GHIVAILE*. Godric teneƀ T.R.E.7 geldƀ ꝓ dimid hida. Ibi tam.ē una hida. Tra.VI.car. Ibi st.V.car.7 VIII.serui. 7 V.uitti 7 XIII.bord.7 V.ac̄ siluæ.7 C.ac̄ pasturæ. Olim.XL.solid. Modo ual.XXX.solid.

Idē ten *POLDVH*. Aluuin teneƀ T.R.E.7 geldƀ ꝓ.I.hida. Tra.ē.X.car. Ibi st.V.car.7 VIII.serui.7 VIII.uitti.7 XIIII. bord.7 XV.ac̄ siluæ. Pastura.III.leū lḡ.7 una leū lat. Olim.XL.sol. Modo ual.XXX.solid.

Idē ten *WODERON*. Aluuin teneƀ T.R.E.7 geldƀ ꝓ una virg træ. Ibi tam.ē dimid hida. Tra.III.car. Ibi.ē car 7 dim. 7 II.serui.7 II.uitti 7 IIII.bord.7 LX.ac̄ siluæ. Pastura.V.leū lḡ.7 una leū lat. Olī.XX.solid. Modo ual.X.solid.

Idē ten *KEVERBIN*. Aluuin teneƀ T.R.E.7 geldƀ ꝓ dimid virg træ. Ibi tam.ē una v træ. Tra.III.car. Ibi.ē car 7 dimid. 7 II.serui 7.II.uitti 7 III.bord.7 II.ac̄ siluæ.7 XX.ac̄ pasturæ Olim.X.solid. Modo ual.V.solid.

He also holds

9 BODIGGO. Aelfric held it before 1066, and paid tax for ½ h; 1 h. there, however. Land for 7 ploughs; as many there; 9 slaves.
  10 villagers and 22 smallholders.
  Pasture, 1 league.
  Formerly 40s; value now 30s. 11 cattle; 3 pigs; 80 sheep.

10 BODRUGAN. Alwin held it before 1066, and paid tax for 3 v. of land; 1 h. there, however. Land for 10 ploughs; 3 ploughs there; 4 slaves.
  4 villagers and 12 smallholders.
  Woodland, 4 acres; pasture, 200 acres.
  Formerly 60s; value now 30s. 1 cob; 6 pigs; 40 sheep; 20 goats.

11 TUCOYSE. Godric held it before 1066, and paid tax for 1 v. of land. Land for 5 ploughs; 3 ploughs there; 5 slaves.
  4 villagers and 8 smallholders.
  Woodland, 8 acres; pasture, 40 acres.
  Formerly 30s; value now 20s. 2 cattle; 40 sheep; 20 goats.

12 GOVILEY. Godric held it before 1066, and paid tax for ½ h; 1 h. there, however. Land for 6 ploughs; 5 ploughs there; 8 slaves.
  5 villagers and 13 smallholders.
  Woodland, 5 acres; pasture, 100 acres.
  Formerly 40s; value now 30s. 9 cattle; 8 pigs; 232 sheep.

13 POLSUE. Alwin held it before 1066, and paid tax for 1 h. Land for 10 ploughs; 5 ploughs there; 8 slaves.
  8 villagers and 14 smallholders.
  Woodland, 15 acres; pasture, 3 leagues long and 1 league wide.
  Formerly 40s; value now 30s. 10 pigs; 100 sheep; 10 goats.

14 GOODERN. Alwin held it before 1066, and paid tax for 1 v. of land; ½ h. there, however. Land for 3 ploughs; 1½ ploughs there; 2 slaves.
  2 villagers and 4 smallholders.
  Woodland, 60 acres; pasture, 5 leagues long and 1 league wide.
  Formerly 20s; value now 10s. 5 cattle; 20 sheep; 10 goats.

15 TREVERBYN. Alwin held it before 1066, and paid tax for ½ v. of land; 1 v. of land there, however. Land for 3 ploughs; 1½ ploughs there; 2 slaves.
  2 villagers and 3 smallholders.
  Woodland, 2 acres; pasture, 20 acres.
  Formerly 10s; value now 5s.

Idē teñ *BRETHEI*. Aïlbriht teneb T.R.E.7 geldb ꝑ.ıı.ferlings.
Tra.ē.ıııı.car̄.Ibi.ē.car̄ 7 dim̄.7 v.ſerui.7 v.bord.7 xx.ac̄
paſturæ.Olī.xx.ſolid.Modo ual.x.ſolid.

Idē teñ *LISNESTOCH*. Aïlbric teneb T.R.E.7 geldb ꝑ uno fer
ling.Tra.v.car̄.Ibi ſt.ıı.car̄.7 ıı.ſerui.7 ıııı.bord.7 una ac̄
ſiluæ.7 xx.ac̄ paſturæ.Olī.xv.ſot.modo ual.x.ſolid.

Idē Ricard teñ *WICH*. Colo teneb T.R.E.7 geldb ꝑ.dimid.
hida.Ibi tam̄.ē.ı.hida.Tra.vıı.car̄.Ibi ſt.ııı.car̄.7 ıııı.
ſerui.7 vı.uilli 7 x.bord.7 ıı.ac̄ ſiluæ.7 Paſtura.ı.leū lḡ.7 tntd
lat.Olī.xx.ſolid.Modo ual.xxx.ſolid.

Idē teñ *PENHALVN*. Erneis teneb T.R.E.7 geldb ꝑ dimid
hida.Ibi tam̄.ē hida 7 dim̄.Tra.x.car̄.Ibi ſt.vı.car̄.7 vı.
ſerui.7 vııı.uilli 7 xxıı.bord.7 vı.ac̄ ſiluæ.Paſtura.ı.leū lḡ.
7 tntd.lat.Olim.xL.ſolid.Modo ual.xxx.ſolid.

Idē teñ *DONECHENIV*. Merleſuain teneb T.R.E.7 geldb
ꝑ una hida.Ibi tam̄ ſt.ıı.hidæ.Tra.ē.xıı.car̄.Ibi ſt.x.
car̄.7 x.ſerui.7 x.uilli 7 xx.bord.Paſtura.ı.leū lḡ.7 tntd
lat.Olim.Lx.ſolid.Modo ual.xL.ſolid.

Idē teñ *OTRHAM*. Eduui teneb T.R.E.7 geldb ꝑ dimid hida.
Ibi tam̄.ē una hida.Tra.vı.car̄.Ibi ſt.ıııı.car̄.7 vı.ſerui.

122 d

7 vı.uilli 7 vııı.bord.Paſturæ.ı.leū lḡ 7 lat.Olī.xxx.ſot.m̄ ual *7 xx.ſolid.*

Idē Ricard teñ *HAMOTEDI*. Alric teneb T.R.E.7 geldb ꝑ dimid
hida.Ibi tam̄.ē.ı.hida.Tra.vı.car̄.Ibi ſt.ıııı.car̄.7 ııı.ſerui.
7 ıııı.uilli 7 vııı.bord.7 ıı.ac̄ ſiluæ.7 Paſtura.v.leū lḡ.7 ıı.leū
lat.Olī.xL.ſot.Modo ual.xxx.ſolid.

16 BURTHY. Albert held it before 1066, and paid tax for 2 f. Land
for 4 ploughs; 1½ ploughs there; 5 slaves.
    5 smallholders.
    Pasture, 20 acres.
Formerly 20s; value now 10s. 6 cattle; 4 pigs; 60 sheep.

                                                           L
   248
   b 1

17 LANESCOT. Albert held it before 1066, and paid tax for 1 f. Land
for 5 ploughs; 2 ploughs there; 2 slaves.
    4 smallholders.
    Woodland, 1 acre; pasture, 20 acres.
Formerly 15s; value now 10s. 4 cattle; 2 pigs; 40 sheep; 12 goats.

 L
 248
 b 2

18 Richard also holds WEEK (St. Mary). Cola held it before 1066, and
paid tax for ½ h.; 1 h. there, however. Land for 8 ploughs; 3
ploughs there; 4 slaves.
    6 villagers and 10 smallholders.
    Woodland, 2 acres; pasture, 1 league long and as wide.
Formerly 20s; value now 30s. 2 cattle; 8 pigs; 40 sheep; 15 goats.

 L
 259
 a 1
 E

19 He also holds PENHALLYM. Erneis held it before 1066, and paid
tax for ½ h; 1½ h. there, however. Land for 10 ploughs; 6
ploughs there; 6 slaves.
    8 villagers and 22 smallholders.
    Woodland, 6 acres; pasture, 1 league long and as wide.
Formerly 40s; value now 30s. 9 cattle; 2 pigs; 80 sheep; 20 goats.

 L
 259
 a 2

20 He also holds DOWNINNEY. Merleswein held it before 1066, and
paid tax for 1 h; 2 h. there, however. Land for 12 ploughs;
10 ploughs there; 10 slaves.
    10 villagers and 20 smallholders.
    Pasture, 1 league long and as wide.
Formerly 60s; value now 40s. 4 unbroken mares; 12 cattle; 5 pigs; 80 sheep.

 L
 259
 a 3

21 He also holds OTTERHAM. Edwy held it before 1066, and paid tax
for ½ h; 1 h. there, however. Land for 6 ploughs; 4 ploughs
there; 6 slaves.
    6 villagers and 8 smallholders.
    Pasture, 1 league long and wide.
Formerly 30s; value now 20s. 5 cattle; 40 sheep.

 L
 259
 b 1
 122 d

22 Richard also holds HAMATETHY. Alric held it before 1066, and
paid tax for ½ h; 1 h. there, however. Land for 6 ploughs;
4 ploughs there; 3 slaves.
    4 villagers and 8 smallholders.
    Woodland, 2 acres; pasture, 5 leagues long and 2 leagues wide.
Formerly 40s; value now 30s. 6 unbroken mares; 6 cattle; 40 sheep; 6 goats.

 L
 259
 b 2

Idē ten CHILCOIT. Colo teneƀ T.R.E. 7 geldƀ ᵽ una hida 7 dimiđ.
Tra.ē.x.caŕ.Ibi sŧ.III.caŕ.7 III.ſerui.7 VI.uiłłi 7 VIII.borđ
7 xx.ãc ſiluæ.7 XL.ãc paſturæ.Olĩ.XL.ſoł.M̊ uał.xx.ſoliđ.

Idē ten KAWISCOIT.Merleſuain teneƀ T.R.E.7 geldƀ ᵽ una
hida.Ibi tãm sŧ.II.hidæ.Ţra.xII.caŕ.Ibi sŧ.VI.caŕ.7 VIII.
ſerui.7 VIII.uiłłi 7 IX.borđ.7 moliñ redđ.II.ſoliđ.7 xx.ãc
ſiluæ.7 L.ãc paſturæ.Olĩ.xxx.ſoliđ.Modo uał.xxv.ſoliđ.

Idē ten TEWARDEVI.Britnod teneƀ T.R.E.7 geldƀ ᵽ dim ᵈⁱᵃ
ferling træ.Ibi tãm.ē una v̄ træ.Tra.I.caŕ.Ibi.ē un
uiłłs 7 II.borđ.7 xxx.ãc paſturæ.Olĩ.v.ſoł.Modo uał.II.ſoł.

Idē ten LANDELECH.Alnod teneƀ T.R.E.7 geldƀ ᵽ una
virg træ.Ibi tãm.ē dimiđ hida.Ţra.ē.v.caŕ.Ibi.ē.I.caŕ.
7 II.ſerui.7 II.uiłłi 7 v.borđ.7 x.ãc paſturæ.
Olim.xv.ſoliđ.Modo uał.x.ſoliđ.

Idē ten LVDVHA.Aluuin teneƀ T.R.E.7 geldƀ ᵽ.I.hida.
Ibi tãm sŧ.III.hidæ.Tra.xv.caŕ.ℓ xxx.caŕ.Ibi.III.hidæ.
Ibi sŧ.xII.caŕ 7 IX.ſerui.7 xIIII.uiłłi 7 xL.borđ.7 ccc.ãc
paſturæ.Olim.c.ſoliđ.Modo uał.Lx.ſoliđ.

Idē ten CHELENOCH.Godric teneƀ T.R.E.7 geldƀ ᵽ dimiđ
hida.Ibi tãm.ē.I.hida.Tra.vIII.caŕ.Ibi sŧ.v.caŕ.7 v.
ſerui.7 x.borđ.7 vI.uiłłi.7 c.ãc paſturæ.
Olim.xxx.ſoliđ.Modo uał.xx.ſoliđ.

TVRSTIN ten de comite KELAND.Toiſuuald teneƀ T.R.E.
7 geldƀ ᵽ una v̄ træ.Ibi tãm.ē.I.hida.Tra.ē.v.caŕ.Ibi sŧ
III.caŕ.7 IIII.ſerui.7 II.uiłłi 7 vI.borđ.7 III.leū paſturæ lḡ.
7 II.leū'łat.Olim.xxx.ſoliđ.Modo uał.xxv.ſoliđ.

He also holds

23 COLQUITE. Cola held it before 1066, and paid tax for 1½ h. Land   L
for 10 ploughs; 3 ploughs there; 3 slaves.   259
    6 villagers and 8 smallholders.   b 3
    Woodland, 20 acres; pasture, 40 acres.
Formerly 40s; value now 20s. 4 cattle; 8 pigs; 60 sheep.

24 TREVISQUITE. Merleswein held it before 1066, and paid tax for   L
1 h; 2 h. there, however. Land for 12 ploughs; 6 ploughs there;
8 slaves.   260
    8 villagers and 9 smallholders.   a 1
    A mill which pays 2s; woodland, 20 acres; pasture, 50 acres.
Formerly 30s; value now 25s. 5 cattle; 5 pigs; 100 sheep.

25 TRETHEVY. Brictnoth held it before 1066, and paid tax for ½ f.
of land; 1 v. of land there, however. Land for 1 plough.   260
    1 villager and 2 smallholders.   a 2
    Pasture, 30 acres.
Formerly 5s; value now 2s.

26 LANDULPH. Alnoth held it before 1066, and paid tax for 1 v.
of land; ½ h. there, however. Land for 5 ploughs; 1 plough   L
there; 2 slaves.   260
    2 villagers and 5 smallholders.   a 3
    Pasture, 10 acres.
Formerly 15s; value now 10s. 13 sheep.

27 LUDGVAN. Alwin held it before 1066, and paid tax for 1 h; 3 h.   E
there, however. Land for 15 ploughs or 30 ploughs. 3 h. 12   L
ploughs there; 9 slaves.   260
    14 villagers and 40 smallholders.   a 4
    Pasture, 300 acres.
Formerly 100s; value now 60s. 27 unbroken mares; 22 cattle; 17 pigs; 140 sheep.

28 KELYNACK. Godric held it before 1066, and paid tax for ½ h;   L
1 h. there, however. Land for 8 ploughs; 5 ploughs there; 5   260
slaves.   b 1
    10 smallholders and 6 villagers.
    Pasture, 100 acres.
Formerly 30s; value now 20s. 2 unbroken mares; 6 cattle; 1 pig; 25 sheep.

5,4

1 **Thurstan** holds TRELAN from the Count. Tortwald held it before   E
1066, and paid tax for 1 v. of land; 1 h. there, however. Land   L
for 5 ploughs; 3 ploughs there; 4 slaves.   224
    2 villagers and 6 smallholders.   a 3
    Pasture, 3 leagues long and 2 leagues wide.
Formerly 30s; value now, 25s. 2 cattle; 40 sheep.

Turſtin ten⁹ de.co. *PENGVARE* . Briſmar teneƀ T.R.E.7 geldƀ
�ariſtin ten⁹ de.co. *PENGVARE* . Briſmar teneƀ T.R.E.7 geldƀ
đp dimiđ ferling.Ibi.ē un⁹ ager.Tra.ɪ.caſ.Ibi ſꝉ.ɪɪ.borđ.7 ɪɪ.
ſerui.7 x.ac̄ ſiluæ.7 vɪɪ.ac̄ paſturæ.Olı̄.x.ſoꝉ.m̄ uaꝉ.ɪɪɪ.ſoꝉ.

Turſtin ten⁹ de.co. *CHENOWEN* . Vlnod teneƀ T.R.E.7 geldƀ
đp uno ferling.Ibi.ē tam̄.ɪ.uirg træ.Tra.ɪɪ.caſ.Ibi.ē dim
caſ.cū.ɪ.ſeruo 7 ɪɪ.borđ.7 xɪɪ.ac̄ ſiluæ.7 xx.ac̄ paſturæ.
Olim 7 modo uaꝉ.v.ſoliđ.

Idē ten de.co. *NANTVAT* .Briſmar teneƀ T.R.E.7 geldƀ pro
dimiđ ferling.Ibi tam̄.ē una virg træ.Tra.ɪɪ.caſ.Ibi ſꝉ.ɪɪ.
ſerui cū.ɪ.borđ.7 vɪ.ac̄ paſturæ.Olı̄.ɪɪ.ſoꝉ.M̊ uaꝉ.xɪɪ.den.

Idē ten de co. *KEWINEDOI* .Merleſuain teneƀ T.R.E.
7 geldƀ đp uno ferling.Ibi tam̄.ē una v træ.Tra.ē.ɪɪ.caſ.
Ibi.ē una caſ.7 ɪɪ.ſerui.cū.ɪ.uiꝉꝉo 7 ɪɪ.borđ.7 xv.ac̄ ſiluæ.
Olim.v.ſoliđ.Modo uaꝉ.ɪɪɪ.ſoliđ.

Turſtin ten⁹ de.co. *SANGVILAND* .Eduui teneƀ T.R.E.7 geldƀ
đp uno ferling.Ibi tam̄.ē una v træ.Tra.ɪɪɪ.caſ.Ibi eſt
dimiđ caſ.7 ɪɪ.ſerui.7 ɪɪ.uiꝉꝉi.7 xxx.ac̄ paſturæ.
Olim.vɪɪ.ſoliđ.Modo uaꝉ.v.ſoliđ.

Idē ten *WILEVVRDE* .Cheniſi teneƀ T.R.E.7 geldƀ đp dim
ferling.Ibi.ē tam̄ una virg træ.Tra.ē.ɪɪ.caſ.Ibi.ē.ɪ.caſ
cū.ɪ.ſeruo.7 ɪɪ.uiꝉꝉi 7 vɪ.borđ.7 ɪɪɪɪ.ac̄ ſiluæ.7 c.ac̄ paſturæ.
Olim.vɪɪ.ſoliđ.Modo uaꝉ.v.ſoliđ.

Idē ten *TREVERBET* .Eduuin⁹ teneƀ T.R.E.7 geldƀ đp.ɪɪɪ.fer
lings.Ibi tam̄.ē.ɪ.hida.Tra.ɪɪɪ.caſ.Ibi ſꝉ.ɪɪ.caſ.7 vɪɪ.ſerui.

2 Thurstan holds PENCARROW from the Count. Brictmer held it
before 1066, and paid tax for ½ f; 1 acre there.
Land for 1 plough.
   2 smallholders and 2 slaves.
   Woodland, 10 acres; pasture, 7 acres.
Formerly 10s; value now 3s.

L
233
a 3

3 Thurstan holds TRENEWEN? from the Count. Wulfnoth held it
before 1066, and paid tax for 1 f; 1 v. of land there, however.
Land for 2 ploughs; ½ plough there, with 1 slave.
   2 smallholders.
   Woodland, 12 acres; pasture, 20 acres.
Value formerly and now 5s.

L
234
a 2

4 He also holds 'LANTIVET' from the Count. Brictmer held it before
1066, and paid tax for ½ f; 1 v. of land there, however.
Land for 2 ploughs, 2 slaves, with
   1 smallholder.
   Pasture, 6 acres.
Formerly 2s; value now 12d.

236
b 2

5 He also holds TRENDERWAY? from the Count. Merleswein held it
before 1066, and paid tax for 1 f; 1 v. of land there, however.
Land for 2 ploughs; 1 plough there; 2 slaves, with
   1 villager and 2 smallholders.
   Woodland, 15 acres.
Formerly 5s; value now 3s. 2 pigs; 15 sheep.

L
236
b 3

6 Thurstan holds ST. JULIOT from the Count. Edwy held it before
1066, and paid tax for 1 f; 1 v. of land there, however.
Land for 3 ploughs; ½ plough there; 2 slaves.
   2 villagers.
   Pasture, 30 acres.
Formerly 7s; value now 5s. 2 cows.

L
238
b 4

He also holds

7 WILLSWORTHY. Cynesi held it before 1066, and paid tax for ½ f;
1 v. of land there, however. Land for 2 ploughs; 1 plough there,
with 1 slave.
   2 villagers and 6 smallholders.
   Woodland, 4 acres; pasture, 100 acres.
Formerly 7s; value now 5s. 10 sheep.

E
239
a 1

8 TREBARFOOTE. Edwin held it before 1066, and paid tax for 3 f;
1 h. there, however. Land for 3 ploughs; 2 ploughs there;
7 slaves.

L
239
a 2

7 vi . bord . 7 xl . ac pasturæ . Oli 7 modo ual . xx . solid.

Idē ten TALGAR . Eduuin teneb T.R.E. 7 geldb p uno ferling.
Ibi . ē tam dimid hida . Tra . iii . car . Ibi . ii . uilli 7 vi . bord
hnt . i . car . 7 xx . ac pasturæ . Oli 7 m ual . v . solid.

Idē ten AMAL . Grim teneb T.R.E. 7 geldb . p . ii . ferlings . Ibi
tam . ē dimid hida . Tra . iii . car . Ibi . ē . i . car . 7 iiii . bord . 7 v.
serui . 7 xx . ac pasturæ . Olim . x . solid . Modo ual . vi . solid.

123 a

Idē Turstin ten de . com CARNETONE . Brihferd teneb
T.R.E. 7 geldb p uno ferling . Ibi tam ē . i . virg træ.
Tra . ē . ii . car . Ibi st . vi . bord . 7 iiii . serui . 7 x . ac siluæ.
7 c . ac pasturæ . Olim . x . solid . Modo ual . x . solid.

Idē ten ARGANLIS . Brismer teneb T.R.E. 7 geldb p uno
ferling . Ibi . ē tam di|hida . Tra . ē . iii . car . Ibi . ē dimid car.
7 vii . bord cū . i . seruo . 7 x . ac siluæ . 7 una leu pasturæ
Olim . xx . solid . Modo ual . ii . solid.

Idem ten BOTHARDER . Grim teneb T.R.E. 7 geldb p una
uirg træ . Ibi tam . ē una hida . Tra . ē . viii . car . Ibi st . iiii.
car . 7 vii . serui . 7 x . uilli 7 xxiiii . bord . 7 xx . ac siluæ . 7 xxx.
ac pasturæ . Olim . xxxv . solid . Modo . ual . xx . solid.

Idē ten KELWI . Aluuard teneb T.R.E. 7 geldb p una v
træ . Ibi tam . ē dim hida . Tra . ē . iiii . car . Ibi st . ii . car . 7 iii.
serui . 7 iii . uilli 7 vi . bord . 7 xx . ac siluæ . 7 ccc . ac pasturæ.
Olim . xxv . solid . Modo ual . xv . solid.

6 smallholders.
Pasture, 40 acres.
Value formerly and now 20s. 1 cow; 3 pigs.

9 MINSTER. Edwin held it before 1066, and paid tax for 1 f; ½ h.
there, however. Land for 3 ploughs.
   2 villagers and 6 smallholders have 1 plough.
   Pasture, 20 acres.
Value formerly and now 5s.

239
a 3

10 AMBLE. Grim held it before 1066, and paid tax for 2 f; ½ h.
there, however. Land for 3 ploughs; 1 plough there.
   4 smallholders and 5 slaves.
   Pasture, 20 acres.
Formerly 10s; value now 6s.

L
239
a 4

11 Thurstan also holds CARADON from the Count. Brictferth
held it before 1066, and paid tax for 1 f; 1 v. of land there,
however. Land for 2 ploughs.
   6 smallholders and 4 slaves.
   Woodland, 10 acres; pasture, 100 acres.
Formerly 10s; value now 10s. 6 sheep; 5 goats.

123a
L
245
a 4

E

He also holds

12 ARRALLAS. Brictmer held it before 1066, and paid tax for 1 f;
½ h. there, however. Land for 3 ploughs; ½ plough there.
   7 smallholders with 1 slave.
   Woodland, 10 acres; pasture, 1 league.
Formerly 20s; value now 2s. 1 cow; 6 pigs; 12 sheep; 6 goats.

L
249
b 2

13 BODARDLE. Grim held it before 1066, and paid tax for 1 v. of
land; 1 h. there, however. Land for 8 ploughs; 4 ploughs
there, 7 slaves.
   10 villagers and 24 smallholders.
   Woodland, 20 acres; pasture, 30 acres.
Formerly 35s; value now 20s. 2 cobs; 1 bull; 17 sheep.

L
249
b 3

14 TRELOWTH. Alfward held it before 1066, and paid tax for 1 v. of
land; ½ h. there, however. Land for 4 ploughs; 2 ploughs
there; 3 slaves.
   3 villagers and 6 smallholders.
   Woodland, 20 acres; pasture, 300 acres.
Formerly 25s; value now 15s. 2 cows; 2 pigs; 20 sheep; 10 goats.

L
250
a 1

Idem ten ꞌTᴿᴇᴛʜᴀᴄ. Alric teneb T.R.E.꞉7 geldb ꝑ una

virg ꞌꞌtræ. Ibi tam̃ . ẽ . ɪ . hida . Tꞌra . vɪɪ . car̃ . Ibi sꞇ̃ . ɪɪ . car̃ꞌ.

7 vɪ . ſerui. 7 ɪɪɪɪ . uiħi 7 vɪɪɪ . borđ. 7 xʟ . ãc̃ paſturæ.

Olim . xx . ſoliđ . Modo uaꞁ . xv . ſoliđ.

Iđẽ ten ꞌꞰᴇᴡᴏʀᴏᴄ. Alric teneb T.R.E. 7 geldb ꝑ dimiđ

uirg ꞌꞌtræ. Ibi tam̃ . ẽ . ɪ . hida . Tꞌra . ẽ . v . car̃ . Ibi . ẽ . ɪ . car̃.

7 ɪɪ . ſerui. 7 ɪɪ . uiħi 7 vɪɪɪ . borđ. 7 xx . ãc̃ ſiluæ. 7 ʟx . ãc̃ paſturæ.

Olim . x . ſoliđ . Modo uaꞁ . v . ſoliđ.

Iđẽ ten ꞌEɢʟᴇsʜᴏs . Herald comes⁹ teneb T.R.E. 7 geldb ꝑ uno

ferling. Ibi . ẽ tam̃ . ɪ . uirg ꞌtræ . Tꞌra . ɪɪ . car̃ . Ibi . ẽ dimiđ

car̃ꞌ. 7 ɪɪɪ . ſerui. 7 ɪɪɪ . borđ 7 xx . ãc̃ paſturæ. Oliꞌ 7 m̊ uaꞁ . x . ſoꞁ.

Turſtin⁹ ten ꞌde . co . ꞌᴡᴏʀᴇsʟɪɴ . Dodo teneb T.R.E. 7 geldb

ꝑ una v ꞌtræ. Ibi tam̃ . ẽ una hida . Tꞌra . ẽ . v . car̃ . Ibi . ẽ una

car̃ 7 vɪɪ . ſerui. 7 xvɪ . borđ. 7 ɪɪ . ãc̃ ſiluæ minutæ. 7 c . ãc̃

paſturæ. Olim . xxv . ſoliđ . Modo uaꞁ . xv . ſoliđ.   ☞

Hᴀᴍᴇʟɪɴ ten ꞌde comite ᴄᴀʀɪᴏʀɢᴇʟ . Eduui teneb T.R.E꞉

7 geldb ꝑ uno ferling. Tꞌra . ẽ . ɪɪɪ . car̃ꞌ. Ibi sꞇ̃ . ɪɪ . car̃ꞌ. 7 ɪɪɪɪ . borđ.

7 vɪ . ãc̃ ſiluæ. 7 c . ãc̃ paſturæ. Olim. xv . ſoliđ. M̊ uaꞁ . x . ſoꞁ.

Hᴀᴍᴇʟɪɴ ten ꞌde . co . ᴍɪᴅᴇʟᴛᴏɴᴇ . Aluuin teneb T.R.E.

7 geldb ꝑ . ɪɪ . hiđ 7 dimiđ . Ibi sꞇ̃ tam̃ . v . hidæ . Tꞌra . xx . car̃ꞌ.

Ibi sꞇ̃ . vɪɪɪ . car̃ . 7 vɪɪ . ſerui. 7 xɪɪɪɪ . uiħi 7 xx . borđ 7 vɪ . ãc̃ ſiluæ.

7 c . ãc̃ paſturæ. Olim. ʟx . ſoliđ . Modo uaꞁ . ʟ . ſoliđ.

Idem Ham̃ ten ꞌꞌʟᴇɢᴇ . Aluuin⁹ teneb T.R.E. 7 geldb ꝑ . ɪ . hida

7 dimiđ . Ibi tam̃ sꞇ̃ . ɪɪɪ . hidæ. Tꞌra . xv . car̃ . Ibi sꞇ̃ . vɪ . car̃ꞌ. 7 vɪ . ſerui.

7 vɪɪɪ . uiħi 7 xɪɪ . borđ. 7 x . ãc̃ ſiluæ. 7 xxx . ãc̃ paſturæ.

Olim. xʟ . ſoliđ. Modo uaꞁ. xxx . ſoliđ.

15 TRETHEAKE. Alric held it before 1066, and paid tax for 1 v. of land; 1 h. there, however. Land for 7 ploughs; 2 ploughs there; 6 slaves.
    4 villagers and 8 smallholders.
    Pasture, 40 acres.
Formerly 20s; value now 15s. 30 sheep; 1 cow; 2 goats.

L
250
a 2

16 TREWORRICK. Alric held it before 1066, and paid tax for ½ v. of land; 1 h. there, however. Land for 5 ploughs; 1 plough there, 2 slaves.
    2 villagers and 8 smallholders.
    Woodland, 20 acres; pasture, 60 acres.
Formerly 10s; value now 5s. 1 cow; 30 sheep; 3 goats.

L
250
a 3

17 PHILLEIGH. Earl Harold held it before 1066, and paid tax for 1 f; 1 v. of land there, however. Land for 2 ploughs; ½ plough there; 3 slaves.
    3 smallholders.
    Pasture, 20 acres.
Value formerly and now 10s.

L
250
b 1

18 Thurstan holds GURLYN from the Count. Doda held it before 1066, and paid tax for 1 v. of land; 1 h. there, however.
Land for 5 ploughs; 1 plough there; 7 slaves.
    16 smallholders.
    Underwood, 2 acres; pasture, 100 acres.
Formerly 25s; value now 15s. 4 unbroken mares; 2 cobs; 1 cow; 30 sheep.

E
L
255
b 1

† *5, 4, 19 & 20 are entered in the opposite column, after 5, 5, 17 & 5, 5, 22,*
directed to their proper place by transposition signs.

5,5

1 **Hamelin** holds 'CRAWLE' from the Count. Edwy held it before 1066, and paid tax for 1 f. Land for 3 ploughs; 2 ploughs there.
    4 smallholders.
    Woodland, 6 acres; pasture, 100 acres.
Formerly 15s; value now 10s. 1 cow.

L
224
b 1

2 Hamelin holds MILTON from the Count. Alwin held it before 1066, and paid tax for 2½ h; 5 h. there, however.
Land for 20 ploughs; 8 ploughs there; 7 slaves.
    14 villagers and 20 smallholders.
    Woodland, 6 acres; pasture, 100 acres.
Formerly 60s; value now 50s. 10 cattle; 6 pigs; 60 sheep; 12 goats.

L
232
a 3
E

3 Hamelin also holds LEE. Alwin held it before 1066, and paid tax for 1½ h; 3 h. there, however. Land for 15 ploughs; 6 ploughs there; 6 slaves.
    8 villagers and 12 smallholders.
    Woodland, 10 acres; pasture, 30 acres.
Formerly 40s; value now 30s. 6 cattle; 4 pigs; 40 sheep.

L
232
b 1

Idē teñ *Boietone*. Alnod teneb̃ T.R.E. 7 geldb̃ p una virg̃ træ.
Ibi tam̃.ē dimid̃ hida.Tra.ē. IIII. car̃. Ibi st̃. II. car̃.7 III. ſerui.
7 II. uitti 7 III. bord̃.7 v. ac̃ ſiluæ.7 LX. ac̃ paſturæ.
Olim. xx. ſolid̃. Modo uat. xv. ſolid̃.

Idē teñ *Maronecirche*. Brodre teneb̃ T.R.E.7 geldb̃ p uno
ferling 7 dimid̃.Ibi tam̃.ē una v̆ træ.Tra.ē. II.car̃. Ibi.ē. I. car̃
cū. I. ſeruo.7 I. uitto 7 II. bord̃.7 xx. ac̃ paſturæ.
Olim. x. ſolid̃.Modo uat. vi.ſolid̃.

Idē teñ *Orcert*.Sauuin teneb̃ T.R.E.7 geldb̃ p. II. ferlings
7 dim̃. Ibi tam̃.ē dimid̃ hida. Tra. III. car̃. Ibi st̃. II. car̃. cū. I.
ſeruo.7 I. uitto 7 v. bord̃.7 II. ac̃ ſiluæ.7 xx. ac̃ paſturæ.
Olim. xx. ſolid̃. Modo uat. xv. ſolid̃.

Idē teñ *Wadefeste*. Siuuard teneb̃ T.R.E.7 geldb̃ p una
virg̃ træ 7 dimid̃. Ibi tam̃.ē una hida. Tra. vi, car̃. Ibi st̃. IIII.
car̃.7 III. ſerui. cū. I. uitto 7 v. bord̃.7 xv. ac̃ ſiluæ.7 c. ac̃ pa
ſturæ. Olim 7 modo uat. xx. ſolid̃.

Idē teñ *Torne*. Vluric teneb̃ T.R.E.7 geldb̃ p dim̃ v̆ træ.
Ibi tam̃ ē una v̆ træ.Tra. I. car̃; Ibi st̃. IIII; bord̃ cū. I. ſeruo.
7 xx. ac̃ paſturæ.Olim 7 modo uat. II.ſolid̃.

Hamelin teñ de.co: *Recharedoc*.Goduin teneb̃ T.R.E.
7 geldb̃ p. I. hida.Ibi tam̃ st̃. II. hidæ. Tra. xv. car̃. Ibi st̃. IIII.
car̃ 7 dimid̃.7 vi.ſerui.7 vii. uitti 7 xvi. bord̃.7 vi. ac̃ ſiluæ.
Paſtura. III. leū lg̃.7 II. leū lat: Oli. LX. ſot. m̃ uat:XL. ſolid̃.

Idē teñ *Kewallen*. Briſtric teneb̃ T.R.E.7 geldb̃ p: I. agro.
Tra. II.car̃. Ibi.ē. I. car̃.7 II.ſerui. cū. I. uitto 7 II. bord̃.7 x. ac̃
paſturæ. Olim. v. ſolid̃.Modo uat. III.ſolid̃.

He also holds

4 BOYTON. Alnoth held it before 1066, and paid tax for 1 v. of
land; ½ h. there, however. Land for 4 ploughs; 2 ploughs
there; 3 slaves.

    2 villagers and 3 smallholders.

    Woodland, 5 acres; pasture, 60 acres.

Formerly 20s; value now 15s. 6 cattle; 20 sheep.

L
232
b 2

5 MARHAMCHURCH. Broder held it before 1066, and paid tax for
1½ f. 1 v. of land there, however. Land for 2 ploughs; 1 plough
there, with 1 slave and

    1 villager and 2 smallholders.

    Pasture, 20 acres.

Formerly 10s; value now 6s. 20 sheep.

L
232
b 3

6 (Week) ORCHARD. Saewin held it before 1066, and paid tax for 2½
f; ½ h. there, however. Land for 3 ploughs; 2 ploughs there, with
1 slave and

    1 villager and 5 smallholders.

    Woodland, 2 acres; pasture, 20 acres.

Formerly 20s; value now 15s. 5 cattle; 10 sheep.

L
232
b 4

7 WADFAST. Siward held it before 1066, and paid tax for 1½ v. of
land; 1 h. there, however. Land for 6 ploughs; 3 ploughs
there; 3 slaves, with

    1 villager and 5 smallholders.

    Woodland, 15 acres; pasture, 100 acres.

Value formerly and now 20s. 8 cattle; 30 sheep; 6 pigs; 15 goats.

L
233
a 1

8 THORNE. Wulfric held it before 1066, and paid tax for ½ v. of land.
1 v. of land there, however. Land for 1 plough.

    3 smallholders with 1 slave.

    Pasture, 20 acres.

Value formerly and now 2s. 20 sheep; 4 goats.

123 b
L
233
a 2

9 Hamelin holds ROSECRADDOC from the Count. Godwin held it
before 1066, and paid tax for 1 h; 2 h. there, however.
Land for 15 ploughs; 4½ ploughs there; 6 slaves.

    7 villagers and 16 smallholders.

    Woodland, 6 acres; pasture, 3 leagues long and 2 leagues wide.

Formerly 60s; value now 40s. 4 unbroken mares; 7 cattle; 20 sheep; 10 goats.

L
234
a 4

He also holds

10 TREWOLLAND. Brictric held it before 1066, and paid tax for 1 acre.
Land for 2 ploughs; 1 plough there; 2 slaves, with

    1 villager and 2 smallholders.

    Pasture, 10 acres.

Formerly 5s; value now 3s. 2 cattle; 2 pigs; 37 sheep.

L
234
b 1

Idē ten̄ KELOEN . Eduui teneɓ T.R.E.7 geldɓ ꝓ uno agro.
Tra.ē.ıı.car̄.Ibi.ē dimiđ car̄ 7 ıı.ſerui.7 x.ac̄ ſiluæ.7 x.ac̄
paſturæ.Olim.v.ſoliđ.Modo ual.ııı.ſoliđ.
Idē ten̄ KEGEMELIN.Eduui teneɓ T.R.E.7 geldɓ ꝓ uno agro.
Tra.ē.ıı.car̄.Ibi.ē.ı.car̄.7 ıı.borđ cū.ı.ſeruo.7 x.ac̄ paſturæ.
Olim 7 modo ual.v.ſoliđ.
Idē ten̄ TREDHAC. Aluuin teneɓ T.R.E.7 geldɓ ꝓ una v træ.
Tra.ē.ıı.car̄.Ibi.ē car̄ 7 dimiđ.cū.ı.ſeruo.7 ı.uilło 7 vıı.borđ
7 xx.ac̄ paſturæ.Olim.xv.ſoliđ.Modo ual.x.ſoliđ.
Idem ten̄ DOVENOT.Bric̄tric teneɓ T.R.E.7 geldɓ ꝓ.ı.ferling.
Ibi tam̄.ē una v træ.Tra.ı.car̄.Ibi.ē dimiđ car̄ cū.ı.ſeruo.
7 ıı.borđ.7 v.ac̄ ſiluæ.7 xL.ac̄ paſturæ.Oli.x.ſoł.m̄ ual.v.ſoł.
Hamelin ten̄ de.co.PENPEL.Bric̄tric teneɓ T.R.E.7 geldɓ
ꝓ una v træ.Ibi tam̄.ē dimiđ hida.Tra.ē.ııı.car̄.Ibi.ē una
car̄.7 ıı.ſerui.7 ıııı.borđ.7 ıı.ac̄ ſiluæ.7 Lx.ac̄ paſturæ.
Olim.x.ſoliđ.Modo ual.v.ſoliđ.
Idē ten̄ KEMODRET.Goduin teneɓ T.R.E.7 geldɓ ꝓ.ı.hida.
Ibi tam̄.ē hida 7 dimiđ.Tra.xv.car̄.Ibi ſt.v.car̄.7 vıı.
ſerui.7 vııı.uilłi 7 xvıı.borđ.7 una ac̄ ſiluæ.Paſtura.ıııı.leū
lḡ.7 ıı.leū lat̄.Olim.Lx.ſoliđ.Modo ual.xL.ſoliđ.
Idē ten̄ KEGOIN.Briſmar teneɓ T.R.E.7 geldɓ ꝓ una v træ.
Ibi tam̄.ē dimiđ hida.Tra.ıııı.car̄.Ibi.ē.ı.car̄ 7 dimiđ
7 ıı.ſerui 7 v.borđ.Paſtura.ı.leū lḡ.7 dimiđ leū lat̄.
Olim.x.ſoliđ.modo ual.vıı.ſoliđ.

11 TRELOWIA. Edwy held it before 1066, and paid tax for 1 acre.
Land for 2 ploughs; ½ plough there; 2 slaves.   E
    Woodland, 10 acres; pasture, 10 acres.   234
Formerly 5s; value now 3s. 10 goats.   b 2

12 TREGAMELLYN. Edwy held it before 1066, and paid tax for 1 acre.
Land for 2 ploughs; 1 plough there.   L 234
    2 smallholders with 1 slave.   b 3
    Pasture, 10 acres.
Value formerly and now 5s. 2 cattle; 6 pigs; 20 sheep.

13 TRETHAKE. Alwin held it before 1066, and paid tax for 1 v. of   E
land. Land for 2 ploughs; 1½ ploughs there, with 1 slave and   L
    1 villager and 7 smallholders.   235
    Pasture, 20 acres.   a 1
Formerly 15s; value now 10s.

14 DAWNA. Brictric held it before 1066, and paid tax for 1 f. 1 v. of
land there, however. Land for 1 plough; ½ plough there, with 1   E
slave.   235
    2 smallholders.   a 2
    Woodland, 5 acres; pasture, 40 acres.
Formerly 10s; value now 5s.

15 Hamelin holds PENPELL from the Count. Brictric held it before 1066,
and paid tax for 1 v. of land; ½ h. there, however.   L
Land for 3 ploughs; 1 plough there; 2 slaves.   250
    4 smallholders.   b 2
    Woodland, 2 acres; pasture, 60 acres.
Formerly 10s; value now 5s. 20 sheep.

16 He also holds TREMODDRETT. Godwin held it before 1066, and paid
tax for 1 h; 1½ h. there, however. Land for 15 ploughs; 5   L
ploughs there; 7 slaves.   250
    8 villagers and 17 smallholders.   b 3
    Woodland, 1 acre; pasture, 4 leagues long and 2 leagues wide.
Formerly 60s; value now 40s. 10 cattle; 12 pigs; 80 sheep.

17 He also holds TREWOON. Brictmer held it before 1066, and paid
tax for 1 v. of land; ½ h. there, however.
Land for 4 ploughs; 1½ ploughs there; 2 slaves.   L 251
    5 smallholders.   a 1
    Pasture, 1 league long and ½ league wide.
Formerly 10s; value now 7s. 5 cattle; 4 pigs; 15 sheep; 10 goats.

⊙ Turſtin ten de.com .*CLVNEWIC* . Wine teneð T.R.E. 7 geldð
ꝑ dimið ferling . Ibi ſt . ii . ac̃ træ . Tra . ii . car̃ . Ibi ſt . ii . borð
cũ . i . ſeruo . 7 iiii . ac̃ ſiluæ . 7 xv . ac̃ paſturæ . Oli . v . ſot . Ṁ uat . iii . ſot.

Hamelin ten de , co . *KEGANMEDAN* . Brictric teneð T.R.E.
7 geldð ꝑ . ii . ferlings . Ibi tã . e dim hida . Tra . ii . car̃ . Ibi
eſt . i . car . cũ . i . ſeruo . 7 iiii . borð . Paſtura . i . leũ lg̃ . 7 dim leũ lat.
Olim . x . ſolið . Modo uat . vii . ſolið . 7 vi . denar.

Idē ten *PENFONTENIO* . Alſi teneð T.R.E. 7 geldð ꝑ una v̄ træ.
Ibi tã . e una hida . Tra . iiii . car̃ . Ibi ſt . ii . car̃ . 7 ii . ſerui.
7 vi . borð . 7 v . ac̃ ſiluæ . 7 x . ac̃ paſturæ . Oli . xx . ſolið . Ṁ uat . x . ſot.

Idē ten *TRENANT* . Briſmar teneð T.R.E. 7 geldð ꝑ una
virg̃ træ . Ibi tã . e . i . hida . Tra . v . car̃ . Ibi ſt . iii . car̃ . 7 iii.
ſerui . 7 vi . borð . 7 x . ac̃ paſturæ . Oli . xx . ſot . m̃ uat . xv . ſot.

Idem ten *KEGAVRAN* . Leuric teneð T.R.E. 7 geldð ꝑ una
ac̃ træ . Tra . i . car̃ . Ibi . e . i . borð cũ . i . ſeruo . 7 xl . ac̃ paſturæ.
Olim 7 modo uat . xii . denar.

Idē ten *BETNECOTE* . Almer teneð T.R.E. 7 geldð ꝑ dim ferling.
Tra . e . i . car̃ . Ibi . e un uitts cũ . i . borð . 7 xl . ac̃ paſturæ.
Olim . v . ſolið . Modo uat . iii . ſolið.

⊙ Turſtin ten de . co . *KIBERTHA* . Vlnod teneð T.R.E. 7 geldð
ꝑ uno ferling . Ibi tã . e dimið hida . Tra . iiii . car̃ . Ibi ſt . iii.
car̃ 7 dimið . 7 ii . uitti 7 vi . borð . Oli 7 modo uat . xv . ſolið.

5,4 *directed to its proper place by transposition signs.*

† 19 Thurstan holds CLINNICK? from the Count. Wine held it before 1066, and paid tax for ½ f; 2 acres of land there. Land for 2 ploughs.
    2 smallholders with 1 slave.
    Woodland, 4 acres; pasture, 15 acres.
    Formerly 5s; value now 3s.

L 231
b 3

5,5

18 Hamelin holds TREGAVETHAN from the Count. Brictric held it before 1066, and paid tax for 2 f; ½ h. there, however. Land for 2 ploughs; 1 plough there, with 1 slave.
    4 smallholders.
    Pasture, 1 league long and ½ league wide.
    Formerly 10s; value now 7s 6d. 20 sheep; 4 goats.

L 251
a 2

He also holds

19 PENVENTINUE. Alfsi held it before 1066, and paid tax for 1 v. of land; 1 h. there, however. Land for 4 ploughs; 2 ploughs there; 2 slaves.
    6 smallholders.
    Woodland, 5 acres; pasture, 10 acres.
    Formerly 20s; value now 10s.

L 251
b 1

20 TRENANCE? Brictmer held it before 1066, and paid tax for 1 v. of land; 1 h. there, however. Land for 5 ploughs; 3 ploughs there; 3 slaves.
    6 smallholders.
    Pasture, 10 acres.
    Formerly 20s; value now 15s. 6 cattle; 30 sheep.

L
251
b 2

21 'TREHAVERNE'. Leofric held it before 1066, and paid tax for 1 acre of land. Land for 1 plough.
    1 smallholder with 1 slave.
    Pasture, 40 acres.
    Value formerly and now 12d.

251
b 3

22 BARNACOTT? Aelmer held it before 1066, and paid tax for ½ f. Land for 1 plough.
    1 villager with 1 smallholder.
    Pasture, 40 acres.
    Formerly 5s; value now 3s.

264
b 4

5,4 *transferred to its proper place by transposition signs.*

20 Thurstan holds TREBARTHA from the Count. Wulfnoth held it before 1066, and paid tax for 1 f; ½ h. there, however. Land for 4 ploughs; 3½ ploughs there.
    2 villagers and 6 smallholders.
    Value formerly and now 15s.

L 264
a 2

Nigellvs ten̄ de comite *Vlnodestone* . Elric teneb̄
T.R.E.7 geldb̄ p̄ dimid̄ hida. Ibi tam̄.ē una hida. Tra.vi.
car̄. Ibi st̄ . iiii . car̄ 7 dimid̄.7 v .ſerui.7 iiii . uiłłi 7 xii . bord̄
7 una ac̄ ſiluæ.7 x . ac̄ paſturæ . Olim 7 modo ual.xx . ſolid̄.
Idem . N . ten̄ *Gverdevalan* . Briſmer teneb̄ T.R.E.

7 geldb̄ p̄ dim̄ hida. Tra .ē.viii . car̄ . Ibi st̄.vi.car̄.7 xii .
ſerui.7 x . uiłłi 7 xxi . bord̄.7 una ac̄ ſiluæ minutæ.7 una
ac̄ p̄ti.7 xx . ac̄ paſturæ. Olim . iiii . lib̄. Modo ual.xl . ſol.
Id̄e Nigel ten̄ de . co . *Kevoet* . Alric teneb̄ T.R.E.7 geldb̄
p̄ dimid̄ hida. Ibi tam̄.ē una hida. Tra .ē.iiii.car̄ . Ibi st̄
ii.car̄ 7 dimid̄.7 v . ſerui.7 iiii . uiłłi 7 vi . bord̄.7 una ac̄
p̄ti.7 xxx.ac̄ paſturæ . Olim . xl . ſolid̄ . Modo ual.xxv . ſol.
Id̄e.N . ten̄ *Rosminvet* . Ednod teneb̄ T.R.E.7 geldb̄
p̄ una virḡ træ . Ibi tam̄.ē dimid̄ hida. Tra.ē.iii . car̄ . ⌐Val
Ibi .ē car̄ 7 dim̄.7 iii . ſerui.7 vi . bord̄.7 xx.ac̄ paſturæ. ⌊ x.ſol.
Id̄e.N . ten̄ *Roscaret* . Aluuin teneb̄ T.R.E.7 geldb̄ pro
una uirḡ træ . Ibi tam st̄ . iii . Virḡ træ. Tra.ē.iiii . car̄.
Ibi st̄ . ii . car̄.7 iiii . ſerui.7 ii . uiłłi 7 v . bord̄.7 una ac̄ p̄ti.
7 x . ac̄ paſturæ . Olim 7 modo ual . xv . ſolid̄.
Id̄e ten̄ *Lancharet* . Aluuold̄ teneb̄ T.R.E. Ibi .ē una
uirḡ træ q̄ nunq̄ geldauit. Tra .ē.ii . car̄ . q̄ ibi st̄.7 ii.ſerui.
7 x . bord̄.7 xxx.ac̄ ſiluæ.7 x . ac̄ paſturæ. ⌐Petroci . +
Olim . xx . ſolid̄ . Modo ual . x . ſol. H̄ terra .ē de honore Ʃ

5,6

1 **Nigel** holds WOOLSTONE from the Count. Alric held it before 1066, and paid tax for ½ h; 1 h. there, however. Land for 6 ploughs; 4½ ploughs there; 5 slaves.
    4 villagers and 12 smallholders.
Woodland, 1 acre; pasture, 10 acres.
Value formerly and now 20s. 5 cattle; 6 pigs; 50 sheep.

L
240
b 4

2 **Nigel** also holds WORTHYVALE. Brictmer held it before 1066, and paid tax for ½ h. Land for 8 ploughs; 6 ploughs there; 12 slaves.
    10 villagers and 21 smallholders.
Underwood, 1 acre; meadow, 1 acre; pasture, 20 acres.
Formerly £4; value now 40s.
    6 unbroken mares; 16 cattle; 2 pigs; 180 sheep; 12 goats.

123 c
E
L
241
a 1

3 **Nigel** also holds TRENUTH? from the Count. Alric held it before 1066, and paid tax for ½ h; 1 h. there, however. Land for 4 ploughs; 2½ ploughs there; 5 slaves.
    4 villagers and 6 smallholders.
Meadow, 1 acre; pasture, 30 acres.
Formerly 40s; value now 25s. 1 unbroken mare; 4 cattle; 8 pigs; 73 sheep.

E
L 241
a 2

4 **Nigel** also holds ROSEBENAULT. Ednoth held it before 1066, and paid tax for 1 v. of land; ½ h. there, however. Land for 3 ploughs; 1½ ploughs there; 3 slaves.
    6 smallholders.
Pasture, 20 acres.
Value 10s; when acquired 20s. 8 cattle; 1 unbroken mare; 100 sheep.

L
241
a 3

5 **Nigel** also holds ROSCARROCK? Alwin held it before 1066, and paid tax for 1 v. of land; 3 v. of land there, however.
Land for 4 ploughs; 2 ploughs there; 4 slaves.
    2 villagers and 5 smallholders.
Meadow, 1 acre; pasture, 10 acres.
Value formerly and now 15s. 1 unbroken mare; 4 cattle; 4 pigs; 30 sheep.

L
241
b 1

6 He also holds LANCARFFE. Alfwold held it before 1066. 1 v. of land, which never paid tax. Land for 2 ploughs, which are there; 2 slaves.
    10 smallholders.
Woodland, 30 acres; pasture, 10 acres.
Formerly 20s; value now 10s. 6 cattle; 4 pigs; 47 sheep.
This land is of the Honour of St. Petroc's.

L
241
b2

7 *is placed in the opposite column, after 5,7,13, directed to its proper place by transposition signs.*

Idem.N.ten̄ *KEVAGAV*. Aluuin teneƀ T.R.E.7 geldƀ
p una v̄ træ.Ibi.ē tam̄ dimiđ hida.T̄ra.ē.vɪ.car̄.Ibi sꝯ
ɪɪɪɪ.car̄ 7 dimiđ 7 vɪ.ſerui.7 vɪɪɪ.uiꞇꞇi 7 xvɪɪɪ.borđ.7 una
ac̄ ſiluæ minutæ.Paſtura.ɪɪ.leū l̄g.7 una leū la�.
Olim.xʟ.ſoliđ.Modo uaꞇ.xxx.ſoliđ.
Idē.N.ten̄ *POLEFAND*.Vluric teneƀ T.R.E.7 geldƀ p una
virḡ træ.Ibi.ē tam̄ dimiđ hida.T̄ra.ē.ɪɪɪ.car̄.Ibi sꝯ.ɪɪ.car̄
7 ɪɪɪ.ſerui.7 ɪɪɪ.uiꞇꞇi 7 vɪ.borđ.7 ɪɪ.ac̄ p̄ti.7 una ac̄ ſiluæ.
7 x.ac̄ paſturæ.Olim 7 modo uaꞇ.xv.ſoliđ.
Idē.N.ten̄ *GLOERET*.Saulf teneƀ T.R.E.7 geldƀ p uno ferling.
Ibi tam̄.ē una virḡ træ.T̄ra.ē.ɪɪ.car̄.Ibi.ē.ɪ.car̄ 7 ɪɪ.ſerui.
7 ɪɪ.borđ.7 ɪɪɪɪ.ac̄ ſiluæ.7 x.ac̄ paſturæ.Olī 7 m̄ uaꞇ.vɪɪ.ſoliđ.
Jovin̄ ten de comite *ROSCARNAN*.Grifin teneƀ T.R.E.
7 geldƀ p uno ferling træ.T̄ra.ē.ɪɪ.car̄.Ibi.ē dim̄iđ car̄
7 ɪɪ.ſerui.7 ʟx.ac̄ paſturæ.Olim.x.ſoꞇ.Modo uaꞇ.v.ſoliđ.
Idem.Jo.ten̄ *LANTMATIN*.Alfeg teneƀ T.R.E.7 geldƀ
p dimiđ ferling.Ibi.ē un̄ ager træ.T̄ra.ɪ.car̄.q̄ ibi eſt
cū.ɪ.ſeruo.7 ɪɪɪ.borđ.7 ɪɪɪ.ac̄ ſiluæ.Olī.ɪɪɪ.ſoꞇ.M̄ uaꞇ.ɪɪɪɪ.ſoꞇ.
Idē ten̄ *NORTONE*.Almer teneƀ T.R.E.7 geldƀ p una v̄
træ.Ibi tam̄.ē dimiđ hida.T̄ra.ē.v.car̄.Ibi sꝯ.ɪɪɪ.car̄
7 dim̄.7 ɪɪɪ.ſerui.7 ɪɪɪ.uiꞇꞇi 7 v.borđ.7 vɪɪ.ac̄ ſiluæ.7 ʟx.ac̄
paſturæ.Olim.xx.ſoliđ.Modo uaꞇ.xxv.ſoliđ.
Idē teū *MORTVNE*.Briſmer teneƀ T.R.E.7 geldƀ p uno
ferling.Ibi tam̄.ē una v̄ træ.T̄ra.ɪɪɪ.car̄.Ibi sꝯ.ɪɪ.car̄.7 ɪɪ.
ſerui.7 v.borđ.7 xx.ac̄ paſturæ.Olī 7 m̄ uaꞇ.x.ſoliđ.

8 Nigel also holds TREVAGUE. Alwin held it before 1066, and paid   L
tax for 1 v. of land; ½ h. there, however. Land for 6 ploughs; 4½   242
ploughs there; 6 slaves.   b 2
    8 villagers and 18 smallholders.
    Underwood, 1 acre; pasture, 2 leagues long and 1 league wide.
Formerly 40s; value now 30s. 6 unbroken mares; 7 cattle; 12 pigs; 50 sheep.

9 Nigel also holds POLYPHANT. Wulfric held it before 1066, and
paid tax for 1 v. of land; ½ h. there, however. Land for 3 ploughs;   L
2 ploughs there; 3 slaves.   243
    3 villagers and 6 smallholders.   a 1
    Meadow, 2 acres; woodland, 1 acre; pasture, 10 acres.
Value formerly and now 15s. 7 cattle; 30 sheep.

10 Nigel also holds GALOWRAS. Saewulf held it before 1066, and
paid tax for 1 f; 1 v. of land there, however.   L
Land for 2 ploughs; 1 plough there; 2 slaves.   252
    2 smallholders.   b 1
    Woodland, 4 acres; pasture, 10 acres.
Value formerly and now 7s. 2 pigs; 30 sheep.

5,7

1 **Iovin** holds ROSCARNON from the Count. Griffin held it before 1066,
and paid tax for 1 f. of land. Land for 2 ploughs; ½ plough   L
there; 2 slaves.   224
    Pasture, 60 acres.   b 2
Formerly 10s; value now 5s.

2 Iovin also holds LAMETTON. Alfheah held it before 1066, and
paid tax for ½ f; 1 acre of land there. Land for 1 plough,   L
which is there, with 1 slave.   235
    3 smallholders.   a 3
    Woodland, 3 acres.
Formerly 3s; value now 4s. 3 cattle; 20 sheep.

He also holds
3 NORTON. Aelmer held it before 1066, and paid tax for 1 v. of
land; ½ h. there, however. Land for 5 ploughs; 3½ ploughs   L
there; 3 slaves.   237
    3 villagers and 5 smallholders.   a 4
    Woodland, 7 acres; pasture, 60 acres.
Formerly 20s; value now 25s. 10 cattle; 30 sheep.

4 MORETON. Brictmer held it before 1066, and paid tax for 1 f; 1 v. of   L
land there, however. Land for 3 ploughs. 2 ploughs there;
2 slaves.   237
    5 smallholders.   b 2
    Pasture, 20 acres.
Value formerly and now 10s. 8 cattle; 6 pigs; 6 sheep.

Idē teñ *BELLESDONE* . Chitel teneƀ T.R.E. 7 geldƀ ꝓ dimid

ferling. Ibi tañ . ē uñ ferł træ . Tra . ē . I . car̄ . Ibi . ē dim̄ car̄

cū . I . uiłło. 7 II . bord . 7 xx . ac̄ pasturæ . Oli 7 m̄ uał . v . solid.

Idē teñ *PONDESTOCH* . Ghida teneƀ T.R.E. 7 geldƀ ꝓ una

uirg træ . Ibi tañ . ē una hida . Tra . VI . car̄ . Ibi sƚ . II . car̄ .

cū . I . seruo . 7 I . uiłło 7 v . bord . 7 x . ac̄ siluæ . 7 xL . ac̄ pasturæ.

Oli 7 m̄ uał . xx . solid . Ħ terra . ē de Lantloho.

Idē teñ *ROSPERVET* . Brixi teneƀ T.R.E. 7 geldƀ ꝓ . II . ferlings.

Ibi tañ . ē dimid hida . Tra . VI . car̄ . Ibi . ē . I . car̄ 7 dimid.

cū . I . seruo . 7 I . uiłło 7 IIII . bord . 7 ccc . ac̄ pasturæ.

Olim 7 modo uał . xII . solid.

Idem teñ . *TREBLERI* . Brixi teneƀ T.R.E. 7 geldƀ ꝓ uno ferling.

Ibi tañ . ē una virg træ . Tra . II . car̄ . Ibi . ē . I . car̄ . cū . I . seruo.

7 uno uiłło 7 IIII . bord . 7 xL . ac̄ pasturæ.

Olim . v . solid . Modo uał . x . solid.

123 d

Idē . Jo. teñ de . co . *SANWINAS* . Gudda teneƀ . T.R.E.

7 geldƀ ꝓ una virg træ . Ibi tañ . ē dimid hida . Tra . x . car̄.

Ibi sƚ . III . car̄ . 7 III . serui . 7 II . uiłłi 7 VIII . bord . 7 xL . ac̄ pa

sturæ . Olim 7 modo uał . xx . solid.

Idem teñ *LISART* . Brixi teneƀ T.R.E. 7 geldƀ ꝓ uno ferling.

Ibi tañ . ē una virg træ . Tra . II . car̄ . Ibi . ē . I . car̄ . 7 III . bord.

7 Lx . ac̄ pasturæ . Oli . x . solid . Modo uał . v . solid.

Jouin teñ de . co . *KEVRET* . Ipse teneƀ T.R.E. 7 geldƀ ꝓ uno

ferling . Ibi tañ . ē . I . uirg træ . Tra . II . car̄ . Ibi . ē . I . car̄ 7 dim̄.

7 IIII . serui . cū . I . uiłło 7 II . bord . 7 xx . ac̄ pasturæ.

Olim 7 modo uał . xx . solid.

5 BALSDON. Ketel held it before 1066, and paid tax for ½f; 1 f. of land there, however. Land for 1 plough. ½ plough there, with
   1 villager and 2 smallholders.
   Pasture, 20 acres.
Value formerly and now 5s.

      L
    237
    b 3

6 POUNDSTOCK. Gytha held it before 1066, and paid tax for 1 v. of land; 1 h. there, however. Land for 6 ploughs; 2 ploughs there, with 1 slave and
   1 villager and 5 smallholders.
   Woodland, 10 acres; pasture, 40 acres.
Value formerly and now 20s. 10 cattle; 50 sheep.
   This land is of St. Kew's.

      E
      L
    238
    a 1
    101
    a 2

7 TRESPARRETT. Brictsi held it before 1066, and paid tax for 2 f; ½ h. there, however. Land for 6 ploughs; 1½ ploughs there, with 1 slave and
   1 villager and 4 smallholders.
   Pasture, 300 acres.
Value formerly and now 12s. 10 cattle; 30 sheep.

      L
    238
    a 2

8 TREMBLARY. Brictsi held it before 1066, and paid tax for 1 f; 1 v. of land there, however. Land for 2 ploughs; 1 plough there, with 1 slave and
   1 villager and 4 smallholders.
   Pasture, 40 acres.
Formerly 5s; value now 10s. 3 cattle; 30 sheep.

      E
      L
    238
    a 3

9 Iovin also holds ST. GENNYS from the Count. Gytha held it before 1066, and paid tax for 1 v. of land; ½ h. there, however. Land for 10 ploughs; 3 ploughs there; 3 slaves.
   2 villagers and 8 smallholders.
   Pasture, 40 acres.
Value formerly and now 20s. 7 cattle; 40 sheep; 6 goats.

    123 d
      E
      L
    238
    b 1
    101
    a 2

10 He also holds DIZZARD. Brictsi held it before 1066, and paid tax for 1 f; 1 v. of land there, however. Land for 2 ploughs; 1 plough there.
   3 smallholders.
   Pasture, 60 acres.
Formerly 10s; value now 5s. 2 cattle; 12 sheep.

      L
    238
    b 2
      E

11 Iovin holds TRERICE from the Count. He held it himself before 1066, and paid tax for 1 f; 1 v. of land there, however. Land for 2 ploughs; 1½ ploughs there; 4 slaves, with
   1 villager and 2 smallholders.
   Pasture, 20 acres.
Value formerly and now 20s. 2 cows; 40 sheep.

      L
    253
    a 4

Idẽ ten̄ *ḰEVRGEN*. Eiulf teneb̄ T.R.E. 7 geldb̄ p uno ferlig̃ træ. Tra. ii. car̄. Ibi. ē. i. car̄. cū. i. feruo 7 ii. bord̄. 7 xl. ac̄ pafturæ. Oli. iiii. fol. Modo ual. viii. folid.

Idẽ ten̄ *CHORI*. Goduin teneb̄ T.R.E. 7 geldb̄ p dim̄ ferling træ. Tra. ē dim car̄. Ibi. ē un feruus 7 c. ac̄ pafturæ. . Olim. iiii. folid. Modo ual. ii. folid.

+ Nigel ten̄ de com̄ *TREDAVAL*. Aluuold teneb̄ T.R.E. 7 geldb̄ p dim̄ hida. Ibi tam̄. ē una hida. Tra. viii. car̄. Ibi s̄t. vi. car̄. 7 viii. ferui. 7 vii. uil̄ti 7 xx. bord̄. 7 una ac̄ p̄ti. 7 una ac̄ filuæ. Paftura. ii. leū lḡ. 7 tn̄td̄ lat̄. Olim. lx. folid. Modo ual. xl. folid.

Bernervs ten̄ de comite *HORNIECOTE*. Edzi teneb̄ T.R.E. 7 geldb̄ p dimid̄ virg̃. Ibi tam̄. ē una v̄ træ. Tra. ē. iiii. car̄. Ibi. ē car̄ 7 dimid̄ cū. i. feruo. 7 ii. uil̄ti 7 iii. bord̄. 7 x. ac̄ filuæ minutæ. 7 xxx. ac̄ pafturæ. Olim. xx. fol. Modo ual. xii. folid.

Idẽ ten̄ *ALVEVACOTE*. Aluiet teneb̄ T.R.E. 7 geldb̄ p dimid̄ uirg̃ træ. Ibi tam̄ eft uirg̃. Tra. ē. iii. car̄. Ibi eft car̄ 7 dimid̄. cū. i. feruo. 7 i. uil̄to. 7 iii. bord̄. 7 iii. ac̄ filuæ. 7 xxx. ac̄ pafturæ. Olim. xx. folid. Modo ual. xii. folid.

Idẽ ten̄ *WESCOTE*. Vlnod teneb̄ T.R.E. 7 geldb̄ p dimid̄ ferling. Ibi tam̄. ē un ferling. Tra. ē dimid̄ car̄. Ibi s̄t. ii. uil̄ti cū. i. bord̄. 7 xxx. ac̄ pafturæ. Oli. x. fol. M ual. v. fol. Idẽ. ten̄ *ROSCHEL*. Eduui teneb̄ T.R.E. 7 geldb̄ p uno ferling. Ibi tam̄. ē una v̄ træ. Tra. ii. car̄. Ibi. ē. i. car̄. cū. i. feruo. 7 ii. bord̄. 7 v. ac̄ pafturæ. Oli 7 m̄ ual. vii. folid 7 vi. den̄.

12   He also holds TREWORYAN. Aiulf held it before 1066, and paid
tax for 1 f. of land. Land for 2 ploughs; 1 plough there,   L
with 1 slave;
    2 smallholders.   264
    Pasture, 40 acres.   b 2
Formerly 4s; value now 8s. 3 cattle; 20 sheep.

13   He also holds CURRY. Godwin held it before 1066, and paid tax
for ½ f. of land. Land for ½ plough. 1 slave.
    Pasture, 100 acres.   264
Formerly 4s; value now 2s.   b 3

†5,6 *directed to its proper place by transposition signs.*

7   **Nigel** holds TREDAULE from the Count. Alfwold held it before 1066,
and paid tax for ½ h; 1 h. there, however. Land for 8 ploughs;   L
6 ploughs there; 8 slaves.   242
    7 villagers and 20 smallholders.   b 3
    Meadow, 1 acre; woodland, 1 acre; pasture, 2 leagues long
      and as wide.   E
Formerly 60s; value now 40s. 3 unbroken mares; 12 pigs; 10 cattle; 100 sheep.

5,8

1   **Berner** holds HORNACOTT from the Count. Edsi held it before 1066,
and paid tax for ½ v; 1 v. of land there, however.   L
Land for 4 ploughs; 1½ ploughs there, with 1 slave.
    2 villagers and 3 smallholders.   239
    Underwood, 10 acres; pasture, 30 acres.   b 1
Formerly 20s; value now 12s. 10 cattle; 7 pigs; 40 sheep; 10 goats.

He also holds

2   ALVACOTT. Alfgeat held it before 1066, and paid tax for ½ v. of
land; a v. there, however. Land for 3 ploughs; 1½ ploughs   L
there, with 1 slave and   239
    1 villager and 3 smallholders.   b 2
    Woodland, 3 acres; pasture, 30 acres.
Formerly 20s; value now 12s. 8 cattle; 2 pigs; 40 sheep; 8 goats.

3   WESTCOTT? Wulfnoth held it before 1066, and paid tax for ½ f;
1 f. there, however. Land for ½ plough.   E 239
    2 villagers with 1 smallholder.   b 3
    Pasture, 30 acres.
Formerly 10s; value now 5s. 10 cattle; 40 sheep.

4   ROSECARE. Edwy held it before 1066, and paid tax for 1 f; 1 v.
of land there, however. Land for 2 ploughs. 1 plough there,   L
with 1 slave.   240
    2 smallholders.   a 1
    Pasture, 5 acres.
Value formerly and now 7s 6d. 5 cattle; 30 sheep.

Idē ten̄ *TRERIHQC*. Waſo teneƀ T.R.E.⁊ geldƀ ꝑ uno ferling.
Ibi tam̄.ē una virḡ træ.Tra.ɪ.caʀ.Ibi ſt.ɪɪɪ.borđ.⁊ c.ac̄
paſturæ.Olꭵ.v.ſoliđ.Modo ual.ɪɪɪ.ſoliđ.

Idē ten̄ *CRACHENWE*. Eduui teneƀ T.R.E.⁊ geldƀ ꝑ una v̄ træ.
Ibi tam̄.ē dim̄ hida.Tra.ē.ɪɪɪ.caʀ.Ibi.ē.ɪ.caʀ.⁊ ɪɪ.ſerui.
⁊ vɪ.borđ.⁊ ɪɪɪɪ.ac̄ ſiluæ minutæ.⁊ xx.ac̄ paſturæ
Olim.xx.ſoliđ.Modo ual.x.ſoliđ.

Idē ten̄ *ROSLECH*. Eduui teneƀ T.R.E.⁊ geldƀ ꝑ dimiđ,ac̄
træ.Ibi.ē una ac̄ træ tam̄.Tra.ē.ɪ.caʀ.Ibi ſt.ɪɪɪ.borđ cū
dimiđ caʀ.⁊ xxx.ac̄ paſturæ.Olim ⁊ modo ual.v.ſoliđ.

Idē ten̄ *TREWIN*.Eduui teneƀ T.R.E.⁊ geldƀ ꝑ una ac̄ træ.
Ibi.ē una virḡ træ.Tra.ɪ.caʀ.Ibi ſt.ɪɪ.borđ.⁊ xxx.ac̄ pa
ſturæ.Olim.v.ſoliđ.Modo ual.xl.denaʀ.

Idē ten̄ *LANDMANVEL*.Eduui teneƀ T.R.E.⁊ geldƀ ꝑ una
virḡ træ.Ibi tam̄.ē dim̄ hida.Tra.ɪɪɪɪ.caʀ.Ibi.ē caʀ ⁊ dim̄.
⁊ ɪɪ.ſerui.⁊ v.borđ.⁊ xx.ac̄ paſturæ.Olꭵ ⁊ m̄ ual.xv.ſoliđ.

Idē ten̄ *KEGREBRI*.Eduui teneƀ T.R.E.Ibi.ē.ɪ.hida
q̄ nunq̄ geldau.Tra.ē.ɪɪɪɪ.caʀ.Ibi.ē caʀ ⁊ dimiđ.cū.ɪ.
ſeruo ⁊ ɪɪɪɪ.borđ.⁊ xxx.ac̄ paſturæ.Olꭵ.xx.ſol.M̄ ual.x.ſol.
H̄ tra.ē de poſſeſſione S PIÉRAN.

124 a

BRIEND ten̄ de com̄ite *WITEMOT*.Vluiet teneƀ
T.R.E.⁊ geldƀ ꝑ una virḡ træ.Ibi tam̄.ē dim̄ hida.
Tra.ɪɪɪɪ.caʀ.Ibi ſt.ɪɪ.caʀ ⁊ dimiđ ⁊ ɪɪ.ſerui.⁊ ɪɪɪ.uiłłi ⁊ ɪɪɪ.
borđ.⁊ una ac̄ p̄ti.⁊ x.ac̄ paſturæ.Olꭵ.xx.ſol.m̄ ual
Idē ten̄ *WALESBRAV*.Sauuin teneƀ T.R.E.ꝼxv.ſoliđ.
⁊ geldƀ ꝑ dimiđ v̄ træ.Ibi tam̄.ē una virḡ.Tra.ɪɪɪ.caʀ.

5 TREVIGUE. Wace held it before 1066, and paid tax for 1 f; 1 v. of land there, however. Land for 1 plough.
   3 smallholders.
   Pasture, 100 acres.
Formerly 5s; value now 3s.

240
a 2

6 CRACKINGTON. Edwy held it before 1066, and paid tax for 1 v. of land; ½ h. there, however. Land for 3 ploughs; 1 plough there; 2 slaves.
   6 smallholders.
   Underwood, 4 acres; pasture, 20 acres.
Formerly 20s; value now 10s. 4 cattle; 3 pigs; 25 sheep.

L
240
a 3

7 TRESLAY. Edwy held it before 1066, and paid tax for ½ acre of land; 1 acre of land there, however. Land for 1 plough.
   3 smallholders with ½ plough.
   Pasture, 30 acres.
Value formerly and now 5s.

240
a 4

8 TREWEN? Edwy held it before 1066, and paid tax for 1 acre of land; 1 v. of land there. Land for 1 plough.
   2 smallholders.
   Pasture, 30 acres.
Formerly 5s; value now 40d.

240
b 1

9 LAMELLEN. Edwy held it before 1066, and paid tax for 1 v. of land; ½ h. there, however. Land for 4 ploughs; 1½ ploughs there; 2 slaves.
   5 smallholders.
   Pasture, 20 acres.
Value formerly and now 15s. 8 cattle; 60 sheep.

L
240
b 2

10 'GENVER?' Edwy held it before 1066. 1 h. which never paid tax. Land for 3 ploughs; 1½ ploughs there, with 1 slave.
   4 smallholders.
   Pasture, 30 acres.
Formerly 20s; value now 10s. 30 sheep.
   This land is of the possessions of St. Piran's.

L
240
b 3

E

5,9

1 **Brian** holds WIDEMOUTH from the Count. Wulfgeat held it before 1066, and paid tax for 1 v. of land; ½ h. there, however. Land for 4 ploughs; 2½ ploughs there; 2 slaves.
   3 villagers and 3 smallholders.
   Meadow, 1 acre; pasture, 10 acres.
Formerly 20s; value now 15s. 4 cattle; 50 sheep.

124 a

L

241
b 3

2 He also holds WHALESBOROUGH. Saewin held it before 1066, and paid tax for ½ v. of land; 1 v. there, however.

L

Ibi st̄.ii.car̄.cū.i.feruo.7 ii.uilli 7 iii.borð.7 ii.ac̄ p̄ti.

7 x.ac̄ pafturæ.Olim 7 modo ual̄.xv.foliđ.

Idē ten PENFOV.Eddeua teneb̄ T.R.E.7 geldb̄ ᵱ dimiđ v̄

træ.Ibi tam̄.ē una uirg.Tr̄a.ii.car̄.Ibi.ē.i.car̄ cū.i.feruo.

7 ii.borđ.7 ii.ac̄ p̄ti.7 x.ac̄ pafturæ.Oli 7 m̄ ual̄.xx.fol̄.

Briend ten de comite TRENANT.Ailmer teneb̄ T.R.E.

7 geldb̄ ᵱ uno ferling træ.Ibi tam̄.ē dimiđ hida.Tr̄a.iii.car̄.

Ibi.ē.i.car̄ 7 ii.ferui.7 vii˙.borđ.7 ccc.ac̄ pafturæ.

Olim 7 modo ual̄.xxv.foliđ.

Willts ten de comite POCHEHELLE.Aluuard teneb̄ T.R.E.

7 geldb̄ ᵱ dim̄ hida.Ibi tam̄.ē.i.hida.Tr̄a.xvi.car̄.Ibi st̄.v.

car̄.7 ii.ferui.7 viii.uilli 7 xiii.borđ.7 xl.ac̄ filuæ minutæ.

7 c.ac̄ pafturæ.Olim.c.foliđ.Modo ual̄.xl.foliđ.

Alvred ten de comite HILTONE.Sþern teneb̄ T.R.E.7 geldb̄

ᵱ.iii.uirg træ.Ibi tam̄ st̄.ii.hidæ.Tr̄a.ē.x.car̄.Ibi st̄.v.

car̄.7 iii.ferui.7 vii.uilli 7 xi.borđ.7 x.ac̄ filuæ.7 l.ac̄ pafturæ.

Olim.c.foliđ.Modo ual̄.l.foliđ.

Idē ten TIRLEBERE.Sauuin teneb̄ T.R.E.7 geldb̄ ᵱ una virg

7 Ibi tam' st̄.iii.v˙.terre.

træ.|Tr̄a.ē.vii.car̄.Ibi st̄.ii.car̄.7 iii.ferui.7 iii.uilli 7 vii.borđ.

7 viii.ac̄ filuæ minutæ.7 xxx.ac̄ pafturæ.Oli.xl.fol̄.m̄ ual̄

Idē ten BRECELESBEORGE.Aluui teneb̄ T.R.E.ꝉxxx.foliđ.

7 geldb̄ ᵱ dim̄ ferling.Ibi.ē tam̄ dimiđ v̄ træ.Tr̄a.ē.i.car̄.

q̄ ibi.ē cū.i.feruo.7 iiii.ac̄ filuæ.7 x.ac̄ pafturæ.

Olim.x.foliđ.Modo ual̄.vii.fol̄ 7 vi.denar̄.

Land for 3 ploughs; 2 ploughs there, with 1 slave. 242
   2 villagers and 3 smallholders. a 1
   Meadow, 2 acres; pasture, 10 acres.
Value formerly and now 15s. 2 cows; 15 sheep.

3 He also holds PENFOUND. Edeva held it before 1066, and paid tax
for ½ v. of land; 1 v. there, however. Land for 2 ploughs; 1   L
plough there, with 1 slave. 242
   2 smallholders. a 2
   Meadow, 2 acres; pasture, 10 acres.
Value formerly and now 20s.

4 Brian holds 'TRENANCE?' from the Count. Aelmer held it before 1066,
and paid tax for 1 f. of land; ½ h. there, however.   L
Land for 3 ploughs; 1 plough there; 2 slaves. 252
   7 smallholders. b 2
   Pasture, 300 acres.
Value formerly and now 25s. 3 cattle; 40 sheep.

5,10

1 **William** holds POUGHILL from the Count. Alfward held it before   E
1066, and paid tax for ½ h; 1 h. there, however.   L
Land for 16 ploughs; 5 ploughs there; 2 slaves. 233
   8 villagers and 13 smallholders. b 1
   Underwood, 40 acres; pasture, 100 acres.
Formerly 100s; value now 40s. 3 cattle; 60 sheep; 10 goats.

5,11

1 **Alfred** holds HILTON from the Count. Osbern held it before 1066,
and paid tax for 3 v. of land; 2 h. there, however.   L
Land for 10 ploughs; 5 ploughs there; 3 slaves. 233
   7 villagers and 11 smallholders. b 2
   Woodland, 10 acres; pasture, 50 acres.
Formerly 100s; value now 50s. 6 cattle; 2 pigs; 70 sheep; 11 goats.

He also holds.
2 THURLIBEER. Saewin held it before 1066, and paid tax for 1 v. of
land; 3 v. of land there, however. Land for 7 ploughs; 2   L
ploughs there; 3 slaves. 233
   3 villagers and 7 smallholders. b 3
   Underwood, 8 acres; pasture, 30 acres.   E
Formerly 40s; value now 30s. 10 cattle; 7 pigs; 60 sheep; 40 goats.

3 BUTTSBEAR. Alfwy held it before 1066, and paid tax for ½ f; ½ v.
of land there, however. Land for 1 plough, which is there,   E
with 1 slave. 244
   Woodland, 4 acres; pasture, 10 acres. a 1
Formerly 10s; value now 7s 6d. 18 sheep; 8 goats.

Idē teñ *LANDSEV*. Aluric teneƀ T.R.E.7 geldƀ p una v̄ træ
7 dimiđ.Ibi tam̄ st̄.ii.hidæ.Tra.ix.car̄.Ibi st̄.iii.car̄ 7 dim.
7 ii.ſerui.7 iii.uilli.7 xi.borđ.7 xxx.aͨ ſiluæ minutæ.7 l.aͨ
paſturæ.Olim.xx.ſoliđ.Modo ual.xl.ſoliđ.
Idē teñ *ORCET*.Aluric teneƀ T.R.E.7 geldƀ p uno ferling.
Ibi tam̄.ē una v̄ træ.Tra.ii.car̄.q̄ ibi st̄ cū.i.uillo.7 iiii.
borđ 7 ii.ſerui.7 ii.aͨ ſiluæ.7 x.aͨ paſturæ.Olī.xv.ſoliđ.
Modo ual.xii.ſoliđ.
Idē teñ *BORGE*.Algar teneƀ T.R.E.7 geldƀ p dim̄ ferling.
Ibi tam̄.ē una virḡ træ.Tra.iii.car̄.Ibi st̄.ii.car̄.cū.i.ſeruo.
7 ii.uilli 7 ii.borđ.7 v.aͨ ſiluæ minutæ.7 xv.aͨ paſturæ.
Olim.x.ſoliđ.Modo ual.xv.ſoliđ.
Idē teñ *ROSCARET*.Aluuiñ teneƀ T.R.E.7 geldƀ p dimiđ
ferling.Ibi tam̄.ē una virḡ træ.Tra.i.car̄.Ibi st̄.ii.borđ.
Olim.x.ſoliđ.Modo ual.ii.ſoliđ.
Erchenbalđ teñ *BODBRAN*.Alnod teneƀ T.R.E.7 geldƀ
p uno ferling.Ibi tam̄.ē una v̄ træ.Tra.ii.car̄.Ibi.ē dim̄
car̄.7 ii.ſerui.7 ii.uilli.7 xii.aͨ ſiluæ.7 x.aͨ paſturæ
Olim.x.ſoliđ.Modo ual.vii.ſoliđ.7 vi.denar̄.
Idē teñ *AVALDE*.Dodo teneƀ.T.R.E.7 geldƀ p uno terling.
Ibi tam̄.ē una virḡ træ.Tra.iii.car̄.Ibi.ē.i.car̄.7 iii.ſerui.
7 ii.uilli 7 i.borđ.7 lx.aͨ paſturæ.Silua.iii.q̄ʒ lḡ.7 una
q̄ʒ lat̄.Olim.xx.ſoliđ.Modo ual.x.ſoliđ.
Idē teñ *BRET*.Dodo teneƀ T.R.E.7 geldƀ p uno ferling.
Ibi tam̄.ē dimiđ hida.Tra.iii.car̄.Ibi.ē.i.car̄ 7 dimiđ.
7 iii.ſerui.cū.i.uillo 7 v.borđ.7 xl.aͨ paſturæ.
Olim.xx.ſoliđ.Modo ual.xii.ſoliđ 7 vi.denar̄.

4 LAUNCELLS. Aelfric held it before 1066, and paid tax for 1½ v. of
land; 2 h. there, however. Land for 9 ploughs; 3½ ploughs   L
there; 2 slaves.   244
   3 villagers and 11 smallholders.   a 2
   Underwood, 30 acres; pasture, 50 acres.
Formerly 20s; value now 40s. 10 cattle; 12 pigs; 50 sheep; 50 goats.

5 (Cann) ORCHARD. Aelfric held it before 1066, and paid tax for 1 f;
1 v. of land there, however. Land for 2 ploughs, which are there,   L
with   244
   1 villager; 4 smallholders and 2 slaves.   a 3
   Woodland, 2 acres; pasture, 10 acres.
Formerly 15s; value now 12s. 30 sheep; 20 goats.

6 BOROUGH? Algar held it before 1066, and paid tax for ½ f; 1 v. of
land there, however. Land for 3 ploughs; 2 ploughs there, with
1 slave.   244
   2 villagers and 2 smallholders.   L a 4
   Underwood, 5 acres; pasture, 15 acres.
Formerly 10s; value now 15s. 15 cattle; 8 pigs; 45 sheep; 20 goats.

7 ROSCARROCK? Alwin held it before 1066, and paid tax for ½ f; 1 v.
of land there, however. Land for 1 plough.
   2 smallholders.   245
Formerly 10s; value now 2s.   a 2

5,12

1 **Erchenbald** holds BODBRANE. Alnoth held it before 1066, and paid
tax for 1 f; 1 v. of land there, however.   L
Land for 2 ploughs; ½ plough there; 2 slaves.   229
   2 villagers.   a 3
   Woodland, 12 acres; pasture, 10 acres.
Formerly 10s; value now 7s 6d. 1 cow; 2 pigs; 24 sheep; 12 goats.

2 He also holds LEVALSA. Doda held it before 1066, and paid tax
for 1 f; 1 v. of land there, however.   L
Land for 3 ploughs; 1 plough there; 3 slaves.   234
   2 villagers and 1 smallholder.   a 3
   Pasture, 60 acres; woodland, 3 f. long and 1 f. wide.
Formerly 20s; value now 10s. 1 cow; 12 sheep; 1 pig.

3 He also holds BREA. Doda held it before 1066, and paid tax for 1 f;
½ h. there, however. Land for 3 ploughs; 1½ ploughs there; 3   L
slaves, with   255
   1 villager and 5 smallholders.   b 2
   Pasture, 40 acres.
Formerly 20s; value now 12s 6d. 4 cattle; 4 pigs; 25 sheep.

Offers teñ de com̄ *Mingeli*. Alric teneƀ T.R.E. 7 geldƀ
p dimiđ hida. Ibi tam̄ sƚ. ii. hidæ. Tra. xii. car̄. Ibi sƚ. iii. car̄.
7 iiii. ſerui. 7 v. uitti 7 xvi. borđ. 7 viii. ac̄ ſiluæ. Paſtura. i. leu̗
lḡ. 7 dimiđ leū laƚ. Olim. iiii. liƀ. Modo uaƚ. xxx. ſoliđ.

Idē teñ *Bochenod*. Idē teneƀ T.R.E. 7 geldƀ p una v̄ træ. Ibi
tam̄. ē dimiđ hida. Tra. viii. car̄. Ibi. ē. i. car̄. cū. i. ſeruo.
7 ii. uitti 7 vi. borđ. 7 c. ac̄ ſiluæ. 7 xl. ac̄ paſturæ
Olim. xl. ſoliđ. Modo uaƚ. x. ſoliđ.

Idē teñ *Tremeteret*. Eduui teneƀ T.R.E. 7 geldƀ p una
uirg træ. Ibi tam̄. ē dimiđ hida. Tra. vi. car̄. Ibi sƚ car̄. ii.
7 dimiđ. 7 ii. ſerui. 7 iii. uitti 7 ix. borđ. 7 x. ac̄ ſiluæ. 7 xl. ac̄
paſturæ. Olim. lx. ſoliđ. Modo uaƚ. xv. ſoliđ.

Idē teñ *Trenand*. Offerd teneƀ T.R.E. 7 geldƀ p una v̄ træ
Ibi tam̄. ē dimiđ hida. Tra. viii. car̄. Ibi sƚ. ii. car̄. 7 ii. ſerui.
7 iiii. uitti 7 xii. borđ. 7 vi. ac̄ ſiluæ. 7 xl. ac̄ paſturæ
Olim. lx. ſoliđ. Modo uaƚ. xv. ſoliđ.

Idem teñ *Glin*. Ipſe teneƀ T.R.E. 7 geldƀ p una virg træ.
Tra. ē. ii. car̄. Ibi. ē. i. car̄ cū. i. ſeruo. 7 ii. uitti 7 vi. borđ.
7 c. ac̄ ſiluæ. 7 xl. ac̄ paſturæ. Olim. xl. ſoƚ. M uaƚ. x. ſoliđ.

Idē teñ *Bowidoc*. Offers ipſe teneƀ T.R.E. 7 geldƀ p uno
ferling. Tra. ē. ii. car̄. Ibi. ē uñ uitƚs 7 ii. borđ.
Olim. v. ſoliđ. Modo uaƚ. ii. ſoliđ.

Idē teñ *Pennalt*. Ipſe teneƀ T.R.E. 7 geldƀ p dim uirg træ.
Ibi tam̄ ē una v̄ træ. Tra. iiii. car̄. Ibi sƚ. vi. borđ. 7 x.
ac̄ paſturæ. Olim. xx. ſoliđ. Modo uaƚ. iii. ſoliđ.

Idē teñ *Penponte*. Ipſe teneƀ T.R.E. 7 geldƀ p dim hida.
Ibi tam̄. ē una hida. Tra. xvi. car̄. Ibi sƚ. ii. car̄ 7 dimiđ.
7 v. ſerui. 7 iiii. uitti 7 xviii. borđ. 7 lx. ac̄ paſturæ.
Olim. c. ſoliđ. Modo uaƚ. xxv. ſoliđ.

5,13

1 **Osferth** holds MANELY from the Count. Alric held it before 1066, and paid tax for ½ h; 2 h. there, however. Land for 12 ploughs; 3 ploughs there; 4 slaves.
>5 villagers and 16 smallholders.
>Woodland, 8 acres; pasture, 1 league long and ½ league wide.

Formerly £4; value now 30s. 3 cattle; 1 pig; 5 sheep.

124 b
L
229
b 3

He also holds

2 BOCONNOC. He also held it before 1066, and paid tax for 1 v. of land; ½ h. there, however. Land for 8 ploughs; 1 plough there, with 1 slave.
>2 villagers and 6 smallholders.
>Woodland, 100 acres; pasture, 40 acres.

Formerly 40s; value now 10s. 2 unbroken mares; 2 cattle; 20 sheep; 7 goats.

L
229
E b 4

3 TREMADART. Edwy held it before 1066, and paid tax for 1 v. of land; ½ h. there, however. Land for 6 ploughs; 2½ ploughs there; 2 slaves.
>3 villagers and 9 smallholders.
>Woodland, 10 acres; pasture, 40 acres.

Formerly 60s; value now 15s. 15 goats.

L
230
E a 1

4 TRENANT. Osferth held it himself before 1066, and paid tax for 1 v. of land; ½ h. there, however. Land for 8 ploughs; 2 ploughs there; 2 slaves.
>4 villagers and 12 smallholders.
>Woodland, 6 acres; pasture, 40 acres.

Formerly 60s; value now 15s. 2 cows; 2 pigs; 8 goats.

L
230
a 2

5 GLYNN. He held it himself before 1066, and paid tax for 1 v. of land. Land for 2 ploughs; 1 plough there, with 1 slave.
>2 villagers and 6 smallholders.
>Woodland, 100 acres; pasture, 40 acres.

Formerly 40s; value now 10s. 4 unbroken mares; 2 cows; 24 sheep; 7 goats.

L
230
a 3

6 BOWITHICK. Osferth held it himself before 1066, and paid tax for 1 f. Land for 2 ploughs.
>1 villager and 2 smallholders.

Formerly 5s; value now 2s.

243
b 2

7 PENHALT. He held it himself before 1066, and paid tax for ½ v. of land; 1 v. of land there, however. Land for 4 ploughs.
>6 smallholders.
>Pasture, 10 acres.

Formerly 20s; value now 3s.

L
243
b 3

8 PENPONT. He held it himself before 1066, and paid tax for ½ h; 1 h. there, however. Land for 16 ploughs; 2½ ploughs there; 5 slaves.
>4 villagers and 18 smallholders.
>Pasture, 60 acres.

Formerly 100s; value now 25s. 30 sheep.

L
243
b 1

Idē ten *LANTHIEN*. Ipſe teneƀ T.R.E. 7 geldƀ ꝑ una
uirg træ. Ibi tā̃.ē. I. hida. Tra. VIII. car̃. Ibi.ē. I. car̃
7 dimiđ. 7 IIII. ſerui. 7 II. uiłłi 7 VI. borđ. 7 VIII. ac̃ ſiluæ.
7 XX. ac̃ paſturæ. Olim. LX. ſoliđ. Modo uał. XX. ſoliđ.

Idē ten *TREVELIEN*. Bretel teneƀ T.R.E. 7 geldƀ ꝑ uno
ferling. Ibi tā̃ ſt̃. II. ferlings. Tra.ē. II. car̃. Ibi eſt
un uiłłs 7 III. borđ. 7 v. ac̃ paſturæ. Olĩ. x. ſoł. M̃ uał

Offels ten de comite *KELOSCH*. Ipſe teneƀ ⨍ II. ſoliđ.
T.R.E. 7 geldƀ ꝑ una v̄ træ. Ibi tā̃.ē dim̃ hida. Tra
VIII. car̃. Ibi ſt̃. II. car̃ 7 dimiđ. 7 II. ſerui. 7 III. uiłłi
7 XII. borđ. 7 x. ac̃ ſiluæ. 7 L. ac̃ paſturæ.
Olim. LX. ſoliđ. Modo uał. XX. ſoliđ.

Idē ten *KEGRIL*. Alric teneƀ T.R.E. 7 geldƀ ꝑ una
uirg træ. Ibi tā̃.ē. I. hida. Tra.ē. VII. car̃. Ibi ſt̃. II.
car̃ 7 II. ſerui. 7 IIII. uiłłi 7 XVI. borđ. 7 una ac̃ ſiluæ.
7 LX. ac̃ paſturæ. Olim. LX. ſoliđ. Modo uał. XX. ſoliđ.

Odo ten de comite *BOTILED*. Oſulf teneƀ T.R.E. 7 geldƀ
ꝑ una virg træ. Ibi tā̃ ſt̃. II. hidæ. Tra. VIII. car̃. Ibi ſt̃. II.
car̃ 7 dimiđ. 7 IIII. ſerui. 7 IIII. uiłłi 7 XII. borđ. 7 LX. ac̃ ſiluæ.
7 L. ac̃ paſturæ. Olim. XL. ſoliđ. Modo uał. L. ſoliđ.

Idē ten *NIETESTOV*. Godric teneƀ T.R.E. Ibi eſt una hida
ꝗ nunꝗ geldau. Tra. v. car̃. Ibi.ē. I. car̃. 7 III. ſerui. 7 III. uiłłi
7 VI. borđ. 7 LX. ac̃ paſturæ. Olim. XX. ſoliđ. M̃ uał. v. ſoliđ.

Odo ten de. co. *KELVGE*. Briſmar teneƀ T.R.E. 7 geldƀ ꝑ uno
ferling. Ibi tā̃.ē. I. hida. Tra. II. car̃. Ibi.ē. I. car̃. 7 II. ſerui.
cū. I. uiłło 7 II. borđ. 7 vI. ac̃ paſturæ. Olĩ. x. ſoł. M̃ uał. v. ſoliđ.

9 LANTYAN. He held it himself before 1066, and paid tax for 1 v. of
land; 1 h. there, however. Land for 8 ploughs; 1½ ploughs
there; 4 slaves.   L 252
    2 villagers and 6 smallholders.   a 2
    Woodland, 8 acres; pasture, 20 acres.
    Formerly 60s; value now 20s. 5 cattle; 30 sheep; 1 pig.

10 TREVILLYN. Bretel held it before 1066, and paid tax for 1 f; 2 f.
there, however. Land for 2 ploughs.   L 252
    1 villager and 3 smallholders.   a 3
    Pasture, 5 acres.
    Formerly 10s; value now 2s.

11 Osferth holds TRELASKE from the Count. He held it himself
before 1066, and paid tax for 1 v. of land; ½ h. there,   L
however. Land for 8 ploughs; 2½ ploughs there; 2 slaves.   263
    3 villagers and 12 smallholders.   b 4
    Woodland, 10 acres; pasture, 50 acres.
    Formerly 60s; value now 20s.   5 cattle; 4 pigs; 60 sheep.

12 He also holds TREGRILL. Alric held it before 1066, and paid tax
for 1 v. of land; 1 h. there, however. Land for 7 ploughs; 2   L
ploughs there; 2 slaves.   263
    4 villagers and 16 smallholders.   b 5
    Woodland, 1 acre; pasture, 60 acres.
    Formerly 60s; value now 20s.

5,14

1 **Odo** holds BOTELET from the Count. Oswulf held it before 1066,   L
and paid tax for 1 v. of land; 2 h. there, however.
Land for 8 ploughs; 2½ ploughs there; 4 slaves.   230
    4 villagers and 12 smallholders.   b 1
    Woodland, 60 acres; pasture, 50 acres.
    Formerly 40s; value now 50s. 4 cattle; 30 sheep; 6 pigs; 12 goats.   E

2 He also holds ST. NEOT. Godric the priest held it before 1066. 1 h.
there, which has never paid tax. Land for 5 ploughs; 1 plough   L
there; 3 slaves.   E 230
    3 villagers and 6 smallholders.   b 2
    Pasture, 60 acres.
    Formerly 20s; value now 5s. 2 cattle; 2 pigs; 30 sheep.

3 Odo holds TRELIGGA from the Count. Brictmer held it before 1066,
and paid tax for 1 f; 1 h. there, however. Land for 2 ploughs;   L
1 plough there; 2 slaves, with   244
    1 villager and 2 smallholders.   b 2
    Pasture, 6 acres.
    Formerly 10s; value now 5s.   E

Idē ten *TREVINIEL*.Briſmar teneb̄ T.R.E.7 geldb̄ ꝑ uno
★ ferling.Ibi tā̄.ē dimiđ hida.Ťra.ɪ.caɍ.Ibi.ē.ɪ.caɍ.
7 ɪɪ.ſerui.7 ɪɪ.uiłłi 7 ɪɪɪɪ.borđ.7 ɪɪ.a͡c ſiluæ minutæ.7 xx.a͡c
paſturæ.Olim.xx.ſoliđ.Modo uał.x.ſoliđ.

124 c

Idem Odo teñ *KEWALE*.Oſulf teneb̄ T.R.E.7 geldb̄ ꝑ uno
ferling.Ibi tā̄.ē dimiđ hida.Ťra.ɪɪ.caɍ.Ibi ſ̄t.ɪɪ.uiłłi 7 ɪɪɪɪ.
borđ cū̄.ɪ.ſeruo.7 x.a͡c paſturæ.Olim.xv.ſoł.m̄ uał.v.ſoł.
Odo teñ de.co.*PORTATLANT*.Leueron teneb̄ T.R.E.7 geldb̄
ꝑ uno ferling.Ťra.ē.ɪɪ.caɍ.Ibi ſ̄t.ɪɪ.borđ cū̄.ɪ.ſeruo.7 ɪɪɪɪ.
a͡c paſturæ.Olim.vɪɪ.ſoliđ.Modo uał.ɪɪ.ſoliđ.
Algar teñ de Comite *KENANT*.Oſulf teneb̄ T.R.E.7 geldb̄
ꝑ uno ferling.Ibi tā̄.ē.ɪ.hida.Ťra.vɪ.caɍ.Ibi ſ̄t.ɪɪ.caɍ.7 ɪɪɪ.
ſerui.7 ɪɪ.uiłłi 7 ɪx.borđ.7 c.a͡c paſturæ.Olĩ.xʟ.ſoł.M̄ uał.xv.ſoł.
Idē ten *KEWENT*.Oſulf teneb̄ T.R.E.7 geldb̄ ꝑ.ɪɪ.ferlings.
Ibi tā̄.ē una hida.Ťra.vɪ.caɍ.Ibi ſ̄t.ɪɪ.caɍ.7 ɪɪɪ.ſerui.7 ɪɪɪ.uiłłi
7 vɪɪ.borđ 7 q̄ngentæ a͡c paſturæ.Olĩ.xxx.ſoliđ.m̄ uał.xv.ſoliđ.
Algar teñ *PLVNENT*.Oſulf teneb̄ T.R.E.7 geldb̄ ꝑ una v̇ ťræ.
Ibi tā̄.ē dimiđ hida.Ťra.vɪɪɪ.caɍ.Ibi ſ̄t.ɪɪɪ.caɍ 7 dimiđ.
7 vɪ.ſerui.7 ɪɪɪɪ.uiłłi 7 xɪɪ.borđ.7 xxx.a͡c ſiluæ.7 xʟ.a͡c paſturæ.
Olim.ʟ.ſoliđ.Modo uał.xx.ſoliđ.
Algar ten *BENTEWOIN*.Oſulf teneb̄ T.R.E.7 geldb̄ ꝑ.ɪɪ.fer
lings.Ibi tā̄.ē dim̄ hida.Ťra.ē.ɪɪɪ.caɍ.Ibi ſ̄t.ɪɪ.caɍ.7 ɪɪ.ſerui.
7 ɪɪɪ.uiłłi 7 vɪɪ.borđ.7 ɪɪɪɪ.a͡c ſiluæ.7 x.a͡c paſturæ.Olĩ.xx.ſoliđ.
Idē ten *TREFITENT*.Oſulf teneb̄ T.R.E.7 geldb̄ ⌠Modo uał.x.ſoł.
ꝑ.ɪɪ.ferlings.Ibi tā̄.ē dimiđ hida.Ťra.ɪɪɪɪ.caɍ.Ibi ſ̄t.ɪɪ.caɍ.

4 He also holds TREVENIEL. Brictmer held it before 1066, and paid
tax for 1 f; ½ h. there, however. Land for 2 ploughs; 1 plough   L
there; 2 slaves.   244
  2 villagers and 4 smallholders.   b 3
  Underwood, 2 acres; pasture, 20 acres.
Formerly 20s; value now 10s. 3 unbroken mares; 2 cattle; 30 sheep.

5 Odo also holds TREVAL. Oswulf held it before 1066, and paid   124 c
tax for 1 f; ½ h. there, however. Land for 2 ploughs.   245
  2 villagers and 4 smallholders, with 1 slave.   E a 1
  Pasture, 10 acres.
Formerly 15s; value now 5s.

6 Odo holds PORTHALLOW? from the Count. Leofrun held it before
1066, and paid tax for 1 f. Land for 2 ploughs.   264
  2 smallholders, with 1 slave.   b 5
  Pasture, 4 acres.
Formerly 7s; value now 2s.

5,15

1 **Algar** holds TRENANCE from the Count. Oswulf held it before 1066,
and paid tax for 1f; 1 h. there, however.   L
Land for 6 ploughs; 2 ploughs there; 3 slaves.   224
  2 villagers and 9 smallholders.   a 1
  Pasture, 100 acres.
Formerly 40s; value now 15s. 2 cattle; 37 sheep.

2 He also holds TREWINCE. Oswulf held it before 1066, and paid
tax for 2 f; 1 h. there, however. Land for 6 ploughs; 2   L
ploughs there; 3 slaves.   224
  3 villagers and 7 smallholders.   a 2
  Pasture, 500 acres.
Formerly 30s; value now 15s. 3 cattle; 25 sheep.

3 Algar holds PELYNT. Oswulf held it before 1066, and paid tax
for 1 v. of land; ½ h. there, however.   L
Land for 8 ploughs; 3½ ploughs there; 6 slaves.   230
  4 villagers and 12 smallholders.   b 3
  Woodland, 30 acres; pasture, 40 acres.
Formerly 50s; value now 20s. 2 cattle; 14 pigs; 57 sheep.

4 Algar holds PENTEWAN. Oswulf held it before 1066, and paid
tax for 2 f; ½ h. there, however. Land for 3 ploughs; 2   L
ploughs there; 2 slaves.   253
  3 villagers and 7 smallholders.   b 1
  Woodland, 4 acres; pasture, 10 acres.
Formerly 20s; value now 10s. 2 cattle; 6 pigs; 18 sheep.

5 He also holds TREVESSON? Oswulf held it before 1066, and
paid tax for 2 f; ½ h. there, however. Land for 4 ploughs; 2   L 253
ploughs there; 3 slaves.   b 2

7 III.ſerui.7 III.uilti 7 IIII.borđ.7 xx.ac̃ ſiluæ.7 totiđ paſturæ.
Oli.xx.ſol.Modo ual.x.ſolid.

Idẽ ten EDELET.Oſulf teneƀ T.R.E.7 geldƀ p una virg træ.
Ibi tam̃.ē.I.hida.Tra.VI.car̃.In dñio sᵵ.III.car̃.7 IIII.ſerui.
7 IIII.uilti 7 VII.borđ 7 XL.ac̃ ſiluæ.Paſtura.II.leũ lg̃.7 una
leũ lat̃.Olim.XL.ſolid.Modo ual.xv.ſolid.

ALWARD ten de comite KAGARADVC.Ipſe teneƀ T.R.E.7 gẽldƀ
p.III.ferlings.Ibi tam̃.ē dimiđ hida.Tra.III.car̃.Ibi sᵵ.II.
car̃ 7 dimiđ.7 II.ſerui.7 IIII.uilti 7 VI.borđ.7 x.ac̃ paſturæ.
Olim.xx.ſolid.Modo ual.x.ſolid.

Idem ten CHENMERCH.Ipſe teneƀ T.R.E.7 geldƀ p dimiđ
uirg træ.Ibi tam̃.ē una uirg.Tra.I.car̃.q̃ ibi.ē.cũ.uno
ſeruo 7 III.borđ.Ibi.x.ac̃ paſturæ.Olĩ.x.ſol.M̃ ual.VII.ſol.

ALNOD ten de comite TALGOLLE.Idẽ teneƀ T.R.E.7 geldƀ
p.II.ferlings.Tra.ē.III.car̃.Ibi.ē.I.car̃ 7 dimiđ.7 III.ſerui.
7 IIII.borđ.7 II.ac̃ ſiluæ.7 LX.ac̃ paſturæ.Oli.xx.ſol.M̃ ual

Idẽ ten KESCAV.7 ipſe teneƀ T.R.E.7 geldƀ ┌IIII.ſol.
p uno ferling.Tra.III.car̃.Ibi.ē.I.car̃ cũ.I.ſeruo.7 III.borđ.
7 III.ac̃ ſiluæ.7 c.ac̃ paſturæ.Oli.xxv.ſol.M̃ ual.v.ſolid.

ALnod ten DISART.Aluric teneƀ T.R.E.7 geldƀ p uno agro.
Ibi tam̃.ē una v træ.Tra.I.car̃.Ibi.ē dimiđ car̃.7 II.uilti.
cũ.I.ſeruo.7 I.ac̃ p̃ti.7 x.ac̃ paſturæ.Oli.x.ſol.M̃ ual.v.ſol.

ALnod ten TREWDERET.Merleſuain teneƀ T.R.E.7 geldƀ
p uno ferling.Ibi tam̃.ē una v træ.Tra.II.car̃.Ibi.ē.I.car̃.

3 villagers and 4 smallholders.
Woodland, 20 acres; pasture, as many.
Formerly 20s; value now 10s. 3 cattle; 6 pigs; 15 sheep.

6 He also holds IDLESS. Oswulf held it before 1066, and paid tax
for 1 v. of land; 1 h. there, however. Land for 6 ploughs;   E
in lordship 3 ploughs; 4 slaves; 1/3 v.   254
    4 villagers and 7 smallholders & the rest of the land.   a 1
    Woodland, 40 acres; pasture, 2 leagues long and 1 league wide.
Formerly 40s; value now 15s. 23 sheep; 7 goats.

5,16

1 **Alfward** holds TREGARDOCK from the Count. He held it himself
before 1066, and paid tax for 3 f; ½ h. there, however.   L
Land for 3 ploughs; 2½ ploughs there; 2 slaves.   263
    4 villagers and 6 smallholders.   b 1
    Pasture, 10 acres.
Formerly 20s; value now 10s. 50 sheep.

2 He also holds KILMARTH. He held it himself before 1066, and
paid tax for ½ v. of land; 1 v. there, however.   L
Land for 1 plough, which is there, with 1 slave.   263
    3 smallholders.   b 2
    Pasture, 10 acres.
Formerly 10s; value now 7s. 40 sheep.

5,17

1 **Alnoth** holds TOLGULLOW from the Count. He also held it before
1066, and paid tax for 2 f. Land for 3 ploughs; 1½ ploughs   L
there; 3 slaves.   225
    4 smallholders.   a 2
    Woodland, 2 acres; pasture, 60 acres.
Formerly 20s; value now 4s. 2 cows; 15 sheep.

2 He also holds TRESCOWE; he held it himself before 1066, and
paid tax for 1 f. Land for 3 ploughs; 1 plough there,   L
with 1 slave.   225
    3 smallholders.   a 3
    Woodland, 3 acres; pasture, 100 acres.
Formerly 25s; value now 5s.

3 Alnoth holds DIZZARD. Aelfric held it before 1066, and paid
tax for 1 acre; 1 v. of land there, however. Land for 1   L
plough; ½ plough there.   243
    2 villagers, with 1 slave.   a 2
    Meadow, 1 acre; pasture, 10 acres.
Formerly 10s; value now 5s. 3 cattle; 30 sheep; 10 goats.

4 Alnoth holds TREHUDRETH. Merleswein held it before 1066, and
paid tax for 1 f; 1 v. of land there, however. Land   245
for 2 ploughs; 1 plough there.   E   b 3

7 II.uilli 7 IIII.borđ.7 c.ac̄ pasturæ.Olī.xv.sol.m̄ ual.x.sol.

Ednod ten PENGELLE.Idem teneb̄ T.R.E.7 geldb̄ ꝑ dimiđ
ferling.Ibi.e̅ un̄ ager.Tra.I.car̄.Ibi s̄t.II.borđ.7 xx.ac̄
pasturæ.Olim.v.soliđ.Modo ual.II.soliđ.

Alnod ten VLLAVESTONE.Saulf teneb̄ T.R.E.7 geldb̄ ꝑ uno
ferling.Ibi tam̄.e̅ una virg trǣ.Tra.I.car̄.q̄ ibi.e̅ cū uno
uillo 7 III⁝borđ.Ibi.c.ac̄ pasturæ.Olim 7 m̄ ual.v.soliđ.

Alric ten de comite LANLAWERNEC.Idē teneb̄ T.R.E.7 geldb̄
ꝑ uno ferling.Ibi tam̄.e̅ una virg trǣ.Tra.II.car̄.Ibi.e̅ dim̄
car̄ cū.I.seruo.7 II.uilli 7 III.borđ.7 x.ac̄ siluæ.7 LX.ac̄ pasturæ.
Olim.xx.soliđ.Modo ual.VIII.soliđ.

Alric ten DRAINOS.Idē teneb̄ T.R.E.7 geldb̄ ꝑ dim̄ ferling.
Ibi tam̄.e̅ un̄ ferling trǣ.Tra.I.car̄.Ibi.e̅ dimiđ car̄.7 II.uilli
7 II.borđ.7 III.ac̄ siluæ minutæ.7 xxx.ac̄ pasturæ.
Olim.xx.soliđ.Modo ual.III.soliđ.

Alsi ten de com̄ KELAMAR.Idē tenẹb̄ T.R.E.7 geldb̄ ꝑ dimiđ
124 d
ferling trǣ.Ibi.e̅ un̄ ager trǣ.Tra.I.car̄.Ibi.e̅.I.seruus.7 pa'
stura dimiđ leū lḡ.7 tntđ lat̄.Valet.XII.denar.

Almar ten de comite CABVLIAN.Idē teneb̄ T.R.E.7 geldb̄
ꝑ dimiđ uirg Ibi tam̄ s̄t.III.uirg trǣ.Tra.e̅.vi.car̄.Ibi.e̅ una
car̄.7 III.serui.7 III.uilli 7 VII.borđ.7 xl.ac̄ siluæ.7 l.ac̄ pasturæ
Olim.xl.soliđ.Modo ual.x.soliđ.

2 villagers and 4 smallholders & the rest of the land.
Pasture, 100 acres.
Formerly 15s; value now 10s. 2 cows; 15 sheep.   E

5,18
1 **Ednoth** holds PENGELLY. He also held it before 1066, and
paid tax for ½ f; 1 acre there. Land for 1 plough.   L 245
2 smallholders.   a 3
Pasture, 20 acres.
Formerly 5s; value now 2s.

5,19
1 **Alnoth** holds WOOLSTON. Saewulf held it before 1066, and paid
tax for 1 f; 1 v. of land there, however. Land for 1 plough,   L
which is there, with   263
1 villager and 3 smallholders.   b 3
Pasture, 100 acres.
Value formerly and now 5s. 20 sheep; 5 goats.

5,20
1 **Alric** holds LANWARNICK from the Count. He also held it before
1066, and paid tax for 1 f; 1 v. of land there, however.   L
Land for 2 ploughs; ½ plough there, with 1 slave.   231
2 villagers and 3 smallholders.   a 1
Woodland, 10 acres; pasture, 60 acres.
Formerly 20s; value now 8s. 5 pigs; 15 sheep; 15 goats.
2 **Alric** holds DRAYNES. He also held it before 1066, and paid tax
for ½ f; 1 f. of land there, however.   L
Land for 1 plough; ½ plough there.   231
2 villagers and 2 smallholders.   a 3
Underwood, 3 acres; pasture, 30 acres.
Formerly 20s; value now 3s. 1 cattle; 10 sheep; 10 goats.

5,21
1 **Alfsi** holds _TRELAMAR_ from the Count. He also held it before 1066,
and paid tax for ½ f. of land; 1 acre of land there.   234
Land for 1 plough. 1 slave.   a 1
Pasture, ½ league long and as wide.   124 d
Value 12d. 1 ox; 8 sheep.   234
a 1

5,22
1 **Aelmer** holds CABILLA from the Count. He also held it before 1066,
and paid tax for ½ v; 3 v. of land there, however.   L
Land for 6 ploughs; 1 plough there; 3 slaves.   231
3 villagers and 7 smallholders.   b 1
Woodland, 40 acres; pasture, 50 acres.
Formerly 40s; value now 10s. 10 goats.

Brictric ten de com̅ *Lisniwen*. Ipfe teneƀ T.R.E.7 geldƀ
ᵱ dimiđ ac̅. Ibi tam̅ e una uirg̅ træ.Tra.ii.car̅.Ibi.e̅.i.car̅
cu̅.i.feruo 7 iii.borđ.7 ii.ac̅ ᵽti.7 xv.ac̅ pafturæ.
Olim.xxv.foliđ.Val.x.foliđ.

Ide̅ ten *Kegal*.Burgered teneƀ T.R.E.7 geldƀ ᵱ una ac̅ træ.
Tra.e̅.ii.car̅.Ibi.e̅ dimiđ car̅.7 ii.borđ.7 una ac̅ filuæ.7 ii.ac̅
ᵽti.7 x.ac̅ pafturæ.Oli.xx.fol.Modo ual.viii.foliđ.

Brictric ten *Kegingale*.Ipfe teneƀ T.R.E.7 geldƀ ᵱ.i.ferling
Ibi tam̅.e̅ dimiđ hida.Tra.e̅.iii.car̅.Ibi.e̅ un uitts.7.i.borđ.
cu̅.i.feruo.7 viii.ac̅ filuæ.7 xx.ac̅ pafturæ.
Olim.xv.foliđ.Modo ual.v.foliđ.

Brictric ten *Ketweret*.Leuric teneƀ T.R.E.7 geldƀ ᵱ uno
ferling.Ibi tam̅.e̅ una v træ.Tra.ii.car̅.Ibi.e̅.i.borđ cu̅.i.
feruo.7 iiii.ac̅ filuæ.7 xl.ac̅ pafturæ.Oli.xx.fol.M ual.v.fol.

Brictric ten *Odenol*.Haemar teneƀ T.R.E.7 geldƀ ᵱ una
virg̅ træ.Ibi tam̅.e̅.i.hida.Tra.iiii.car̅.Ibi.e̅.i.car̅ 7 dim̅.
7 iii.ferui.7 vii.uitti 7 viii.borđ.7 xxx.ac̅ pafturæ
Olim.xxx.foliđ.Modo ual.x.foliđ.

Vlsi ten de comite *Drainos*.Ide̅ teneƀ T.R.E.7 geldƀ pro
dimiđ ferling.Ibi tam̅ st.ii.ferlings træ.Tra.ii.car̅.Ibi.e̅
una car̅.cu̅.i.feruo.7 ii.uitti 7 iii.borđ.7 iii.ac̅ filuæ.7 xxx.
ac̅ pafturæ.Olim.x.foliđ.Modo ual.v.foliđ.

Ide̅ ten *Kevilivd*.Ipfe teneƀ T.R.E.7 geldƀ ᵱ uno ferling.
Ibi tam̅ st.ii.ferlings.Tra.iii.car̅.Ibi.e̅.i.car̅.cu̅.i.feruo.7 ii.

5,23

1 **Brictric** holds LESNEWTH from the Count. He held it himself
before 1066, and paid tax for ½ acre; 1 v. of land there,   L
however. Land for 2 ploughs; 1 plough there, with 1 slave.   242
  3 smallholders.   a 3
  Meadow, 2 acres; pasture, 15 acres.
  Formerly 25s; value 10s. 3 unbroken mares; 3 cattle; 20 sheep.

2 He also holds *TREGAL*. Burgred held it before 1066, and paid
tax for 1 acre of land. Land for 2 ploughs; ½ plough there.   L 242
  2 smallholders.   b 1
  Woodland, 1 acre; meadow, 2 acres; pasture, 10 acres.
  Formerly 20s; value now 8s. 4 cattle; 30 sheep.

3 Brictric holds TREGEAGLE? He held it himself before 1066,
and paid tax for 1 f; ½ h. there, however.
Land for 3 ploughs.   L 253
  1 villager and 1 smallholder with 1 slave.   a 3
  Woodland, 8 acres; pasture, 20 acres.
  Formerly 15s; value now 5s. 1 cattle; 15 sheep; 5 goats.

4 Brictric holds TREVERRAS. Leofric held it before 1066, and
paid tax for 1 f; 1 v. of land there, however.   254
Land for 2 ploughs.   a 3
  1 smallholder, with 1 slave.
  Woodland, 4 acres; pasture, 40 acres.
  Formerly 20s; value now 5s.   E

5 Brictric holds PERRANUTHNOE. Haemar held it before 1066, and
paid tax for 1 v. of land; 1 h. there, however.   L
Land for 4 ploughs; 1½ ploughs there; 3 slaves.   255
  7 villagers and 8 smallholders.   a 3
  Pasture, 30 acres.
  Formerly 30s; value now 10s. 3 cattle; 6 pigs; 30 sheep.

5,24   [Land of the Count's Other Men]

1 Wulfsi holds DRAYNES from the Count. He also held it before 1066,
and paid tax for ½ f; 2 f. of land there, however.   L
Land for 2 ploughs; 1 plough there, with 1 slave.   232
  2 villagers and 3 smallholders.   a 1
  Woodland, 3 acres; pasture, 30 acres.
  Formerly 10s; value now 5s. 2 cattle.

2 He also holds TREVILVETH? He held it himself before 1066, and
paid tax for 1 f; 2 f. there, however. Land for 3 ploughs; 1   L 232
plough there, with 1 slave.   a 2

uilli 7 ıı . borđ . 7 xx . ac̃ filuæ . 7 v . ac̃ pafturæ . Olĩ . xx . foliđ .

Coᴌo teñ de . Co . ʜᴇ\ʟᴀ . Ipfe teneƀ T . R . E. ⌐ Modo ual . v . foł .
7 geldƀ ꝓ una ac̃ . Ibi . ē una virg̃ træ . Tra . ē . ıı . car̃ . Ibi . ē di
miđ car̃ . 7 ıııı . borđ . 7 una ac̃ p̃ti . 7 ıı . ac̃ filuæ . 7 v ac̃ pafturæ .
Olim . x . foliđ . Modo ual . v . foliđ .

Lᴇᴠᴇɴᴏᴛ teñ ᴇᴌᴇʀᴄʜɪ de comite . Merlefuain teneƀ T . R . E.
7 geldƀ ꝓ . ı . hida . Ibi tam̃ sꝉ . ıııı . hidæ . Tra . ē . xx . car̃ . Ibi sꝉ
. v . car̃ . 7 x . ferui . 7 xvıı . uilli . 7 xvııı . borđ . 7 xxx . ac̃ filuæ .
7 c . ac̃ pafturæ . Olim . c . foliđ . Modo ual . ʟ . foliđ .

Lᴇᴜᴇɴᴏᴛ teñ ᴇʀᴍᴇɴʜᴇᴠ . Idē teneƀ T . R . E . 7 geldƀ ꝓ dimiđ
uirg̃ træ . Ibi tam̃ . ē una v̄ træ . Tra . ē . vı . car . Ibi . ē dimiđ
car̃ . 7 ıı . ferui . 7 v . borđ . 7 xv . ac̃ filuæ . 7 xx . ac̃ pafturæ
Olim . xv . foliđ . Modo ual . v . foliđ .

Wᴌuuard teñ de com̃ uñ ferling træ in ʀᴇɴᴛɪɴ . Aluuiñ
teneƀ T . R . E . Ibi . ē uñ uilƚs 7 x . ac̃ pafturæ . Valet . v . foliđ .

Vᴌsɪ teñ ᴘᴏᴌʜᴀᴌ . Vluuiñ teneƀ T . R . E . 7 geldƀ ꝓ uno ferlig̃ træ .
Ibi tam̃ . ē una virg̃ . Tra . ıı . car̃ . Ibi . ē . ı . borđ . 7 ııı . ac̃ p̃ti . 7 ʟx .
ac̃ pafturæ . Olĩ . x . foł . Modo ual . xv . denar̃ .

Wᴌuric teñ de Com̃ ʙᴇᴠᴇsʜᴏᴄ . Leuric teneƀ T . R . E . 7 geldƀ
ꝓ uno ferling . Ibi tam̃ . ē una v̄ træ . Tra . ıı . car̃ . Ibi sꝉ . ıı . borđ
cū . ı . feruo . 7 xıı . ac̃ filuæ . Paftura dimiđ leū lg̃ . 7 dim̃ leū
lat̃ . Olim . xx . foliđ . Modo ual . v . foliđ .

Dodo teñ de com̃ ᴋᴀʀsᴀᴌᴀɴ . Ipfe teneƀ T . R . E . 7 geldƀ ꝓ dim̃
ferling . Ibi . ē una ac̃ træ . Tra . ı . car̃ . Ibi sꝉ . ııı . ferui . 7 xxx . ac̃
pafture . Olĩ . x . foliđ . Modo ual . xıı . den .

2 villagers and 2 smallholders.
Woodland, 20 acres; pasture, 5 acres.
Formerly 20s; value now 5s. 2 cattle.

3 Cola holds HELE from the Count. He held it himself before 1066,
and paid tax for 1 acre; 1 v. of land there. Land for 2 ploughs; ½   L
plough there.   243
   4 smallholders.   a 3
   Meadow, 1 acre; woodland, 2 acres; pasture, 5 acres.
Formerly 10s; value now 5s. 3 cattle; 5 sheep; 6 goats.

4 Leofnoth holds VERYAN from the Count. Merleswein held it
before 1066, and paid tax for 1 h; 4 h. there, however.   L
Land for 20 ploughs; 5 ploughs there; 10 slaves.   253
   17 villagers and 18 smallholders.   a 1
   Woodland, 30 acres; pasture, 100 acres.
Formerly 100s; value now 50s. 2 cattle; 30 sheep.

5 Leofnoth holds HALVANA. He also held it before 1066, and
paid tax for ½ v. of land; 1 v. of land there, however.   L
Land for 6 ploughs; ½ plough there; 2 slaves.   264
   5 smallholders.   a 3
   Woodland, 15 acres; pasture, 20 acres.
Formerly 15s; value now 5s.

6 Wulfward holds 1 f. of land from the Count in RINSEY? Alwin
held it before 1066.   262
   1 villager.   b 1
   Pasture, 10 acres.
Value 5s; when acquired 7s.

7 Wulfsi holds PENHOLE. Wulfwin held it before 1066, and paid   E
tax for 1 f. of land; 1 v. there, however.
Land for 2 ploughs.   261
   1 smallholder.   b 3
   Meadow, 3 acres; pasture, 60 acres.
Formerly 10s; value now 15d.

8 Wulfric holds BOSVISACK? from the Count. Leofric held it
before 1066, and paid tax for 1 f; 1 v. of land there, however.   L
Land for 2 ploughs.   254
   2 smallholders, with 1 slave.   a 2
   Woodland, 12 acres; pasture, ½ league long and ½ league wide.
Formerly 20s; value now 5s. 1 cow; 15 sheep.

9 Doda holds CARSELLA from the Count. He held it himself
before 1066, and paid tax for ½ f; 1 acre of land there.
Land for 1 plough. 3 slaves.   254
   Pasture, 30 acres.   a 4
Formerly 10s; value now 12d. 1 cow; 15 sheep.

Sireuuold ten *WIDEWOT*. Ipſe teneб T.R.E. 7 geldб ꝑ uno fer

ling. Ibi ſт. II. aᴄ træ. Tra. I. caᴦ. Ibi. ē. I. uiɫɫs cū. I. ſeruo. Paſ

tura dimid leū lḡ. 7 tntd laᴦ. Olim. x. ſoɫ. Modo uaɫ. III. ſolid.

Gᴠɴʜᴀʀ ten *DIMELIHOC*. Almer teneб T.R.E. 7 geldб ꝑ dimid

ferling. Ibi. ē una aᴄ træ. Tra. I. caᴦ. Ibi ſт. II. bord. 7 paſtura

dimid leū lḡ. 7 tntd laᴦ. Olĭ. x. ſolid. Modo uaɫ. xII. denaᴦ.

Gᴏᴅᴠɪɴ ten *LANDIGHE*. Alſi teneб T.R.E. 7 geldб ꝑ una v̊ træ.

Ibi taм̃. ē. I. hida. Tra. v. caᴦ. Ibi. ē. I. caᴦ 7 dimid. 7 III. ſerui. 7 II.

uiɫɫi 7 IIII. bord. 7 II. aᴄ ꝑti. 7 III. aᴄ ſiluæ. paſtura. I. leū lḡ. 7 tntd

125 a ⌐lat. Olim. xxx. ſolid. Modo uaɫ. x. ſolid.

Wɪʜᴠᴍᴀʀᴄ ten de Comite *TVCOWIT*. Edmer teneб T.R.E.

7 geldб ꝑ uno ferling træ. Tra. IIII. caᴦ. Ibi ſт. II. uiɫɫi 7 III. bord

7 II. aᴄ ſiluæ. 7 una leū paſturæ. Olĭ. Lx. ſoɫ. Modo uaɫ. v. ſolid.

Wɪʜumar ten *ᴋEMARVSTEL*. Edmer teneб T.R.E. ~~7 geldб~~

Ibi ſт. II. aᴄ træ. Tra. ē. I. caᴦ. Ibi ſт. II. ſerui cū. I. bord. 7 una aᴄ

ꝑti. 7 una aᴄ ſiluæ. Olim. x̊. ſoɫ. Modo uaɫ. xxx. denaᴦ.

Ħ tra ꝑtiɳ ad honores. Chei.

Hᴠᴇᴄʜᴇ ten de coм̃ *BOTIVAL*. Idē teneб T.R.E. 7 geldб pro

dimid ferling. Ibi taм̃. ē uɳ ferling træ. Tra. I. caᴦ. Ibi. ē di

midia caᴦ. cū. I. ſeruo. 7 II. uiɫɫi 7 III. bord. 7 x. aᴄ ſiluæ. 7 Lx. aᴄ

paſturæ. Olim. xx. ſolid. Modo uaɫ. vIII. ſolid.

Rᴀʙᴇʟ ten de coм̃ *ᴋEVOCARWINOC*. Alfeg teneб T.R.E.

7 geldб ꝑ dim uirg træ. Ibi taм̃. ē una virg. Tra. III. caᴦ. Ibi. ē

uɳ bord. 7 xx. aᴄ ſiluæ. 7 x. aᴄ paſturæ. Olĭ. v. ſoɫ. m̃ uaɫ. xII. den.

Rᴀʙᴇʟ ten de coм̃ *PANGVOL*. Alſi teneб T.R.E. 7 geldб

ꝑ uno ferling. Ibi taм̃. ē una virg træ. Tra. II. caᴦ. Ibi. IIII.

borд hɴт. I. caᴦ. Ibi. III. aᴄ ſiluæ minutæ. 7 xx. aᴄ paſturæ.

Olim 7 modo uaɫ. v. ſolid.

10 Sheerwold holds GOTHERS. He held it himself before 1066, and
paid tax for 1 f; 2 acres of land there. Land for 1 plough.   254
   1 villager, with 1 slave.   b 1
Pasture, ½ league long and as wide.
Formerly 10s; value now 3s. 2 cattle; 9 sheep.

11 Gunnar holds DOMELLICK. Aelmer held it before 1066, and paid
tax for ½ f; 1 acre of land there. Land for 1 plough.   254
   2 smallholders.   b 2
Pasture, ½ league long and as wide.
Formerly 10s; value now 12d.

12 Godwin holds OLD KEA. Alfsi held it before 1066, and paid tax
for 1 v. of land; 1 h. there, however. Land for 5 ploughs; 1½   L
ploughs there; 3 slaves.   254
   2 villagers and 4 smallholders.   b 3
Meadow, 2 acres; woodland, 3 acres; pasture, 1 league long
   and as wide.
Formerly 30s; value now 10s. 2 cattle; 40 sheep; 15 goats.

13 Wihomarch holds TUCOYSE from the Count. Edmer held it   125 a
before 1066, and paid tax for 1 f. of land. Land for 4 ploughs.   L
   2 villagers and 3 smallholders.   225
Woodland, 2 acres; pasture, 1 league.   a 1
Formerly 60s; value now 5s.

14 Wihomarch holds TREROOSEL. Edmer held it before 1066. 2 acres
of land. Land for 1 plough. 2 slaves, with   245
   1 smallholder.   b 2
Meadow, 1 acre; woodland, 1 acre.
Formerly 10s; value now 30d.
   This land belongs to the Honour of St. Kew.   E

15 Hwata holds BODUEL from the Count. He also held it before 1066,
and paid tax for ½ f; 1 f. of land there, however.   L
Land for 1 plough; ½ plough there, with 1 slave.   231
   2 villagers and 3 smallholders.   a 2
Woodland, 10 acres; pasture, 60 acres.
Formerly 20s; value now 8s. 5 pigs; 15 sheep; 15 goats.

16 Rabel holds TREGUNNICK from the Count. Alfheah held it
before 1066, and paid tax for ½ v. of land; 1 v. there, however.
Land for 3 ploughs.   231
   1 smallholder.   b 2
Woodland, 20 acres; pasture, 10 acres.
Formerly 5s; value now 12d.

17 Rabel holds PENGOLD from the Count. Alfsi held it before 1066, E
and paid tax for 1 f; 1 v. of land there, however.
Land for 2 ploughs.   238
   4 smallholders have 1 plough.   b 3
Underwood, 3 acres; pasture, 20 acres.
Value formerly and now 5s.   E

Bernard teñ de coṁ *TACABERE* . Aluric teneƀ T.R.E.7 geldƀ
ꝑ dim ferling træ.Ibi tam s͞t . II . ferlings . Tra . I . ca͞r . g̅ ibi.e͞
cu͞ . III . borđ . 7 v.a͞c siluæ minutæ .7 XL . a͞c pasturæ.
Olim . IIII . soliđ . Modo ua͞t . VII . soliđ.

Hunfrid teñ de coṁ . *KEFILIES* . Alstan teneƀ T.R.E.7 geldƀ
ꝑ una v̅ træ.Ibi tam.e͞ dimiđ hida.Tra.IIII.ca͞r.Ibi est
un uitts.7 XX.a͞c siluæ.7 XXX.a͞c pasturæ.Oli͞.x.sot.m̊ uat

Seibert teñ de coṁ *HENLAND*.Ailmer teneƀ   ⌐II.soliđ.
T.R.E.7 geldƀ ꝑ uno ferling.Ibi tam.e͞ una virg træ.Tra
IIII . ca͞r.Ibi.e͞.I.ca͞r.7 II.uitti 7 III . borđ.7 IIII.a͞c siluæ.7 XX.a͞c
pasturæ.Olim 7 modo uat.x . soliđ.

Frauuiñ teñ de Coṁ *KELINGAN* . Aluric teneƀ T.R.E.7 geldƀ
ꝑ dimiđ virg træ. Ibi tam.e͞.I . hida.Tra.v.ca͞r.Ibi sͭ.II.ca͞r.
7 v.serui.7 III. uitti 7 VI.borđ.7 XII.a͞c siluæ.7 c.a͞c pasturæ.
Olim.xxv.soliđ.Modo uat.xv.soliđ.

Andreas teñ de coṁ *POLSCAT*. Aluric teneƀ T.R.E.7 geldƀ
ꝑ uno ferling.Ibi tam.e͞ una uirg træ.Tra.I.ca͞r.Ibi.e͞ di
midia ca͞r.7 II.uitti 7 v.borđ.7 III.a͞c siluæ.7 v.a͞c pasturæ.
Olim 7 m̊ uat.III . soliđ.

Andreas teñ de coṁ *CARBIHAN*.Merken teneƀ T.R.E.
7 geldƀ ꝑ uno ferling . Ibi sͭ . IIII.a͞c træ.Tra . IIII . ca͞r . Ibi sͭ
II . ca͞r .7 IIII.serui.7 II. uitti 7 III.borđ.7 v.a͞c siluæ.7 xx . a͞c
pasturæ.Olim 7 m̊ uat.x.soliđ.

18 Bernard the priest holds TACKBEAR from the Count. Aelfric held it
before 1066, and paid tax for ½ f. of land. 2 f. there, however. L
Land for 1 plough, which is there, with 244
   3 smallholders. b 1
   Underwood, 5 acres; pasture, 40 acres.
Formerly 4s; value now 7s. 14 cattle; 11 sheep.

19 Humphrey holds TREVILLIS from the Count. Alstan held it
before 1066, and paid tax for 1 v. of land; ½ h. there, however. L
Land for 4 ploughs. 231
   1 villager. b 4
   Woodland, 20 acres; pasture, 30 acres.
Formerly 10s; value now 2s.

20 Sibert holds HELLAND from the Count. Aelmer held it before 1066,
and paid tax for 1 f; 1 v. of land there, however. L
Land for 4 ploughs; 1 plough there. 252
   2 villagers and 3 smallholders. b 3
   Woodland, 4 acres; pasture, 20 acres.
Value formerly and now 10s.

21 Frawin holds TREGONY from the Count. Aelfric held it before 1066,
and paid tax for ½ v. of land; 1 h. there, however. L
Land for 5 ploughs; 2 ploughs there; 5 slaves. 253
   3 villagers and 6 smallholders. a 2
   Woodland, 12 acres; pasture, 100 acres.
Formerly 25s; value now 15s. 3 cattle; 40 sheep; 20 goats.

22 Andrew holds POLSCOE from the Count. Aelfric held it before 1066,
and paid tax for 1 f; 1 v. of land there, however. 230
Land for 1 plough; ½ plough there. E b 4
   2 villagers and 5 smallholders.
   Woodland, 3 acres; pasture, 5 acres.
Value formerly and now 3s. 3 cattle.

23 Andrew holds CARVEAN? from the Count. Merken held it
before 1066, and paid tax for 1 f; 4 acres of land there. L
Land for 4 ploughs; 2 ploughs there; 4 slaves. 237
   2 villagers and 3 smallholders. b 1
   Woodland, 5 acres; pasture, 20 acres.
Value formerly and now 10s. 6 cattle; 6 pigs; 20 sheep; 7 goats.

Rᴀᴅᴠʟꜰ ten de com̃ *Wɪᴛᴇsᴛᴀɴ*. Aluuold teneð T.R.E.

7 geldð ꝑ dimid ferling trǣ. Ibi tam̃ . ē uñ ferling.

Ibi . ē dimid car̃ cū . ɪ . ſeruo. 7 xɪɪ . ac̃ ſiluæ. Olĩ . xx . ſot. M̊ uał

Hᴇʟᴅʀɪᴄ ten de com̃ *Rɪɢᴠᴇɴ* . Briſmer teneð ⎰xv . ſolid.

T.R.E. 7 geldð ꝑ uno ferling trǣ. Ibi tam̃ . ē una virg̃ . Tra . ɪɪɪ.

car̃. Ibi ſť . ɪɪ . car. 7 ɪɪ . ſerui 7 ᴠɪ . borð. 7 xʟ . ac̃ paſturæ.

Olim . xv . ſolid . Modo uał . x . ſolid.

Bʟᴏʜɪɴ ten de comite *Dᴇʟɪᴀᴠ* . Jaul teneð T.R.E. 7 geldð

ꝑ una uirg̃ trǣ. Ibi tam̃ . ē dimid hida. Tra . ē ɪɪ . car̃ . q̃ ibi ſť

cū . ɪ . ſeruo. 7 ɪɪ . uiłłi 7 ɪɪɪɪ . borð . 7 una ac̃ p̃ti . 7 xx . ac̃ paſturæ.

Olim . xxx . ſolid . Modo uał . xx . ſolid.

Idē ten *Kᴇꜰʀɪᴏᴄ*. Jaulf teneð T.R.E. 7 geldð ꝑ una v̄ trǣ.

Ibi tam̃ . ē dimid hida. Tra . ɪɪ . car̃ . Ibi . ē una car̃ . cu . ɪ . ſeruo.

★ 7 ɪɪ . uiłłi 7 ɪɪɪ . borð . 7 xx . ac̃ paſturæ. Olĩ . xx . ſot. M̊ uał . ſot.

Idē ten *Dᴠᴠᴇɴᴀɴᴛ* . Aluuard teneð T.R.E. 7 geldð ꝑ una v̄

trǣ. Ibi tam̃ . ē.dimid hida . Tra . ē . ɪɪɪ . car̃ . Ibi . ē . ɪ . car̃ 7 dimid.

7 ɪɪɪɪ . ſerui cū . ɪ . uiłło, 7 xʟ . ac̃ paſturæ. Olĩ . xxv . ſot. M̊ uał . xv.

Idem ten *Kᴇᴠᴇʜᴇʀᴇᴛ*. Aluric teneð T.R.E. 7 geldð ⎰ſolid.

ꝑ dimid ferling trǣ. Ibi tam̃ . ē uñ ferling. Tra , ɪɪ . car̃. Ibi . ē uñ

uiłłs . Olim 7 modo uał . ɪɪ . ſolid.

Idem ten *Kᴇᴠᴛʜᴀʟ* . Briſmar teneð T.R.E. Ibi . ē . ɪ , hida trǣ,

125 b

Tra . ᴠɪɪɪ . car . Ibi ſť . ɪɪɪɪ . car̃ . 7 ᴠɪɪ . uiłłi 7 ᴠɪɪ . borð. 7 ɪɪ . ac̃ p̃ti.

7 ʟx . ac̃ paſturæ. Olim . xʟ . ſolid . Modo uał . xx . ſolid.

Hanc trã abſtulit com̃ æcctæ Ŝ Mɪᴄʜᴀᴇʟɪs.

24 Ralph holds WHITSTONE from the Count. Alfwold held it before 1066,
and paid tax for ½ f. of land; 1 f. there, however. ½ plough   E
there, with 1 slave.   255
   Woodland, 12 acres.   b 3
Formerly 20s; value now 15s. 8 cattle; 8 pigs; 40 [sheep]; 40 goats.   E

25 Heldric holds TREDWEN from the Count. Brictmer held it
before 1066, and paid tax for 1 f. of land; 1 v. there, however.   L
Land for 3 ploughs; 2 ploughs there; 2 slaves.   262
   6 smallholders.   b 2
   Pasture, 40 acres.
Formerly 15s; value now 10s. 2 cattle; 40 sheep.

5,25

1 **Blohin** holds DELAMERE from the Count. Iolf held it before 1066, E
and paid tax for 1 v. of land; ½ h. there, however.   L
Land for 2 ploughs, which are there, with 1 slave.   263
   2 villagers and 4 smallholders.   a 1
   Meadow, 1 acre; pasture, 20 acres.
Formerly 30s; value now 20s. 6 unbroken mares; 2 cattle; 5 pigs; 15 sheep.

He also holds
2 TREFREOCK. Iolf held it before 1066, and paid tax for 1 v. of
land; ½ h. there, however. Land for 2 ploughs; 1 plough there,   L
with 1 slave.   263
   2 villagers and 3 smallholders.   a 2
   Pasture, 20 acres.
Formerly 20s; value now [10] s. 3 cattle; 40 sheep.

3 DANNONCHAPEL. Alfward held it before 1066, and paid tax
for 1 v. of land; ½ h. there, however. Land for 3   L
ploughs; 1½ ploughs there; 4 slaves, with   263
   1 villager.   a 3
   Pasture, 40 acres.
Formerly 25s; value now 15s. 3 cattle; 3 pigs; 50 sheep; 20 goats.

4 TREWETHART. Aelfric held it before 1066, and paid tax for ½ f.   E
of land; 1 f. there, however. Land for 2 ploughs.   E
   1 villager.   263
Value formerly and now 2s.   a 4

5 TRUTHWALL. Brictmer held it before 1066. 1 h. of land.   E 258
Land for 8 ploughs; 4 ploughs there.   L b 3
   7 villagers and 7 smallholders.   125 b
   Meadow, 2 acres; pasture, 60 acres.
Formerly 40s; value now 20s. 4 cows; 2 pigs; 50 sheep.
   The Count took this land from St. Michael's Church.

Rogerivs ten de comite *Kavvint*. Borgered teneb T.R.E.

7 geldb ꝑ.ii.ferlings. Ibi tam.e una uirg træ. Tra.i.car.

ꝗ ibi.e cu.i.feruo.7 iiii.bord.7 ii.ac pafturæ.Olim.x.fol.Modo

Ide ten *Deliov*.Leuuin teneb T.R.E.7 geldb ⌐ual.v.folid.

ꝑ.ii.ferlings.Ibi tam.e una hida.Tra.iiii.car.Ibi.e.i.car.

cu.i.feruo.7 i.uillo 7 iii.bord.7 una ac pti.7 xl.ac pafturæ.

Olim.xxx.folid.Modo ual.x.folid.

Idem ten *Legea*.Alnod teneb T.R.E.7 geldb ꝑ.ii.ferlings træ.

Ibi tam.e dimid hida.Tra.iiii.car.Ibi st.ii.car.7 ii.ferui.

7 x.bord.7 ii.ac pti.7 una ac filuæ.7 v.ac pafturæ.

Olim.xx.folid.Modo ual.x.folid.

Idem ten *Hamet*.Alnod teneb T.R.E.7 geldb ꝑ uno ferling.

Ibi st.iii.ac træ.Tra.ii.car.Ibi.e.i.car.7 iii.ferui.7 iiii.bord.

7 una ac filuæ.7 xxx.ac pafturæ.Oli.x.fol.Modo ual.v.folid.

Terra Jvdhel de Totenais.

.VI. Jvdhel de Totenais ten de rege *Forchetestane*.7 Turftin

de eo.Ibi st.iii.ferlings træ.fed geld ꝑ uno ferling.Tra.e.iii.car.

Ibi dimid car.e.7 iiii.ferui.7 ii.bord.7 l.ac pafture.7 xl.ac

filue minute.Oli.xv.folid.Modo ual.xi.folid.

Terra Goscelmi.

.VII. Goscelm tenet *Pigesdone*. Wadel teneb T.R.E.7 geldb

★ ꝑ una virg træ.Tra.e.i.car.ꝗ ibi.e cu.i.bord.Ibi.x.ac

pti.Oli 7 modo ual.v.folid.

5,26

1 **Roger** holds TREWINT from the Count. Burgred held it before 1066,
and paid tax for 2 f; 1 v. of land there, however.　　　　　　　L
Land for 1 plough, which is there, with 1 slave.　　　　　　　　260
　　4 smallholders.　　　　　　　　　　　　　　　　　　　　　b 2
　　Pasture, 2 acres.
Formerly 10s; value now 5s. 10 sheep.

2 He also holds DELABOLE. Leofwin held it before 1066, and
paid tax for 2 f; 1 h. there, however.　　　　　　　　　　　　L
Land for 4 ploughs; 1 plough there, with 1 slave and　　　　　261
　　1 villager and 3 smallholders.　　　　　　　　　　　　E　a 1
　　Meadow, 1 acre; pasture, 40 acres.
Formerly 30s; value now 10s. 5 cattle; 25 sheep.

3 He also holds LEIGH. Alnoth held it before 1066, and paid tax
for 2 f. of land; ½ h. there, however. Land for 4 ploughs; 2　　L
ploughs there; 2 slaves.　　　　　　　　　　　　　　　　　261
　　10 smallholders.　　　　　　　　　　　　　　　　　　　a 2
　　Meadow, 2 acres; woodland, 1 acre; pasture, 5 acres.
Formerly 20s; value now 10s. 5 ... cattle; 30 sheep.　　　　　E

4 He also holds HAMMETT. Alnoth held it before 1066, and paid
tax for 1 f; 3 acres of land there. Land for 2 ploughs; 1　　　L
plough there; 3 slaves.　　　　　　　　　　　　　　　　　261
　　4 smallholders.　　　　　　　　　　　　　　　　　　　a 3
　　Woodland, 1 acre; pasture, 30 acres.
Formerly 10s; value now 5s. 5 cattle; 30 sheep.

6　　　　　**LAND OF IUDHAEL OF TOTNES**

1 Iudhael of Totnes holds FROXTON from the King, and Thurstan　E
from him. 3 f. of land, but it pays tax for 1 f.　　　　　　　E
Land for 3 ploughs; ½ plough there; 4 slaves.　　　　　　　L　334
　　2 smallholders.　　　　　　　　　　　　　　　　　　　b 2
　　Pasture, 50 acres; underwood, 40 acres.　　　　　　　　E
Formerly 15s; value now 11s. 8 cattle; 12 pigs.

7　　　　　**LAND OF GOTSHELM**

1 Gotshelm holds PIGSDON. Waddell held it before 1066, and paid
tax for 1 v. of land. Land for 1 plough, which is there, with　L　397
　　1 smallholder.　　　　　　　　　　　　　　　　　　　b 1
　　Meadow, 10 acres.
Value formerly and now 5s. 3 cattle; 7 sheep.

Notes on the Text and Translation

Notes on Placename Identifications

Exon. Extra Information and Discrepancies

Lordship Detail

Index of Persons

Index of Places

Maps and Map Keys

Systems of Reference

Technical Terms

ABBREVIATIONS used in the notes. DB... Domesday Book. DCNQ... Devon and Cornwall Notes and Queries. DG... H.C. Darby and G.R. Versey *Domesday Gazetteer* Cambridge 1975. Dauzat... A. Dauzat *Dictionnaire Etymologique des noms de famille et prénoms de France*, revised edition by Marie-Thérèse Morlet, Larousse, Paris 1951. EA... C.G. Henderson *Ecclesiastical Antiquities* (see Bibliography in Places Notes). ECH... C.G Henderson *Essays in Cornish History* Oxford 1935. Ellis ... Sir Henry Ellis *Domesday Book* vol. 3 1816. Exon... Exeter Book. Exon Notes... Exon Extra Information and Discrepancies with DB. Forssner... T. Forssner *Continental-Germanic Personal-Names in England in Old and Middle English Times* Uppsala 1916. JRIC... Journal of the Royal Institution of Cornwall. MS... Manuscript. OC... Old Cornwall. OEB... G. Tengvik *Old English Bynames* Uppsala 1938. PNDB... O. von Feilitzen *The Pre-conquest Personal Names of Domesday Book* Uppsala 1937. VCH... Victoria County History, Cornwall Vol.II Part 8 1924.

The manuscript is written on leaves, or folios, of parchment (sheepskin), measuring about 15 by 11 inches (38 by 28 cm) on both sides. On each side, or page, are two columns, making four to each folio. The folios were numbered in the 17th century, and the four columns of each are here lettered a, b, c, d. The manuscript emphasises words and usually distinguishes chapters and sections by the use of red ink. Underlining here indicates deletion.

When quoting from the texts of DB and Exon, this edition extends the abbreviated forms only where there is no reasonable doubt.

CORNWALL. In red, across the top of each folio, spread over both columns, CORNVALGE (CORNVALGIE 120ab).

1,1 THE KING HOLDS. Repeated at the beginning of sections 1,1-12 and 1,14-17.
COUNT OF MORTAIN. Robert, half brother of King William and perhaps the wealthiest man in England after the King. He had holdings in 20 counties, by far the largest being in Cornwall.
BLETCU, *Bletu*, Exon; *Blechu*, DB. Probably the same name as Old Welsh *Bleidcu*, e.g. *Liber Landavensis* 155, Old Cornish *Bledcuf, Bleydcuf, Revue Celtique* 1 (1880-82) 335, 337.
WIHOMARCH. One of the commonest 11th century Breton names; identical with Wymarc (e.g. Robert son of Wymarc, father of Swein of Essex).
£20 10s. DB uses the old English currency system, which endured for a thousand years until 1971. The pound contained 20 shillings, each of 12 pence, and the abbreviations £ s d preserved the DB terms *librae, solidi* and *denarii*.
TREWARNEVAS.. 1 ACRE. The Cornish acre seems to have been larger than the acre of other parts of England, of which there are usually reckoned to be 120 to a hide; possibly a twelfth of a hide. Because in Cornwall the taxable land was generally assessed at half the land there, it would seem from e.g. 5,2,7-8. 5,24,9-11, that an acre was here as much as 1 f., and from e.g. 5,2,15. 5,24,3, as much as ½ v. See Exon Notes for 1,1 (Doda.. Trelan) VCH Introduction p.47 and H.C. Darby and R. Welldon Finn *The Domesday Geography of South-west England* Cambridge 1967, p.306 ff.
GRIFFIN. The ordinary Old Welsh, Cornish and Breton pet-form for *Gruffydd*, but it is used often enough as a distinct personal name to become a separate surname eventually. See Reaney *Dictionary of British Surnames*.
1,2 ALE-MEN. Not elsewhere noted in DB; presumably they paid dues in beer. See ECH p.70. Cf. 2,12 for a customary due of a barrel of ale.
LAND FOR 40 PLOUGHS. The detail amounts to only 20 ploughs. Though in many counties the villagers' and lordship ploughs add up to those in the estimate, in Cornwall they very rarely do; often, as here, they form only half the plough estimate.
1,3 [WIDE]. So, correctly, Exon; DB has "long" in error.
1,4 POUNDSTOCK AND ST. GENNYS. See 5,7,6; 9 for details; also Exon Notes 1,4.
IOVIN. *Ioin*, Exon; other spellings *Iuuinus, Jouuinus, Iouuinus, Jouinus, Ioinus*, PNDB 301 n4. Old French *Jovin*, not, as PNDB 301 and Forssner 286, from Germanic *Gautwin*, but from Latin *Jovinus*; name of an obscure saint cultivated in north and west France in medieval times, see Dauzat 347.
1,7 SMALLHOLDERS. Exon *villani habent*, though only *bordarii* are entered. As in DB, *villanus* is both a specific term, contrasted with *bordarius, cotarius,* etc., and a generic term, including the several categories of unnamed cultivators. Also occurs in 1,1 (for Rinsey held by Wulfward) and 5,4,10.
1,13 BRICTRIC. Son of Algar. Many of his west country lands passed to Queen Matilda, possibly after the fall of Exeter in 1068. A romantic tale, told by the Continuator of Wace and others (Freeman *Norman Conquest* 4, Appendix Note O), alleges that Matilda seized his lands because in youth he had spurned her hand.

1,15	ST. PETROC'S. See 4,22.
	30d OR 1 OX. A common customary due; see Devon 44,1 (col. 116d).
2,2	THE BISHOP HOLDS. Repeated at the beginning of sections 2,2-7.
2,5	BEFORE 1066. MS and Farley have *TRE et*, in error for *et TRE*.
2,6	CASTLE. Probably Trematon Castle, although it is about 3 miles away across the tidal reaches of the R. Tiddy and the R. Lynher. See 5,2,11.
2,10	1½ HIDES THERE. The detail amounts to 2 h. Perhaps there is a scribal error in Exon and the reading for the villagers' land should be 1 h. and 1 v.
4,1	TRUTHWALL.. 2 h.. 20s. The 2 h. are given the same present value as the single hide taken by the Count of Mortain. 1 h. See 5,25,5.
4,2	ST. STEPHENS. It is unusual for there to be no mention of people (nor in Exon), especially in an otherwise full entry.
4,7	LAND FOR 20 PLOUGHS. In the MS the scribe began to write a third x.
4,8	THE COUNT...ST. PETROC'S. Repeated at the beginning of sections 4,8-14.
4,15	FORMERLY 20s. In the MS the scribe seems to have written *xv solid'* first and then altered it to *xx solid'*.
4,22	COSWARTH. See 1,15. LANCARFFE. See 5,6,6.
4,26	FOUR WEEKS' REVENUE. Similar to 'one night's revenue' *(firma unius noctis)*, which was supplied by certain royal manors, and was the amount of food needed to support the King and his household for one night. This custom was adapted by many religious houses. In this case the two lands (possibly with other manors) had originally to supply the Canons with enough provisions to last them four weeks. By the 11th Century, however, these food rents were generally commuted.
	BERNER HOLDS. See 5,8,10.
4,28	ST. NEOT. See 5,14,2.
3,2	ERMENHALD.. CHURCH. Repeated at the beginning of sections 3,2-6.
	LAND FOR 6 PLOUGHS. The detail in DB and Exon totals 7.
3,7	THE ABBOT CLAIMS. There is a gap of about 4 letters due to an erasure, possibly of *abb'*, reproduced by Farley; not in Exon. The Exon MS has *calūniat'(calumniatur)*; Ellis misprints *calūmat' (calummatur)*.
5	LAND OF THE COUNT OF MORTAIN. The beginning of each of the sub-sections in ch.5 is indicated in the MS either by larger capitals for the holder, generally lined through for emphasis and shown by Farley, or (and) by gaps of 1-2 lines between sub-sections, not shown by Farley.
5,1,2	THE COUNT HIMSELF HOLDS. Repeated at the beginning of sections 5,1,2-22.
5,1,3	BISHOP OSBERN. Of Exeter, though he was not consecrated until 1072. Brother of Earl William of Hereford; also Chaplain of King Edward.
	SALT-HOUSES. *Salina* comprehends all kinds of salt workings, from coastal pans to the boilers of Worcester and Cheshire, with their associated sheds and buildings. "Salt-house" is the most comprehensive term.
5,1,5	12 SILVER MARKS. i.e. £8, at 13s 4d for one silver mark. See also 5,1,7-8; 13.
5,1,8	[6] PLOUGHS. As in Exon; DB has *xx*, probably repeated in error from *xx carr'* above.
5,1,14	LANDINNER. See also Devon 1,25 (col. 100d), Lifton: "Two lands, Landinner *(Lanliner)* and Trebeigh *(Trebichen)* (see 5,1,20), belonged to this manor before 1066. The Count of Mortain holds them." See Places Notes under Landinner.
5,1,20	TREBEIGH. See 5,1,14 note.
5,2,2	HE ALSO HOLDS. Repeated at the beginning of sections 5,2,2-15 and 5,2,20-33.
5,2,4	LEWARNE. See 5,2,20. Either a duplicate entry or two very similar holdings at the same place. See Places notes.
5,2,19	VALUE...5s. As MS; Farley misprints *x solid'*.
5,2,20	HE ALSO HOLDS. See 5,2,2 note. LEWARNE. See 5,2,4 note.
5,2,28	SLAVES. Exon. *Ibi habet R. x vill' et xx bord' et habent inter eos omnes i carr' et iii servos.* The classification of slaves with ploughs is unusually explicit.
5,3,3	2 HIDES THERE. The lordship and villagers' land totals only 1 hide.
5,3,9	HE ALSO HOLDS. Repeated at the beginning of sections 5,3,9-17 and 5,3,23-28.
5,3,16	ALBERT. PNDB 182-3 and 143.
5,3,22	VALUE.. 30s. The figure in the MS is squashed, but it is clearly *xxx*, which agrees with Exon.
5,3,23	HE ALSO HOLDS. See 5,3,9 note.
5,3,25	½ f. *Dim'* inserted in the MS above and to the right of *dim' ferling*, in error. Not reproduced by the facsimile, or in Exon.
5,3,28	10 SMALLHOLDERS. Unusual for smallholders to precede villagers; in Exon. the villagers come first as usual.
5,4,1	TORTWALD. PNDB 387.
5,4,7	HE ALSO HOLDS. Repeated at the beginning of sections 5,4,7-10 and 5,4,12-17.

5,4,12	HE ALSO HOLDS. See 5,4,7 note.
	TAX FOR 1 f. The MS and Farley have *pro uno ferling*; the facsimile, however, has not reproduced the *o* of *uno,* which is written in slightly paler ink and on the margin folds of the parchment.
	PASTURE, 1 LEAGUE. The MS has *e (est)* written in paler ink after *pasturae*; not reproduced by facsimile or Farley.
5,5,1	COW. Exon. has *et i vacam* added between the lines, above *vii boves in dominio,* probably in error; insertion at the same place two lines below is the normal place for cows. But see Exon. Notes 5,17,4.
5,5,4	HE ALSO HOLDS. Repeated at the beginning of sections 5,5,4-8 and 5,5,10-14 and 5,5,19-22.
5,5,10	HE ALSO HOLDS. See 5,5,4 note.
5,4,19	WINE. Wulfwin? See PNDB 415; cf. Exon. 261 b 3 = DB 5,24,7.
5,5,19	HE ALSO HOLDS. See 5,5,4 note.
5,6,6	LANCARFFE. See 4,27.
	HONOUR. Equivalent to *feudum,* holding. See also 5,8,10 (Exon. Notes) and 5,24,14.
5,7,3	HE ALSO HOLDS. Repeated at the beginning of sections 5,7,3-8.
	25s. The MS has *xx.v.,* probably a correction of *xx* to *xxv.*
5,7,6	POUNDSTOCK. See 1,4 and Exon. Notes 1,4.
5,7,9	ST. GENNYS. See 1,4 and Exon.Notes 1,4.
5,8,2	HE ALSO HOLDS. Repeated at the beginning of sections 5,8,2-10.
	1½ PLOUGHS THERE. In the MS *est* is written over *st,* in correction.
5,8,10	GENVER. See 4,26.
5,11,2	HE ALSO HOLDS. Repeated at the beginning of sections 5,11,2-7.
5,11,6	PASTURE, 15 ACRES. In the MS the *v* of *xv* is rather smudged, but *xv* is clearly intended; it agrees with Exon.
5,13,1	OSFERTH HOLDS. There is no abbreviation sign over *ten* in the facsimile, though it is in the MS and Farley.
5,13,2	HE ALSO HOLDS. Repeated at the beginning of sections 5,13,2-10.
5,14,2	ST. NEOT. See 4,28.
5,14,4	LAND FOR 2 PLOUGHS. The figure is smudged in the MS, but the scribe probably intended *ii* (which agrees with Exon.). Farley misprints *i.*
5,17-5,19	ALNOTH.. EDNOTH.. ALNOTH. Possibly the same person or only two different people. The personal-names *Alnoth* and *Ednoth* are quite different, of course, and the persons should not be identified with each other unless there is circumstantial evidence. PNDB 233 indicates a confusion of one with the other in a Somerset entry, but this could be simple error. OEB 271 shows clearly there were two *stallers* (constables, marshals, masters of horse) called *Eadnoth* and *Alnoth* and this will have prompted an occasional substitution. In the MS *Alnod* (5,17) is written in larger capitals, lined through in red and with red round the *A,* as is generally the case with the first entry of a new sub-tenant in ch.5. However, *Ednod* (5,18) and *Alnod* (5,19) are not written larger or lined through in red, though the initials are still surrounded by red, as is usually the case for the 1086 holder in second and subsequent entries of a sub-section of ch.5. Exon. has *Alnod'* (for 5,17,1-2 and 5,19,1), *Ailnod'* (for 5,17,3), *Alnoth* (for 5,17,4) and *Ednoth* (for 5,18,1). See PNDB 149 and 233, and OEB 154, 170 and (s.v. *Stallere*) 270-271.
5,23,1	VALUE 10s. *Modo* (now) omitted in error by the scribe.
5,24,7	WULFWIN. See 5,4,19 note above and Exon. Notes 5,24,7.
5,24,14	BEFORE 1066. *et geldb'* written after this and no doubt intended for deletion, though the words are not underlined but lined through, as for emphasis; the ink used is black, however, not red. The tax paid is not mentioned in Exon. either; it may have been the 2 acres stated, as is often the case when the exact size of a holding is mentioned.
	HONOUR OF ST. KEW. Reading *ad honore s. Chei* for *ad honores Chei.* The singular *honor* is more common in this meaning and it agrees with Exon. *de honore s. Chei.* See 5,6,6 note.
5,24,23	MERKEN. Exon. *Merhen.* PNDB 327. Possibly from Old Breton *Merchion, Merhon,* or Old Welsh *Merchiaun, Merchion.*
5,25,2	HE ALSO HOLDS. Repeated at the beginning of sections 5,25,2-5.
	10s. So MS and Exon.; figure omitted in error by Farley.
7,1	WHICH IS THERE. In the MS *quae*; Farley misprints *q̄.*

Notes on Placename Identifications

The editors are indebted to Oliver Padel of the Institute of Cornish Studies, for the placenames research, and he to the Revd. Mr. W.M.M. Picken.

There is no EPNS volume for Cornwall, and the identification of places presents a number of difficulties. Like the other South West Counties, the text of DB contains no Hundred headings, although this lack can in part be made good from Exon, which, without giving Hundred headings, seems to group places by hundred under each major landowner, with a few exceptions. Some help can also be obtained from an analysis of the Tax Return (Exon f 72) which lists the holdings of major landowners under hundred heads but without giving placenames.

But the Cornish Hundreds are large, unlike those of Wilts or Somerset, and locating a place within a hundred does not ensure identification, since each hundred contains a number of places of the same or similar names. Cornwall is also remarkable for the number of names beginning *Tre-*, about thirty per cent of the total, for the quantity of names that survive only as isolated farms rather than as parishes, and for the many 'lost' places which are found on tithe maps or earlier editions of the Ordnance Survey, but are on no modern map: these include the Hundred meeting places of Connerton and Tybesta.

Total and secure identifications depend on a study of early forms of the names and later manorial history, both outside the scope of this edition. The identifications of VCH (Volume II part 8 introduction by L.F. Salzmann, translation by Canon Thomas Taylor 1924) which superseded the pioneering work of J. Carne: *An Attempt to Identify the Domesday Manors* (JRIC I 1865 11-19; II 1867 219-222.), have now been improved by DG, whose identifications have been adopted here except as follows:

	This Edition	Domesday Gazetteer
1,4	St Kew	Lanow
3,4	? Tregrenna	Trewornan
4,8	'Halwyn'	Ellenglaze
4,16	Tregole	Tregolds
5,1,15	*Hela*	South Hill
5,1,21	? Hennett	Hagland
5,2,1	? Trewidland	Torwell
5,2,3	Muchlarnick	Lannear
5,2,4	Lewarne	*Languer*
5,2,9	Castle by Lantyan	Lancallen
5,2,20	Lewarne	Lancare
5,2,29	? Landreyne	Landrake
5,5,20	? Trenance	Trenant in Fowey
5,5,21	'Trehaverne'	St Goran
5,5,22	? Barnacott	Bennacott
5,7,12	Treworyan	*Treurgen*
5,8,5	Trevigue	Trefreock in St Gennys
5,8,10	?'Genver'	*Tregrebri*
5,9,4	?'Trenance'	Trenant in Fowey
5,11,7	? Roscarrock	Tregarrick
5,12,2	Levalsa	Havet
5,14,3	Treligga	Treluggan in Landrake
5,14,5	Treval	Trevallack
5,15,5	? Trevesson	Trewithen
5,17,4	Trehudreth	*Trewderet*
5,21,1	*Trelamar*	Tremar
5,23,2	*Tregal*	Tregole
5,24,2	? Trevilveth	Trewidland
5,24,8	? Bosvisack	Bissick
5,24,14	Treroosel	Trenance in St Austell
5,24,16	Tregunnick	Trevego
5,24,21	Tregony	Treluggan in Gerrans
5,24,23	? Carvean	*Carbihan* lost in St Minver
5,25,1	Delamere	Delabole

A few of these discrepancies are discussed below. The interested reader will consult in addition to VCH and DG:

J.J. Alexander:	The Hundreds of Cornwall	DCNQ 18 (1934) 177-182
H.P.R. Finberg:	A Domesday Identification	DCNQ 22 (1942) 95
J.E.B. Gover:	The Placenames of Cornwall	Typescript deposited at the Royal Institution, Truro
C.G. Henderson:	Essays in Cornish History	Oxford 1935
„ „	Ecclesiastical Antiquites of the Four Western Hundreds	JRIC n.s. 2,3 (1955); 2,4 (1956); 3,2 (1958); 3,4 (1960)
„ „	Manuscript Materials deposited at the Royal Institution	
W.M.M. Picken	Domesday Book and East Cornwall OC 2 (1936) 24-27	
N.J.G. Pounds	The Identification of the Domesday Manors of Cornwall OC 3 (1942) 458-463	

plus the important Bibliography in H.C. Darby and R. Welldon Finn : The Domesday Geography of South West England. Cambridge (1967) 345-347

THE HUNDREDS

The Exon Book provides three lists of Cornish Hundreds, two at f63b and one in the Tax Return f72. If one ignores *Sci Petrocii* written over *Rieltone* in the first list, for this can scarcely have been a geographical hundred, the names of the seven hundreds agree. Connerton is modern Penwith, Stratton is now Trigg, Lesnewth and Stratton, Fawton is Westwivelshire, Pawton is Pydar, Rillaton is Eastwivelshire, Tybesta is Powder and Winnianton now Kerrier. The Exon Book seems to group entries under each major landowner in hundreds. Sometimes all the places in one Hundred appear in a single group of entries, as for Winnianton under the Count of Mortain (224-227b); sometimes a hundred is split between several groups of entries, as Stratton under the Count. In such cases, the division is not geographical and such as to suggest specific subdivisions of a hundred. In some cases the group actually opens with the Hundred meeting places, as Connerton (111b), Tybesta (247), Stratton (237). Such groups of entries are also found in DB, but to a lesser extent as the Exchequer book groups mainly by sub-tenants.

Within the Exon Hundred groupings, a few places stand out as being in the 'wrong' hundred. Sometimes this points to an uncertain identification, or it is because the Exon arrangement itself is not perfect: Rillaton and Stratton places seem to intermingle at 245/245b, and the last few entries under the Count of Mortain seem to be a miscellany (263b-264b). Such discrepancies are noted below. Often places in the 'wrong' Hundred are close to its border, and it is likely that this has subsequently altered. It seems that the 1086 boundary of Fawton was further East (involving Trewolland, Cartuther and perhaps Bonyalva), and that of Tybesta further North (embracing Arrallas and Burthy). Tregrenna, Trewint, Landinner, Halvana, and Polyphant (though not apparently Trevague) on the Rillaton boundary with Stratton appear to have changed their Hundreds. In general the 1086 boundaries seem to have been but slightly disturbed, but since the evidence of DB and Exon, though suggestive, is not full enough to show the 1086 location of every place, places are mapped and indexed in their modern hundreds, with known changes noted below.

CORNWALL Places Notes

1,1   WERRINGTON   EPNS Devon 171. Exchequer DB includes in Devon (101 b = 1,50), Exon. both in Devon (98, 178b) and in the *Terrae Occupatae* of Cornwall (508). Although West of the Tamar and so geographically in Cornwall, it may have been regarded administratively as in Devon since the foundation of Tavistock Abbey (c 970) to which it belonged. See EPNS p. xiii (Devon) and H.P.R. Finberg, *The Early History of Werrington*, English Historical Review LIX (1944) 237-251. Since a recent boundary change (1.1.1966) Werrington is in Cornwall.

1,4   ST KEW. The DB name survives in nearby Lanow. See W.M.M. Picken: *'The Manor of Tremaruustel and the Honour of St Keus'* JRIC n.s. 7 Pt3 (1975-6) 220-230.

1,7   BONYALVA. A dependency of Pendrim and included by Exon among Fawton Hundred places. It is later in Rillaton and was probably a Fawton outlier there in 1086, if the River Seaton was the boundary. See 5,3,5 and 5,5,10 nn.

1.8   CARADON. Possibly Caradon Prior, site at SX 27 70.

1,11   ROSEWORTHY. In DB and in Exon (102b 1) this entry falls between the same Rillaton Hundred places, but the early forms of Roseworthy in Connerton Hundred make the identification secure.

1,14	'CONNERTON'. The manor and Hundred meeting place were near Gwithian village. See Charles Thomas: Gwithian (Redruth 1964) 3-5. The name survives in Connerton Farm (SW 59 39) a nineteenth century antiquarian revival and in Connor Downs (also 59 39)
1,15	COSWARTH. Flanked by two Connerton entries in Exon 111 b 2-3, but it is included correctly in Pawton Hundred at 205 a 1 (= 4,21).
3,4	TREGRENNA. Now in Altarnun parish, Stratton Hundred, but included in Exon (181 a 2) among Rillaton places in which Hundred it probably lay in 1086. See 5,24,5 and 5,26,1 notes.
4	ST. MICHAELS. The church is on St. Michael's Mount, grid ref. SW 51 29.
4,2	ST.STEPHENS. DB *Lanscavetone*. The Church is clearly St Stephens, the DB name surviving in nearby Launceston, which is DB *Dunhevet* 5,1,22.
4,3	BODMIN. Later in Stratton Hundred, but probably regarded as part of Pawton in 1086. In Exon 202 a 1 it begins a list of eight Pawton Places (but see Nancekuke below). The main church of St Petroc was in Bodmin (SX 07 67) with a subsidiary at Padstow (SW 91 75)
4,6	NANCEKUKE. Later in Connerton Hundred. It is a border place and in Exchequer DB and in Exon (202 b 1) it is among Pawton places.
4,8	'HALWYN'. Henderson EA 133.
4,96	TREGOLE. Pounds OC III 463.
4,21	COSWARTH. See 1,15n.
4,22	LANCARFFE. Later in Stratton Hundred and entered there in Exon 241 b 2 (=5,6,6). In Exon (205 a 6) it is among Pawton places and may have had land in both Hundreds. See 4,3n.
4,26	'PERRANZABULOE'. The original site was at St Piran's oratory (SW 76 56), long since engulfed by advancing sand dunes. The modern site is at SW 77 57.
5,1,8	BRANNEL. The centre of the Domesday manor was at Court (SW 95 52)
5,1,11	'ALVERTON' Lost in Penzance. Probably named after the 1066 holder.
5,1,14	LANDINNER. Later in Stratton Hundred, but a border place and included by Exon (261 b 1) in Rillaton where it probably lay in 1086. In the Devon surveys (Exch DB 100d = 1,25. Exon 93) Landinner and Trebeigh are said to have been dependencies of Lifton in Devon before 1066. This arrangement dated back to King Alfred who had divided his lands in Cornwall between his two sons. To the elder he left the lands 'at Stratton in Trigg' and elsewhere, and to the younger lands elsewhere and at ' Lifton and the lands there are administered by it, that is all that I have in Cornwall except Trigg'. W. de G. Birch *Cartularium Saxonicum* no. 553.
5,1,15	*HELA*. Exon includes in Rillaton Hundred (261 b 4). Early spellings of South Hill (*Southull(e)* 1175, 1270 etc) make DG's identification unlikely.
5,1,21	? HENNETT. The identification is not secure. In Exon (262 a 5) it falls between a list of Rillaton and Stratton places, but its immediate environment is uncertain, preceded by Trebeigh, followed by a lacuna then by Rinsey, itself a problem.
5,2,4	LEWARNE. In Fawton Hundred (Exon 236 a 1). A nearly identical entry appears at 5,2,20 (= Exon 257 b 1) where Lewarne is among Rillaton places. If the second entry is a duplicate, a scribal error would account for the place being out of order there.
5,2,11	TREMATON. The castle is at SX 41 58, the modern village at SX 39 59.
5,2,19	? TREMOAN. The identification is not certain. It falls among Rillaton places in Exon 257 a 3, but is followed by the duplicate Lewarne entry (note 5,2,4) 'Tremear' lost in St Ive parish is also possible.
5,2,20	LEWARNE. See 5,2,4 n.
5,3,5	CARTUTHER. Now in Menheniot parish, Rillaton Hundred. It is a border place and included by Exon (228 b 3) in Fawton. The river Seaton was probably the boundary in 1086.
5,3,16	BURTHY. Now in St Enoder parish, Pawton Hundred. It is included by Exon (248 b 1) in Tybesta and was probably there in 1086. See 5,4,12 n.
5,4,6	ST.JULIOT. The church is marked but not named on the OS map. The name survives as a parish.
5,4,9	MINSTER. The church is marked, but not named on the OS map. The names survives as a parish.
5,4,11	CARADON. Probably Caradon Lyer (see 1,8 n.)
5,4,12	ARRALLAS. Now in St Enoder Parish, Pawton Hundred, but probably in Tybesta in 1086 (Exon 249 b 2). See 5,3,16n.
5,5,10	TREWOLLAND. Now in Rillaton Hundred, but probably in Fawton in 1086, with the river Seaton as the boundary (Exon 234 b 1) See 1,7 and 5,5,10 nn. There is a Trewolland at SX 3369 in Rillaton Hundred whose early forms would make it a more likely identification, but for the Exon evidence.

5,5,20 ? TRENANCE. Henderson EA 26
5,5,21 'TREHAVERNE' Lost in Truro. Henderson ECH 2.
5,6,6 LANCARFFE. See 4,22 n.
5,6,9 POLYPHANT. Now in Lewannick parish, Rillaton Hundred, but in both DB and Exon it is included with Stratton places, and was probably there in 1086.
5,7,4 MORETON. Great Moreton is mapped, but M. Mill (SS 28 68) and M. Pound (27 08) are in the locality.
5,7,6 ST KEW. See 1,4n.
5,8,3 WESTCOTT. The choice of location is arbitrary, there being several Westcotts in Stratton Hundred. One, at SX 3099, may have been in Devon in 1086 if the Tamar was the boundary
5,8,10 ? 'GENVER'. See C.Henderson, in G.H. Doble, *St Perran, St Keverne, and St Kerrian* (Long Compton 1931, Cornish Saints 29). The only Stratton place connected with Saint Piran was in Tintagel parish. The chapel is at 'Genver' (1840) probably the same as *Tregenver* (1808), which offers an intermediate spelling between 'Genver' and DB *Tregrebri*.
5,9,4 ? 'TRENANCE'. Henderson EA 26.
5,11,6 BOROUGH. Now in Devon, but the 1086 boundary was probably the Tamar. EPNS Devon 136, does not cite DB. See 5,24,18 n.
5,12,2 LEVALSA. In Tybesta Hundred. Exon places this among Fawton places, (234 a 3) but the early spellings make the identification secure.
5,14,3 TRELIGGA. Pounds OC III 463
5,17,4 TREHUDRETH. Pounds OC III 463
5,21,1 *TRELAMAR*. Exon 234 a 1. Probably in Fawton Hundred. In Exon, *Cornubia* is written above the place. Elsewhere in the Book, it marks the beginning of a new Hundred list as 247 (Tybesta) 255 (Connerton).
5,23,2 *TREGAL*. Placed by Exon 242 b 1 clearly in Stratton Hundred.
5,24,2 ? TREVILVETH. In Tybesta Hundred. The identity is not certain, but the early spellings are suggestive. In Exon it falls between a Fawton Group and a Stratton list (232 a 2)
5,24,5 HALVANA. Later in Stratton Hundred, but it is a border place and probably in Rillaton in 1086 (Exon 264 a 3) See 3,4 and 5,26,1 nn.
5,24,6 ? RINSEY. In Winnianton Hundred. The identity is uncertain. Elsewhere in Exon (99, 100, 225) Rinsey is correctly included in Winnianton, but at 262 b 1 it is among Rillaton or Stratton places. See 5,1,21n.
5,24,14 TREROOSEL. See 1,4n.
5,24,18 TACKBEAR. Now in Devon, but the 1086 boundary was probably the Tamar. EPNS Devon 135. See 5,11,6 n.
5,24,23 ? CARVEAN. The identity is unsure. Carvean is in Tybesta, but Exon (237 b 1) places *Carbihan* in Stratton.
5,24,24 WHITSTONE. In Stratton Hundred. It heads a list of Stratton places in DB, but in Exon (255 b 3) is at the end of Connerton places and before a Rillaton list.
5,25,5 TRUTHWALL. In Connerton Hundred. The identification is hardly in doubt, but it falls between Rillaton and Stratton groups in Exon 258 b 3. As a place recently removed from St. Michael's by the Count of Mortain, it was perhaps inserted out of order by the scribe.
5,26,1 TREWINT. In Exon (260 b 2) it seems to begin a group of Rillaton places, and was probably there in 1086 (see 3,4 and 5,24,5 notes).

E
EXON. EXTRA INFORMATION AND DISCREPANCIES WITH DB

Exon commonly gives an exact number of oxen, whereas DB tends to level up or down to the nearest half plough, at 8 oxen to the plough, so that DB's plough is often the equivalent of Exon's 6 oxen. The details are set forth in the list of lordship entries. References are to the Exon. columns given in the translation, unless otherwise given.

1,1 11 HIDES. So also 99 a 1. 508 b 1 reads "22 manors" (*xx et ii mansiones*) in place of 11 hides.
17 THANES. "They paid customary dues to this manor".. 99 a 1. "Value £9 8s".. 508 b 1.
RINSEY.. VALUE 15s. "When the Count received it 12s".
WULFWARD.. RINSEY. "It paid tax for ½ v.".. 225 b 2.
WULFWARD HAS 1 PLOUGH. "Wulfward and his villagers have 1 plough."
SKEWES FROM THE COUNT. Most of the lands held by the Count of Mortain from the King's manor of Winnianton are entered twice in Exon. Columns 224 - 227 give full detailed entries; columns 99-100 give mainly the plough assessment and value. However, 99 a 2 - 100 a 1 (Skewes Halliggye) have the land taxed also, but the amount is not the same as that given in cols. 224-227 for these places, but the same as the amount of land stated in the DB entries (e.g. Skewes paid tax for 1 v. .. 99 a 2). Here the livestock is, as elsewhere, entered in the translation, and the lordship detail with other such detail in Table L (Lordship Detail). The rest of the entries are given opposite as in 224-227; variants in 99-100 are noted. The variants, chiefly of values, are due perhaps to changes that took place between the entering of the King's and of the Count of Mortain's lands. Places here given references 99 - 100 are not entered in 224 - 227.

DETAIL FOR DB 1,1 GIVEN IN EXON.

a. = acre   f. = furlong   h. = hide   lg. = league   v. = virgate

Exon column	Tax paid for	Land for ploughs	Villagers	Small-holders	Slaves	Woodland	Underwood (*nemusculum*)	Pasture	Meadow	Now	Value when the Count received it (=formerly)
225 b 3 Skewes	1 f.	1	-	-	-	-	-	-	-	waste	15s
225 b 4 Trenance	1 f.	4	-	-	2	-	-	-	-	2s	20s
226 a 1 Garah?	½ f.	1	-	-	1	-	-	½ lg by ½ lg	-	10s	15s
226 a 2 Trembraze	never	-	-	-	-	-	-	-	-	waste	10s
226 a 3 Tregoose	† ⅔ v.	8	2	4	1	-	-	1½ f.	-	30d	40s
224 b 1 'Crawle'	1 f.	3	-	4	-	6 a.	-	100 a.	-	10s	15s
226 a 4 Lizard	½ h.	6	6	6	6	-	-	1½ lg by ½ lg	-	30s	50s
226 a 5 Mawgan	1 f.	4	2	2	1	1 lg by ½ lg	-	20 a.	-	5s	20s
226 b 1 Boden	1 f.	2	2	-	3	-	-	½ lg by 3 f.	1 a.	10s	20s
226 b 2 Trelowarren	1 v.	5	3	6	5	6 a.	-	1 lg by ½ lg	-	15s	30s
226 b 3 Halliggye	1 f.	3	2	-	-	-	6 a.	-	-	5s	10s
227 a 1 Bojorrow	1 f.	2	2	-	1	-	-	½ lg by ½ lg	-	5s	10s
227 a 4 Truthall	½ f.	5	-	-	1	-	5 a.	60 a.	-	10s	2s
227 a 2 Trewarnevas	½ f.	1	-	-	1	-	-	6 a.	-	30d	5s
227 a 3 Trelan	½ f.	2	-	1	-	-	-	½ lg by ½ lg	-	10s	20s
227 a 5 Tredower	1 f.	8	1	-	-	-	-	1 lg by ½ lg	-	30d	10s
100 a 7 Treworder?	-	6	-	-	-	-	-	-	-	3s	40s
224 b 2 Roscarnon	1 f.	2	-	-	2	-	-	60 a.	-	5s	10s
100 a 10 Treal	-	2	-	-	-	-	-	-	-	3s	3s
100 b 1 Trevedor?	-	2	-	-	-	-	-	-	-	5s	10s

Variants: 99 b 2 enters Trembraze with land for 1 plough, omitted in 226 a 2.
Value Now ... Trenance 30d (99 a 3); Garah? 5s (99 b 1);
Mawgan 3s (99 b 6); Roscarnon 10s (100 a 9).
Value Formerly ... Trembraze 15s (99 b 2).

† *ii. part'* (see Lordship Detail note)

E

HAMELIN... CRAWLE. "Edwy held it in 1066."

RICHARD... LIZARD. "He has 2½ ploughs there.." 99 b 5 (see Lordship).

ANDREW... BODEN. "Which two thanes held in 1066.." 99 b 7; so also 226 b 1.

THURSTAN.. TRUTHALL. "Thurstan the Sheriff".. 100 a 3; so also 227 a 4.

DODA... TRELAN. "1 virgate and 1 acre".. 227 a 3, but 4 acres in 100 a 5 and DB. Unless there is a figure error by scribe, three Cornish acres here make 1 virgate. See Notes 1,1.

GRIFFIN ... ROSCARNON . "Griffin holds" .. 100 a 9 and DB 1,1; but "Griffin held in 1066. Iovin now holds" .. 224 b 2 and DB 5,7,1. Either Griffin kept part¹ of Roscarnon and lost part, or the holder changed between the Survey of the King's lands and of the Count's.

1,2   IT PAYS. Here, and commonly with present value, *per annum*.

1,4   POUNDSTOCK AND ST. GENNYS. Also in 507 a 6; 507 b 4; 507 b 5. Fuller details under the Count's holdings in 238 a 1 and 238 b 1 (DB 5,7,6;9). The combined former value is 40s there, however, and the total of the plough assessments is 16, not 12. 507 a 6 agrees with DB 1,4 and 101 a 2. There are no plough assessments or values given in 507 b 4 and 507 b 5,

POUNDSTOCK. "Which was attached to it in 1066" .. 101 a.2. "Which was (part) of the lordship of the King's manor of St. Kew and taken away after 1066" .. 507 b 4.

ST. GENNYS. "Which belonged to the above manor of St. Kew in 1066 and was taken away after 1066" .. 507 b 5.

1,6   PENDAVEY. "Which belonged to the above manor in 1066." So also 507 a 5.

BOIA THE PRIEST. "Of Bodmin." *Boia clericus de bodmine* .. 507 a 5.

1,10   14 SMALLHOLDERS. In the MS *xvi* with *iiii* written above the *vi* which is underlined for deletion; Ellis omits the underlining in error.

1,12   1½ HIDES. The figures do not agree. Exon has *villani habent i hid' et xx carr'* with *et dim'* added above the line. In the MS it looks as though some figure was erased between *i* and *hid'*, (perhaps another *i*, making 2 hides), and the *et dim'* added afterwards. Probably either 1 hide in lordship, or 2 villagers' hides was intended.

1,15   30d OR 1 OX. "30d and 1 ox and 7 sheep... Now it has been taken away." So also 507 b 1. However, "1 ox and 7 sheep" only, in 205 a 1 and 507 b 8, as in DB 4,22.

1,18   PAYS. So 112 a 1 (*reddit*); but 507 b 2 has *reddidit .. quae hactenus retenta est* ("paid .. it is still withheld").

2,2   COUNT OF MORTAIN HAS. "Holds wrongfully" .. 507 b 3.

FAIR. *Annuale forum* .. 199 a 2; *feria* .. 507 b 3.

BISHOP. "Bishop Leofric".

2,3   16 PLOUGHS AND 11½ HIDES. *Villani habent* omitted in error before this.

2,5   TAX. "For 1½ hides"; in agreement with the detail figures.

2,6   IS A MARKET. "Was a market in 1066". So also 507 a 1.

2,10   ROLAND. "Archdeacon Roland". In the MS and Ellis *archididiachon* in error for *archidiachon* - the word is broken after *archidi* by the end of folio 200 b.

2,14   REGINALD. " Of Vautortes" (*de Valletorta* .. OEB 117), held 2,12-13; Hamelin held 2,14. So also 507 a 2-4.

4,1   1 HIDE. "It was (part) of the lordship of St. Michael's in 1066." So also 508 a 6.

1 HIDE. VALUE 20s. "As much when the Count received it". So also 508 a 6. But in 258 b 3 (DB 5,25,5) the former value is given as 40s.

4,2   ST. STEPHENS. "Earl Harold held it in 1066."

3 LEAGUES. "3 leagues in length and 2 in length" (second "length" in error for "width").

4,3   ST. PETROC'S. In 528 b 1 there is a summary of St. Petroc's holdings in Cornwall: "St. Petroc's has in Cornwall 7 lordship manors of 15 hides, which (the hides) do not pay tax; (also) 4 ploughs in lordship; (also) 74 villagers, 74 smallholders, 11 slaves, 68 burgesses, who have 27½ ploughs. Value of this land £8.
The Count of Mortain holds from St. Petroc's Church 10 manors of 16 hides and 1 virgate, which (the hides) do not pay tax; (also) 15½ ploughs; (also) 42 villagers, 74 smallholders, 41 slaves, who have 23½ ploughs. Value of this land £23 3s.
Land for 140 ploughs in all. The Count's part has declined (in value) by £12 5s. The Count of Mortain takes (*aufert*, present) 9 manors from the said Church." See Finn *Liber Exoniensis* p. 126-8, for a discussion of this.

4,4   THE CHURCH. "The Canons of St. Petroc's;" so also hereafter. "They were the holders in 1066." So also in 4,5.

NEVER PAID TAX. "Except for the Church's use (*nisi ad opus aecclesiae*)."

4,7   COUNT OF MORTAIN. "Count Robert."

4,12	GODRIC. "He could not be separated from St. Petroc's".
	WHICH NEVER PAID TAX. Omitted in Exon.
	VALUE.. 20s. In the Exon MS the figure appears to have been corrected from *xx* to *xv*, or vice versa; it is impossible to tell which the scribe finally intended.
4,13	ALFWY. The Exon MS has *Eduuy*, though an attempt seems to have been made to change the *d* to an *l* by partly erasing it. Exon regularly has *y* for DB's *i*.
4,15	2 PLOUGHS THERE. *Ibi habet Comes i carr' et i aliam carr'*. Unusual phrasing; either the Count had both ploughs, or *villani habent* should have taken the place of *i*, between *et* and *aliam*.
4,16	1 HIDE. "It is (part) of St. Petroc's lordship."
4,18	ST. PETROC'S. "They were the holders in 1066." So also for 4,19-20.
4,21	EARL HAROLD. "In 1066."
	EXON. 204 b 4 (also 507 b 6) has "The Count of Mortain has a manor called St. Tudy (*Hecglostudic*) which was St. Petroc's in 1066. It paid 30d (each year.. 507 b 6 only) by custom to St. Petroc's Church." Omitted in DB.
	508 a 5 reads "The King has a manor called Werrington from which ½ hide has been taken, which belonged there in 1066. The Count of Mortain holds it now. Value 40s; when the Count received it £4." The note is part of the entry of Werrington in Devon (1,50 .. col. 101 b, Exon 98 a 3). It was mistakenly entered among the *Terrae Occupatae* (Appropriated Lands) of Cornwall instead of Devon. The place is on the county boundary.
4,22	TREGONA. "Thurstan the Sheriff holds it." So also 507 b 7.
	TREVORNICK. "Edwy held it" (*Edwi*.. 507 b 9; *Edwit*.. 205 a 2). "Brian holds it". (*Brienn*.. 507 b 9; *Brient*.. 205 a 2).
	'TRENHALE'. As for Trevornick.. 205 a 3; 507 b 10. *Brienn* corrected from *Alsi*.. 205 a 3.
	TOLCARNE. "Alfward held it. Alfsi (*Alsinus*) holds it." So also 508 a 1.
	TREMORE. "Thorkell holds it". So also 508 a 2.
	LANCARFFE. "Nigel holds it. A thane held it." So also 508 a 3; DB 5,6,6.
	TRENINNICK. "Roger holds it." So also 508 a 4.
	Edwy, Alfward and the thane "could not be separated from the Church/St. Petroc's." Brian, Alfsi, Thorkell, Nigel and Roger "take the customary dues from the church."
4,23	1 PLOUGH THERE. Omitted in Exon. It is possible that the 8 cattle mentioned form the plough team; see R. Lennard *Domesday Plough-teams: the South-Western Evidence*, English Historical Review LX (1945) p.218.
4,25	IT NEVER PAID TAX. Omitted in Exon.
	THE COUNT. "Of Mortain."
3,1	SHEVIOCK. "Which Abbot Sihtric held in 1066." So also for 3,3-6.
3,7	FOUR MANORS. "Which Abbot Sihtric bought with the Church's goods (*de bonis aecclesiae*) in 1066. The Abbot claims them for the Church's use (*ad opus aecclesiae*)." So also 508 a 7.
	ABBOT CLAIMS. "Abbot Geoffrey (*Gaufridus*)" .. 508 a 7.
5,1,2	WOODLAND, 400 ACRES. "300 acres."
5,1,7	200 SHEEP. So MS; Ellis omits *oves* in error.
5,1,14	EDITH. "Queen Edith."
5,1,16	SIHTRIC. "Abbot Sihtric."
5,2,1	REGINALD. "Of Vautortes", as in 2,14 and 5,2,9; 11.
	TREWIDLAND? "The Count has 1 hide of land called Trewidland?"
5,2,2	VALUE.. 60s. Both values 20s.
5,2,11	CASTLE. "Reginald holds it from the Count."
5,2,12	LORDSHIP. In the MS *i virgis* for *i virgam*; the *is* is squashed, perhaps in an attempt to make an *ā* (= *-am*).
5,2,18	MERLESWEIN. *Merlatona*, in error.
5,2,19	1 v. THERE. The detail totals 2 f. which normally makes only ½ v. (see 5,2,15; 23). Either there is a figure error here or, as apparently also in 5,2,26, 2 f. make 1 v.
5,2,21	1 PLOUGH THERE. *Ibi habet R. ii bord' et inter eos et dominium habent i carr'*. ("Reginald has 2 smallholders there, and between them and the lordship they have 1 plough"). *dm̄n* in the MS; Ellis misprints *dnm̄*.
5,2,26	1 v. THERE. See note to 5,2,19 above.
5,2,27	½ HIDE THERE. Only the ½ v. of Reginald's lordship is mentioned; perhaps the scribe omitted the common phrase "the villagers hold the rest of the land".
	½ PLOUGH. *Habet Raginald'... iii boves inter eum et suos bord'*. ("Reginald has...3 oxen between himself and his smallholders").

5,2,28   AELFRIC. *Ailric*, though an *l* looks as though it may have been erased between the *A* and *i*, thus changing *Alric* to *Ailric*.

5,2,30   PASTURE. "5 acres."

5,2,32   VALUE.. 2s. Both values 3s.

5,3,1   RICHARD. "Richard son of Thorolf."

5,3,6   AELFRIC. *Albric'*, a variant spelling of Aelfric, PNDB 177.

5,3,18   6 VILLAGERS. "3 villagers" in Ellis, but in the MS an attempt has obviously been made to change the *iii* into a *vi*.

5,3,27   LAND FOR 15 PLOUGHS. "3 hides of land there; it paid tax for 1 hide. 15 ploughs there. Richard holds from the Count. 3 hides there; it paid tax for 1 hide. 30 ploughs. Richard holds from the Count." Either the source for both Exon and DB was ambigious, or DB copied Exon here. See Staffs. 1,48;51-53;61;63 for examples of uncertainty in the plough assessments.

5,4,1   THURSTAN. "Thurstan the Sheriff"; so also for 5,4,3; 12.

5,4,7   2 VILLAGERS. "Who have 1 plough."

5,4,11   VALUE NOW 10s. "5s."

5,4,18   GURLYN. *habet t. i agrum in dominio et i carr' et vill' xvi bord' et vii servos*. In the MS *vill'* is underlined for deletion; Ellis omits the underlining in error.

5,5,2   14 VILLAGERS. "13 villagers."

5,5,11   ½ PLOUGH THERE, "Hamelin has 4 oxen in a plough."

5,5,13   TRETHAKE. "½ hide there."

5,5,14   ½ PLOUGH THERE. "Hamelin has 4 oxen in a plough."

5,6,2   6 PLOUGHS THERE. The detail gives 6½. Discrepancies between DB and Exon plough numbers usually only occur when Exon gives the number of oxen. As this is not the case here, perhaps one of the scribes made a mistake, or the information was at fault.

5,6,3   2½ PLOUGHS THERE. The detail gives 3. See 5,6,2 note above.

5,7,6   POUNDSTOCK. See 1,4 note above.

5,7,8   TREMBLARY. *hanc poss' arare ii carr' et habet inde dim' fertinum*. "Iovin holds it from the Count" omitted in error after *ii carr'*.

5,7,9   ST. GENNYS. See 1,4 note above.

5,7,10   3 SMALLHOLDERS. So MS; Ellis misprints "4 smallholders."

5,6,7   VALUE NOW 40s. So MS; Ellis misprints 60s.

5,8,3   2 VILLAGERS. "Who have 2 oxen in a plough."

5,8,10   THIS LAND. "This manor is (part) of the Honour of St. Piran's."

5,10,1   WILLIAM. "William Cheever (*capra*)" .. OEB 360.

5,11,2   UNDERWOOD. *nemoris* ("woodland"), possibly a mistake for *nemusculi* ("underwood"). Ellis misprints *nemori*; in the MS the *s* is written above, as it is in *seruos* in the preceding line. See 6,1 note below.

5,11 3   1 PLOUGH.. THERE. "Alfred has 1 plough."

5,13,2   2 VILLAGERS. *Ibi sunt ii villani* ..., instead of the usual *Osferd habet ii villanos* ...

5,13,3   3 VILLAGERS. *et i carr'* inserted unusually between the villagers and smallholders. The scribe probably forgot to include this plough either with the one held by the villagers or with the ½ plough in lordship (see detail). The total is now 2½ ploughs, as in DB.

5,14,1   VALUE NOW 50s. "20s."

5,14,2   3 SLAVES. *iii seruus* for *iii seruos*. The scribe appears to have attempted to correct the second *u* to an *o*; Ellis does not reproduce this.

5,14,3   FORMERLY 10s. "20s."

5,14,5   2 VILLAGERS. "Who have 2 oxen."

5,15,6   IN LORDSHIP 3 PLOUGHS. "1 plough in lordship and the villagers have .. 2 ploughs."

5,17,4   1 PLOUGH THERE. "Alnoth has .. 1 plough."

      2 COWS. *Habet A. ii vacae*, for *Habet A. ii vacas*. The cows and sheep are written in the normal place for the lordship entry, that is between the present holder and the villagers' holding, rather than as usual after the slaves and before the resources.   See Notes 5,5,1.

5,23,4   VALUE NOW 5s. "3s."

5,24,7   WULFWIN. *Win'*. See Notes 5,4,19.

5,24,14   HONOUR OF ST. KEW. *hec mansio est de honore S. Chei*.

5,24,17   ALFSI. *Ailsi loholt*. See OEB 46 and 126.

      VALUE.. 5s. Both values 10s.

5,24,22   VILLAGERS. "The villagers have all that land and ½ plough."

5,24,24   ½ PLOUGH THERE. *In ea est dim' carr'*. Unusual formula; ploughs are normally stated as held either by the 1086 holder or by the villagers.

      40 [SHEEP]. *pues*, in error for *oves*.

5,25,1   BLOHIN. "Blohin the Breton", as stated in 258 b 3 (DB 5,25,5).

      IOLF. *Iaulus*.

5,25,4	TREWETHART. "Blohin has all the land in lordship." AELFRIC. *Alfic'*. See PNDB 177.
5,25,5	TRUTHWALL. "It paid tax to St. Michael." BRICTMER. "Brictmer the priest."
5,26,2	3 SMALLHOLDERS. Ellis misprints *vi bord'*; in the MS the first two strokes of the *iii* are almost joined together, but the result is unlike the *v* written by the scribe of this part of Exon.
5,26,3	5... CATTLE. *v... animal'*. In the MS a word of 4 or 5 letters has been erased; the *v* probably does refer to the number of cattle.
6,1	JUDHAEL OF TOTNES. "Of Totnes" omitted. FROXTON. "Alfward held it in 1066." THURSTAN. "Thurstan the Sheriff." UNDERWOOD. *nemoris* ("woodland"); possibly a mistake for *nemusculi* ("underwood"). See 5,11,2 note above.

L   LORDSHIP DETAIL

omitted in DB 1,1, given in Exon.

(* indicates that the words *in dominio* have been omitted in Exon. though no doubt intended. Rest = the rest of the land. Note that *tertiam partem* and *iii parte̅* are read as 1/3. *ii part'* (*duae partes* 'two parts') and *iii part'* (*tres partes* 'three parts') are read as 2/3 and 3/4 respectively.

Exon. column		In Lordship land	ploughs	The Villagers have land	ploughs
*225 b 2	Rinsey (Wulfward's)	1 v.	2 oxen	3 v.	1
226 a 3	Tregoose	†2/3 v.	-	Rest	-
224 b 1	'Crawle'	1/3 f.	7 oxen	Rest	6 oxen
*226 a 4	Lizard	1 v.	1½	Rest	1
226 a 5	Mawgan	1 v.	½	Rest	2 oxen
*226 b 1	Boden	‡¾ v.	1	Rest	-
226 b 2	Trelowarren	1 v.	1	3 v.	-
227 a 1	Bojorrow	1 a.	½	Rest	-
*227 a 4	Truthall	-	1	-	-
*227 a 3	Trelan	-	½	-	-
224 b 2	Roscarnon	-	½	-	-

† *ii part'*   ‡ *iii part'*

omitted elsewhere in DB, given in Exon.

(Exon. column references are given on the translation pages.)

DB Chapter and Section		In Lordship land	ploughs	The Villagers have land	ploughs
*4,2	St. Stephens	-	3	-	6
4,6	Nancekuke	1 v.	1	-	-
*4,8	'Halwyn'	1 v.	1½	Rest	1½
*4,11	Treloy	-	1	-	1
*4,13	Bossiney	-	1	-	2 oxen

L

DB Chapter and Section		In Lordship		The Villagers have	
		land	ploughs	land	ploughs
4,14	Tremail	-	2	-	1
*4,16	Tregole	-	1	-	3
*4,17	Fursnewth	-	1	-	3
4,18	Ellenglaze	1 h.	½	1 h.	3½
4,19	Withiel	1 v.	1	3 v.	3
4,20	Treknow	½ h.	½	1½ h.	3
*4,26	'Perranzabuloe'	-	1	-	1
3,4	Tregrenna	1 f.	1	Rest	2
3,5	Penharget	1 f.	1	-	-
5,2,3	Muchlarnick	½ f.	½	Rest	½
5,2,5	Braddock	½ v.	1	Rest	1
5,2,6	Raphael	½ v.	1	Rest	1
5,2,7	Killigorrick	½ a.	2 oxen	Rest	-
5,2,9	Lantyan	½ f.	-	Rest	-
5,2,10	Lanhadron	½ f.	1	Rest	-
5,2,14	Maker	1 v.	-	3 v.	3
5,2,15	Tredinnick?	2 f.	1	2 f.	-
5,2,16	Tregantle	2 f.	1	-	1
5,2,17	Halton	1 v.	1	3 v.	3
5,2,18	Pillaton	1 v.	1	1 v.	2
5,2,19	Tremoan?	2 f.	4 oxen	-	2 oxen
5,2,22	Penpoll	-	1	-	2
5,2,23	Trefrize?	2 f.	½	2 f.	2
5,2,24	Newton Ferrers	1 v.	1	-	1
5,2,25	Appledore	-	1	-	1
5,2,26	Bicton	2 f.	-	-	-
5,2,27	Ashton	½ v.	-	-	-
5,2,29	Landreyne?	-	½	Rest	½
5,3,4	Bosent	½ f.	½	Rest	-
5,3,5	Cartuther	½ v.	2	Rest	2
*5,3,6	Lanreath	-	2	-	1
*5,3,7	Lansallos	-	1	-	1
5,3,9	Bodiggo	1 v.	2	3 v.	5
5,3,10	Bodrugan	1 v.	2	Rest	1
5,3,11	Tucoyse	1 f.	2	3 f.	1
5,3,12	Goviley	1 v.	2	Rest	3
5,3,13	Polsue	1 v.	1	3 v.	4
5,3,14	Goodern	1 f.	1	Rest	3 oxen
5,3,15	Treverbyn	1 f.	½	Rest	1
5,3,16	Burthy	1 f.	1	1 f.	4 oxen
5,3,17	Lanescot	½ f.	1	†½ (f.)	6 oxen
5,3,18	Week St. Mary	1 v.	1½	Rest	1½
*5,3,19	Penhallym	1 v.	2	-	4
5,3,20	Downinney	1 v.	3	Rest	7
5,3,21	Otterham	1 v.	1	Rest	3
5,3,22	Hamatethy	1 v.	2	Rest	2
*5,3,23	Colquite	1 v.	2	Rest	1

† *aliam medietatem (terrae)*

DB Chapter and Section		In Lordship		The Villagers have	
		land	ploughs	land	ploughs
5,3,24	Trevisquite	1 v.	3	Rest	3
5,3,26	Landulph	½ v.	6 oxen	Rest	½
5,3,27	Ludgvan	1 v.	3	Rest	9
*5,3,28	Kelynack	1 v.	1	Rest	4
5,4,1	Trelan	1/3 h.	1½	Rest	1½
5,4,2	Pencarrow	½ f.	3 oxen	-	-
5,4,3	Trenewen?	½ f.	½	Rest	-
5,4,5	Trenderway?	½ f.	½	Rest	½
5,4,6	St. Juliot	½ f.	2 oxen	Rest	2 oxen
5,4,8	Trebarfoote	1 f.	1	Rest	1
5,4,10	Amble	1 f.	1	Rest	-
5,4,11	Caradon	½ f.	3 [oxen]†	Rest	3 oxen
5,4,12	Arrallas	1 v.	3 oxen	1 v.	-
5,4,13	Bodardle	1 v.	-	Rest	4
5,4,14	Trelowth	1 f.	1	Rest	1
5,4,15	Tretheake	½ v.	1	Rest	1
5,4,16	Treworrick	½ v.	-	Rest	1
5,4,17	Philleigh	1 f.	-	Rest	½
5,4,18	Gurlyn	1 a.	1	-	-
5,5,1	'Crawle'	1/3 f.	7 oxen	Rest	6 oxen
5,5,2	Milton	½ h.	3	4½ h.	5
5,5,3	Lee	½ h.	2	Rest	4
5,5,4	Boyton	1 f.	1	Rest	1
*5,5,5	Marhamchurch	½ f.	½	Rest	½
5,5,6	Week Orchard	1 f.	1	Rest	1
*5,5,7	Wadfast	½ v.	2	Rest	1
5,5,8	Thorne	1 f.	-	Rest	2 oxen
5,5,9	Rosecraddoc	1 v.	1½	Rest	3
5,5,10	Trewolland	½ a.	½	½ a.	2 oxen
5,5,12	Tregamellyn	½ a.	1	Rest	-
5,5,13	Trethake	½ v.	1	Rest	3 oxen
5,5,15	Penpell	½ v.	1	Rest	-
5,5,16	Tremoddrett	1 v.	2	Rest	3
5,5,17	Trewoon	½ v.	1	Rest	½
5,4,19	Clinnick?	½ f.	-	Rest	-
5,5,18	Tregavethan	1 f.	1	Rest	-
5,5,19	Penventinue	1 f.	1	Rest	1
5,5,20	Trenance?	2 f.	3	Rest	-
5,4,20	Trebartha	½ f.	½	Rest	3
5,6,1	Woolstone	1 v.	1½	Rest	3
5,6,2	Worthyvale	½ v.	2½	Rest	4
5,6,3	Trenuth?	½ v.	1½	Rest	1½
5,6,4	Rosebenault	1 v.	1	Rest	½
5,6,5	Roscarrock	1 v.	1	Rest	1
5,6,6	Lancarffe	1 a.	1	Rest	7 oxen
5,6,8	Trevague	1 f.	1½	Rest	3
5,6,9	Polyphant	½ v.	1	Rest	1

† *oves*, in error for *boves*

L

DB Chapter and Section		In Lordship land	ploughs	The Villagers have land	ploughs
5,6,10	Galowras	½ f.	1	Rest	-
5,7,1	Roscarnon	-	½	-	-
5,7,2	Lametton	½ f.	½	Rest	½
5,7,3	Norton	1 f.	1½	Rest	2
5,7,4	Moreton	½ f.	1	Rest	1
5,7,5	Balsdon	½ f.	-	Rest	½
5,7,6	Poundstock	1 f.	1	Rest	1
5,7,7	Tresparrett	1 f.	1	Rest	3 oxen
5,7,8	Tremblary	½ f.	½	Rest	½
5,7,9	St. Gennys	½ v.	1	Rest	2
5,7,10	Dizzard	½ f.	½	Rest	½
5,7,11	Trerice	½ f.	1	Rest	½
5,7,12	Treworyan	½ f.	½	Rest	½
5,6,7	Tredaule	1 v.	3	Rest	3
5,8,1	Hornacott	1 f.	1	Rest	3 oxen
5,8,2	Alvacott	1 f.	1	Rest	3 oxen
5,8,4	Rosecare	½ f.	1	Rest	-
5,8,6	Crackington	1 a.	½	Rest	½
5,8,9	Lamellen	½ v.	1	Rest	3 oxen
5,8,10	'Genver?'	1 v.	1	Rest	½
5,9,1	Widemouth	2 a.	1	Rest	1½
5,9,2	Whalesborough	1½ a.	1	Rest	1
5,9,3	Penfound	-	1	-	-
5,9,4	'Trenance?'	½ f.	7 oxen	Rest	-
5,10,1	Poughill	1 v.	2	Rest	3
5,11,1	Hilton	1 v.	3	Rest	2
5,11,2	Thurlibeer	2 f.	2	Rest	-
5,11,4	Launcells	½ v.	2	Rest	1½
5,11,5	Cann Orchard	½ f.	1	Rest	1
5,11,6	Borough?	¼ f.	1	Rest	1
*5,12,1	Bodbrane	-	½	-	2 oxen
5,12,2	Levalsa	½ v.	3 oxen	Rest	3 oxen
*5,12,3	Brea	-	1	-	½
5,13,1	Manely	1 v.	6 oxen	Rest	2
*5,13,2	Boconnoc	†1/3	½	Rest	½
5,13,3	Tremadart	1/3 v.	½	Rest	1
*5,13,4	Trenant	1/3 v.	½	Rest	1½
*5,13,5	Glynn	1/3 v.	½	‡2/3 v.	½
5,13,7	Penhalt	1 f.	-	Rest	-
5,13,8	Penpont	1 v.	½	Rest	2
5,13,9	Lantyan	1 a.	4 oxen	Rest	1
5,13,10	Trevillyn	½ f.	-	Rest	2 oxen
5,13,11	Trelaske	½ v.	½	Rest	2
5,13,12	Tregrill	1 v.	2 oxen	Rest	2
*5,14,1	Botelet	††¾v.	1½	Rest	1
5,14,2	St. Neot	1 v.	½	3 v.	½

† *tertiam partem istius terrae*   ‡ *ii part'*   †† *iii part'*

DB Chapter and Section		In Lordship land	ploughs	The Villagers have land	ploughs
5,14,3	Treligga	½ f.	½	Rest	3 oxen
5,14,4	Treveniel	½ f.	6 oxen	Rest	2 oxen
5,15,1	Trenance	1/3 h.	7 oxen	Rest	1
5,15,2	Trewince	1/3 h.	½	Rest	1 and 2 oxen
5,15,3	Pelynt	1 v.	1½	Rest	2
*5,15,4	Pentewan	1 f.	½	Rest	1 and 2 oxen
5,15,5	Trevesson?	1 f.	1	Rest	1
5,16,1	Tregardock	1 f.	½	Rest	2
5,16,2	Kilmarth	1 f.	½	Rest	½
5,17,1	Tolgullow	1 f.	1	1 f.	½
5,17,2	Trescowe	1/3 f.	1 ox	Rest	1
5,17,3	Dizzard	½ a.	½	Rest	1 ox
5,18,1	Pengelly	¼ f.	2 oxen	-	-
5,19,1	Woolston	1 f.	½	Rest	½
5,20,1	Lanwarnick	½ f.	2 oxen	Rest	2 oxen
5,20,2	Draynes	1/3 f.	1 ox	Rest	4 oxen
5,22,1	Cabilla	½ f.	-	Rest	1
5,23,1	Lesnewth	½ v.	½	Rest	3 oxen
5,23,2	*Tregal*	½ a.	½	Rest	-
5,23,3	Tregeagle?	½ f.	-	Rest	-
*5,23,5	Perranuthnoe	1 v.	5 oxen	-	1
*5,24,1	Draynes	1 f.	½	1 f.	½
5,24,2	Trevilveth	1f.	½	1 f.	½
5,24,3	Hele	½ a.	-	Rest	3 oxen
5,24,4	Veryan	1 h.	1	3 h.	4
5,24,5	Halvana	½ v.	½	Rest	-
5,24,8	Bosvisack?	1 f.	2 oxen	Rest	-
5,24,12	Old Kea	1 a.	1	Rest	½
5,24,13	Tucoyse	½ f.	-	½ f.	-
5,24,15	Boduel	½ f.	2 oxen	Rest	2 oxen
5,24,18	Tackbear	¼ f.	1	Rest	-
5,24,19	Trevillis	½ v.	-	Rest	-
5,24,20	Helland	1 a.	-	Rest	1
5,24,21	Tregony	1 v.	1	Rest	1
5,24,23	Carvean?	½ f.	1½	Rest	½
5,24,25	Tredwen	½ f.	1	Rest	1
5,25,1	Delamere	1½ a.	1	Rest	1
5,25,2	Trefreock	1 v.	1	Rest	2 oxen
5,25,3	Dannonchapel	1 f.	1½	Rest	-
*5,25,5	Truthwall	-	1	-	3
5,26,1	Trewint	1 f.	½	Rest	½

L

DB Chapter and Section		In Lordship		The Villagers have	
		land	ploughs	land	ploughs
5,26,2	Delabole	1 f.	1	Rest	-
5,26,3	Leigh	1 f.	1	Rest	1
5,26,4	Hammett	†½	1	Rest	-
6,1	Froxton	½ f.	½	Rest	-
7,1	Pigsdon	-	1	-	-

† *dimid' partem (terrae)*

INDEX OF PERSONS

Familiar modern spellings are given when they exist. Unfamiliar names are usually given in an approximate late 11th century form, avoiding variants that were already obsolescent or pedantic. Spellings that mislead the modern eye are avoided where possible. Two, however, cannot be avoided: they are combined in the name of 'Leofgeat', pronounced 'Leffyet', or 'Levyet'. The definite article is omitted before bynames except where there is reason to suppose that they described the individual. The chapter numbers of listed landholders are printed in bold type. Names and figures in italics are to be found in Exon. Book only, either in small type in the translation, or in the Exon. notes.

Ketel	5,7,5	Richard *son of Thorolf*	5,3
Leofnoth	1,1. 5,24,4-5	Richard	1,1. 2,8. 4,16
Bishop Leofric	2,2;15	Roger	5,26. *4,22*
Leofric	5,5,21. 5,23,4.	*Archdeacon* Roland	2,10
	5,24,8	Saewin	5,5,6. 5,9,2. 5,11,2
Leofrun	5,2,23, 5,14,6	Saewulf	5,2,29. 5,6,10. 5,19,1
Leofwin	5,26,2	Sheerwold	5,24,10
Loholt, see Alfsi		Sibert	5,24,20
Maccus	4,17	Abbot Sihtric	*3,1;7.* 5,1,7;*16*
Queen Matilda	1,13	Sihtric	5,1,17
Merken	5,24,23	Siward	5,5,7
Merleswein	5,1,1-2;10. 5,2,18	*Thorkell*	*4,22*
	5,3,20;24. 5,4,5	Thorold, see Richard	
	5,17,4. 5,24,4	Thorolf, see Richard	
Robert, Count of Mortain	5,1-5,26. 1,1;4;6-7.	Thurstan *the Sheriff*	5,4. 1,1. *4,22.* 6,1
	2,2;6;14. 3,7. 4,1-2;	Tortwald	5,4,1
	7-15;19-20;22-23;	Uhtred	5,2,7
	25-29	Wace	5,8,5
Nigel	5,6. *4,22*	Waddell	5,1,18. 7,1
Odo	5,14. 4,26;28	Wallo	5,2,30
Ordwulf	5,1,9;12	Walter of Claville	1,18
Bishop Osbern	5,1,3	Wihomarch	1,1. 5,24,13-14
Osbern	5,2,10. 5,11,1	William *Cheever*	**5,10**
Osferth	5,13	Wine	5,4,19
Oswulf	5,1,20. 5,14,1;5.	Wulfgeat	5,9,1
	5,15,1-6	Wulfnoth	5,4,3;20. 5,8,3
Rabel	5,24,16-17	Wulfric	5,5,8. 5,6,9. 5,24,8
Ralph the Constable	5,1,6	Wulfsi	5,24,1-2;7
Ralph	5,24,24	Wulfward	1,1. 5,24,6
Reginald *of Vautortes*	5,2. 2,14	Wulfwin	5,24,7
Richard son of Thorold	2,5	Wymarc, see Wihomarch	

Churches and Clergy. **Abbot** of Horton 3,2; of Tavistock, see Geoffrey; see Sihtric. **Archdeacon** see Roland. **Bishop** of Exeter 2; see Leofric, Osbern. **Canons** of St. Achebran's 4,23; of St. Buryan's 4,27; of St. Carantoc's 4,25; of St. German's 2,6; *of St. Petroc's 4,4*; of St. Piran's 4,26; of St. Probus' 4,24; of St. Stephen's, Launceston 1,7. 4,2. **Clergy** of St. Neot's 4,28. **Dean** of St. Piran's 4,26. **Priests** see Bernard, Boia, Brictmer, Godric. **Saint** Constantine's 4,29. German's 2,12-14. Kew 5,24,14. Michael's 4,1. 5,25,5. Petroc's 1,15;18. 4,3-22. 5,6,6. Piran's 5,8,10. Tavistock Church 3.

Secular Titles. Constable (*stalrus*) ... Ralph. Count (*comes*) ... of Mortain. Earl (*comes*) ... Harold. Marshal (*marescallus*) ... Alfred. Queen (*regina*) ... Edith, Matilda. Sheriff (*vicecomes*) ... Thurstan.

INDEX OF PLACES

The name of each place is followed by (i) the initial of its Hundred and its numbered location on the map in this volume; (ii) its National Grid reference; (iii) the chapter and section references in DB. Bracketed figures denote mention in sections dealing with a different place. Unless otherwise stated in the Places notes, the identifications of the Domesday Gazetteer and the spellings of the Ordnance Survey have been followed for places in Britain; of OEB for places abroad. Inverted commas mark lost places with known modern spelling; unidentified places are given in DB spelling in italics. The National Grid reference system is explained on all Ordnance Survey maps and in the Automobile Association Handbooks: the figures reading from left to right are given before those reading from bottom to top. Grid references beginning with W are in square SW, with X in square SX and with S in square SS. A bracket around a grid reference means that the place does not appear on the Ordnance Survey 1 inch or 1:50,000 maps. Places marked D are in Devon. Places are given exclusively in the 'modern' Hundred in which they lie, but the modern form of the DB Hundred name is used for them. The Cornish Hundreds are Connerton (C); Fawton (F); Pawton (P); Rillaton (R); Stratton (S); Tybesta (T); Winnianton (W). While DB, the Exon Book and the Tax Return do not provide evidence for a full reconstruction of the 1086 Hundred boundaries, their general indications (discussed in the Places Notes) are that, with the exception of a few places on Hundred boundaries, the Hundreds have not greatly altered.

	Map	Grid	Text		Map	Grid	Test
Alvacott	S 1	X 31 95	5,8,2	Cargoll	P 4	W 81 56	4,10
'Alverton'	C 1	(W 46 29)	5,1,11	Carsella	T 6	W 94 57	5,24,9
Amble	S 2	W 99 75	5,4,10	Cartuther	R 9	X 26 63	5,3,5
Antony	R 1	X 39 54	3,2	? Carvean	T 7	W 88 47	5,24,23
Appledore	R 2	X 32 68	5,2,25	Carworgie	P 5	W 90 60	1,18
Arrallas	P 1	W 88 53	5,4,12	Castle	T 8	X 09 58	5,2,9
Ashton	R 3	X 38 68	5,2,27	by Lantyan			
Balsdon	S 3	X 28 98	5,7,5	Climsom	R 10	X 36 74	1,9
? Barnacott	S 4	S 24 09	5,5,22	? Clinnick	F 10	(X 14 65)	5,4,19
Bicton	R 4	X 31 69	5,2,26	Colquite	S 14	X 05 70	5,3,23
Binnerton	C 2	W 60 33	1,16	'Connerton'	C 4	(W 58 41)	1,14
Blisland	S 5	X 10 73	1,6	Constantine	W 3	W 73 29	4,29
Boconnoc	F 1	X 14 60	5,13,2	Cosawes	W 4	(W 76 37)	5,3,1
Bodardle	T 1	(X 09 60)	5,4,13	Coswarth	P 6	W 86 59	1,15. 4,22
Bodbrane	F 2	X 23 59	5,12,1	Crackington	S 15	X 14 96	5,8,6
Boden	W 1	W 77 23	1,1	Crantock	P 7	W 79 60	4,25
Bodigga	F 3	X 27 54	1,7	'Crawle'	W 5	(W 61 31)	1,1. 5,5,1
Bodiggo	T 2	X 04 58	5,3,9	Curry	S 16	X 28 93	5,7,13
Bodmin	S 6	X 07 67	4,3	Dannonchapel	S 17	X 03 82	5,25,3
Bodrugan	T 3	X 01 43	5,3,10	Dawna	F 11	X 14 61	5,5,14
Boduel	F 4	X 22 63	5,24,15	Delabole	S 18	X 06 83	5,26,2
Bojorrow	W 2	(W 70 23)	1,1	Delamere	S 19	X 06 83	5,25,1
Bonyalva	R 5	X 30 59	1,7	Dizzard	S 20	X 16 98	5,7,10. 5,17,3
? Borough (D)	S 7	S 26 02	5,11,6	Domellick	T 9	W 94 58	5,24,11
Bosent	F 5	X 21 63	5,3,4	Downinney	S 21	X 20 90	5,3,20
Bossiney	S 8	X 06 88	4,13	Draynes	F 12	X 21 69	5,20,2. 5,24,1
?Bosvisack	T 4	(W 78 46)	5,24,8	Ellbridge	R 11	X 40 63	5,2,8
Botelet	F 6	X 18 60	5,14,1	Ellenglaze	P 8	W 77 57	4,18
Bowithick	S 9	X 18 82	5,13,6	Fawton	F 13	X 16 68	5,1,1
Boyton	S 10	X 31 91	3,7. 5,5,4	Froxton	S 22	X 25 99	6,1
Braddock	F 7	X 16 62	5,2,5	Fursnewth	F 14	X 22 67	4,17
Brannel	T 5	W 95 51	5,1,8	Galowras	T 10	X 00 44	5,6,10
Brea	C 3	W 37 28	5,12,3	? Garah	W 6	(W 67 18)	1,1
Bucklawren	F 8	X 27 55	1,7	Gear	W 7	W 72 24	5,2,33
Burniere	S 11	W 98 73	2,5	? 'Genver'	S 23	(X 08 88)	5,8,10
Burthy	P 2	W 91 55	5,3,16	Glynn	F 15	X 11 64	5,13,5
Buttsbear	S 12	S 26 04	5,11,3	Goodern	T 11	W 78 43	5,3,14
Cabilla	F 9	X 14 69	5,22,1	Gothers	T 12	W 96 58	5,24,10
Callestick	P 3	W 77 50	4,9	Goviley	T 13	W 94 44	5,3,12
Callington	R 6	X 35 69	1,10	Gulval	C 5	W 48 31	2,10
Calstock	R 7	X 43 68	5,2,12	Gurlyn	C 6	W 56 32	5,4,18
Cann Orchard	S 13	S 23 04	5,11,5	Halliggye	W 8	W 71 23	1,1
Caradon	R 8	X 29 71	1,8. 5,4,11	Halton	R 12	X 40 65	5,2,17

	Map	Grid	Text		Map	Grid	Text
Halvana	S 24	X 21 78	5,24,5	Pencarrow	S 45	X 03 71	5,4,2
'Halwyn'	P 9	(W 78 57)	4,8	Pendavey	S 46	X 00 71	1,6
Hamatethy	S 25	X 09 78	5,3,22	Pendrim	F 28	(X 26 55)	1,7
Hammett	R 13	X 32 65	5,26,4	Penfound	S 47	X 22 99	5,9,3
Hela	- -	- -	5,1,15	Pengelly	R 23	X 31 74	5,18,1
Hele	S 26	X 21 97	5,24,3	Pengold	S 48	X 13 94	5,24,17
Helland	T 14	W 90 49	5,24,20	Penhallym	S 49	X 21 97	5,3,19
Helston	W 9	W 65 27	1,2	Penhalt	S 50	S 19 00	5,13,7
Helstone	S 27	X 08 81	5,1,4	Penharget	R 24	X 29 70	3,5
? Hennett	S 28	X 13 91	5,1,21	Penhawger	R 25	X 28 66	5,2,13
Hilton	S 29	S 23 03	5,11,1	Penheale	R 26	X 26 88	1,12
Hornacott	S 30	X 31 94	5,8,1	Penhole	R 27	X 28 76	5,24,7
Idless	T 15	W 82 47	5,15,6	Penpell	T 22	(W 91 44)	5,5,15
? Illand	R 14	X 28 78	3,7. 5,1,17	Penpoll	R 28	X 33 63	5,2,22
Old Kea	T 16	W 84 41	5,24,12	Penpont	S 51	X 22 81	5,13,8
Kelynack	C 7	W 37 29	5,3,28	Pentewan	T 23	X 01 47	5,15,4
Kilkhampton	S 31	S 25 11	1,5	Penventinue	T 24	X 11 53	5,5,19
Killigorrick	F 16	X 22 61	5,2,7	Perranuthnoe	C 10	W 53 29	5,23,5
Kilmarth	S 32	(X 00 78)	5,16,2	'Perranzabuloe'	P 13	(W 76 56)	4,26
Lamellen	S 33	X 05 77	5,8,9	Philleigh	T 25	W 87 39	5,4,17
Lametton	F 17	X 25 61	5,7,2	Pigsdon	S 52	S 28 09	7,1
Lancarffe	S 34	X 08 68	4,22. 5,6,6	Pillaton	R 29	X 36 64	5,2,18
Landinner	S 35	X 23 83	5,1,14	Polroad	S 53	X 05 78	4,15
? Landreyne	R 15	X 28 76	5,2,29	Polscoe	F 29	X 11 60	5,3,2. 5,2
Landulph	R 16	X 43 61	5,3,26	Polsue	T 26	W 85 46	5,3,13
Lanescot	T 17	X 08 55	5,3,17	Polyphant	R 30	X 26 82	5,6,9
Langunnett	F 18	X 15 57	5,2,31	? Porthallow	F 30	X 22 51	5,14,6
Lanhadron	T 18	W 99 47	5,2,10	Poughill	S 54	S 22 07	5,10,1
Lanherne	P 10	W 87 67	2,7	Poundstock	S 55	X 20 99	1,4. 5,7,6
Lanreath	F 19	X 18 56	5,3,6	Probus	T 27	W 89 47	4,24
Lansallos	F 20	X 17 51	5,3,7	Rame	R 31	X 42 49	3,3
'Lantivet'	F 21	(X 16 51)	5,4,4	Raphael	F 31	X 19 50	5,2,6
Lantyan	T 19	X 10 57	5,13,9	Rialton	P 14	W 84 61	4,5
Lanwarnick	F 22	(X 20 57)	5,20,1	Rillaton	R 32	X 29 73	5,1,13
Launcells	S 36	S 24 05	5,11,4	Rinsey	W 13	W 59 27	1,1. 5,24,
Launceston	R 17	X 33 84	5,1,22	Roscarnon	W 14	(W 77 21)	1,1. 5,7,1
Lawhitton	R 18	X 35 82	2,9	? Roscarrock	S 56	W 98 80	5,6,5. 5,1
Lee	S 37	S 22 12	5,5,3	Rosebenault	S 57	(X 17 84)	5,6,4
Leigh	R 19	X 33 64	5,26,3	Rosecare	S 58	X 16 95	5,8,4
Lesnewth	S 38	X 13 90	5,23,1	Rosecraddoc	F 32	X 26 67	5,5,9
Levalsa	T 20	W 99 48	5,12,2	Roseworthy	C 11	W 61 39	1,11
Lewarne	F 23	X 17 65	5,2,4;20	St. Buryan	C 12	W 40 25	4,27
Liskeard	F 24	X 25 64	5,1,2	St. Enoder	P 15	W 89 56	4,12
Lizard	W 10	W 70 12	1,1	St. Gennys	S 59	X 14 97	1,4. 5,7,9
Ludgvan	C 8	W 50 33	5,3,27	St. Germans	R 33	X 35 57	2,6
Maker	R 20	X 44 52	5,2,14	St. Juliot	S 60	X 12 91	5,4,6
Manely	F 25	X 13 55	5,13,1	St. Keverne	W 15	W 79 21	4,23
Marhamchurch	S 39	S 22 03	5,5,5	St. Kew	S 61	X 02 76	1,4. 5,7,6
Mawgan	W 11	W 70 25	1,1				(5,24,4)
Methleigh	W 12	W 62 26	2,2	St. Neot	F 33	X 18 67	4,28. 5,1
Milton	S 40	S 24 14	5,5,2	St. Stephens	R 34	X 32 85	4,2
Minster	S 41	X 11 90	5,4,9	St. Tudy	S 62	X 06 76	Ex204b,
Moresk	T 21	(W 85 43)	5,1,9	St. Winnow	F 34	X 11 57	2,11
Moreton	S 42	S 27 07	5,7,4	Sheviock	R 35	X 37 55	3,1
Muchlarnick	F 26	X 21 56	5,2,3	Skewes	W 16	(W 69 21)	1,1
Nancekuke	C 9	W 67 45	4,6	Stratton	S 63	S 23 06	5,1,3
Newton Ferrers	R 21	X 34 65	5,2,24;28	Tackbear (D)	S 64	S 25 01	5,24,18
Norton	S 43	S 25 08	5,7,3	Tehidy	C 13	W 64 44	5,1,12
Otterham	S 44	X 16 90	5,3,21	Thorne	S 65	X 27 99	5,5,8
Padstow	P 11	W 91 75	4,4	Thurlibeer	S 66	S 25 04	5,11,2
Patrieda	R 22	X 30 73	5,1,18	Tinten	S 67	X 06 75	2,8
Pawton	P 12	W 95 70	2,4	Tolcarne	P 16	W 88 65	4,22
Pelynt	F 27	X 20 55	5,15,3	Tolcarne	R 36	X 24 78	3,6

Name	Map	Grid	Text
Tolgullow	W 17	W 73 43	5,17,1
Towan	T 28	X 01 49	1,3
Treal	W 18	W 71 16	1,1
Trebarfoote	S 68	X 18 99	5,4,8
Trebartha	R 37	X 26 77	5,4,20
Trebeigh	R 38	X 30 67	3,7. 5,1,20
Trecan	F 35	(X 16 58)	5,2,30
Tredaule	S 69	X 23 81	5,6,7
? Tredinnick	R 39	X 36 59	5,2,15
Tredower	W 19	(W 74 23)	1,1
Tredwen	S 70	X 17 85	5,24,25
Trefreock	S 71	W 99 79	5,25,2
? Trefrize	R 40	X 30 76	5,2,23
Tregaire	T 29	(W 86 37)	2,3
Tregal	- -	- -	5,23,2
Tregamellyn	F 36	X 18 53	5,5,12
Tregantle	R 41	X 39 53	5,2,16
Tregardock	S 72	X 04 83	5,16,1
? Tregarland	F 37	X 25 57	5,2,1
Tregavethan	T 30	W 78 47	5,5,18
? Tregeagle	T 31	W 86 47	5,23,3
Treglasta	S 73	X 18 86	5,1,5
Tregole	S 74	X 19 98	4,16
Tregona	P 17	W 85 69	4,22
Tregony	T 32	W 92 44	5,24,21
Tregoose	W 20	W 68 24	1,1
Tregrenna	S 75	X 23 79	3,4
Tregrill	R 42	X 28 63	5,13,12
Tregunnick	F 38	X 17 54	5,24,16
'Trehaverne'	T 33	(W 82 45)	5,5,21
Trehawke	R 43	X 31 62	5,2,21
Trehudreth	S 76	X 11 72	5,17,4
Treknow	S 77	X 05 86	4,20
Trelamar	- -	- -	5,21,1
Trelan	W 21	W 74 18	1,1. 5,4,1
Trelaske	R 44	X 28 80	5,13,11
Trelawne	F 39	X 21 54	5,2,2
Treliever	W 22	W 76 35	2,1
Treligga	S 78	X 05 84	5,14,3
Trelowarren	W 23	W 72 23	1,1
Trelowia	F 40	X 29 56	5,5,11
Trelowth	T 34	W 98 50	5,4,14
Treloy	P 18	W 85 62	4,11
Tremadart	F 41	(X 21 58)	5,13,3
Tremail	S 79	X 16 86	4,14
Trematon	R 45	X 41 58	5,2,11
Tremblary	S 80	X 15 87	5,7,8
Trembraze	W 24	W 78 21	1,1
? Tremoan	R 46	X 39 65	5,2,19
Tremoddrett	T 35	(X 00 61)	5,5,16
Tremore	P 19	X 01 64	4,22
Trenance	W 25	W 67 18	1,1
? Trenance	T 36	X 00 54	5,5,20
? 'Trenance'	T 37	(X 01 52)	5,9,4
Trenance	W 26	W 80 22	5,15,1
Trenant	F 42	X 24 55	5,13,4
? Trenderway	F 43	X 21 53	5,4,5
? Trenewen	F 44	X 17 53	5,4,3
'Trenhale'	P 20	(W 82 58)	4,22
Treninnick	P 21	W 81 60	4,22
Trenowth	T 38	W 93 50	5,1,7
? Trenuth	S 81	X 12 84	5,6,3
Trerice	T 39	W 93 57	5,7,11
Treroosel	S 82	X 05 80	5,24,14
Trescowe	W 27	W 57 30	5,17,2
Treslay	S 83	X 13 88	5,8,7
Tresparrett	S 84	X 14 91	5,7,7
Trethake	F 45	X 15 52	5,5,13
Tretheake	T 40	W 93 41	5,4,15
Trethevy	S 85	X 03 73	5,3,25
Trevague	S 86	X 23 79	5,6,8
Treval	R 47	X 42 55	5,14,5
Trevalga	S 87	X 08 90	1,17
? Trevedor	W 28	W 74 25	1,1
? Trevell	R 48	X 25 81	5,1,19
? Trevelyan	F 46	X 15 54	5,2,32
Treveniel	R 49	(X 26 77)	5,14,4
Treverbyn	T 41	X 01 57	5,3,15
Treverras	T 42	W 84 38	5,23,4
? Trevesson	T 43	(W 99 41)	5,15,5
Trevigue	S 88	X 13 95	5,8,5
Trevillis	F 47	X 18 61	5,24,19
Trevillyn	T 44	X 04 61	5,13,10
? Trevilveth	T 45	W 94 42	5,24,2
Trevisquite	S 89	X 04 74	5,3,24
Trevornick	P 22	W 92 65	4,22
Trewanta	R 50	X 26 80	3,7. ?5,1,16
Trewarnevas	W 29	W 78 24	1,1
? Trewen	S 90	X 05 76	5,8,8
Trewethart	S 91	(X 01 80)	5,25,4
? Trewidland	F 48	X 25 59	5,2,1
Trewince	W 30	W 73 22	5,15,2
Trewint	S 92	X 22 80	5,26,1
Trewirgie	T 46	W 89 44	5,1,10
Trewolland	R 51	(X 26 65)	5,5,10
Trewoon	T 47	W 99 52	5,5,17
? Treworder	W 31	(W 72 15)	1,1
Treworrick	T 48	W 97 44	5,4,16
Treworyan	T 49	(W 89 50)	5,7,12
Trezance	F 49	X 12 69	5,3,3
Truthall	W 32	W 65 30	1,1
Truthwall	C 14	W 52 32	4,1. 5,25,5
Tucoyse	T 50	W 96 45	5,3,11
Tucoyse	W 33	(W 71 29)	5,24,13
'Tybesta'	T 51	(W 94 48)	5,1,6
Tywardreath	T 52	X 08 54	5,3,8
'Tywarnhayle'	P 23	(W 75 54)	4,7
Veryan	T 53	W 91 39	5,24,4
Wadfast	S 93	X 26 97	5,5,7
Week Orchard	S 94	S 23 00	5,5,6
Week St. Mary	S 95	X 23 97	5,3,18
Werrington (D)	S 96	X 32 87	Exon. 508a
? Westcott	S 97	X 28 95	5,8,3
Whalesborough	S 98	S 21 03	5,9,2
Whitstone	S 99	X 26 98	5,24,24
Widemouth	S 100	S 20 02	5,9,1
Willsworthy	S 101	X 28 96	5,4,7
Winnianton	W 34	W 65 20	1,1
Withiel	P 24	W 99 65	4,19
Woolston	R 52	X 29 68	5,19,1
Woolstone	S 102	S 22 02	5,6,1
Worthyvale	S 103	X 10 86	5,6,2

Places not named

1,19. 2,12 - 14. 4,21; 26

Unidentified (Not mapped)

Hela, Tregal, Trelamar.

Places not in Cornwall

Elsewhere in Britain   Places starred are indexed above.

DEVONSHIRE ... Borough*.   Exeter, see Bishop.   Horton, see Abbot.   Tackbear*.
Tavistock, see Abbot Geoffrey.   Totnes, see Iudhael.   Werrington*.

Outside Britain

Claville ... Walter.   Mortain ... Count Robert.   Vautortes ... Reginald.

Maps and Map Keys

WEST CORNWALL

Connerton (C)
1 'Alverton'
2 Binnerton
3 Brea
4 'Connerton'
5 Gulval
6 Gurlyn
7 Kelynack
8 Ludgvan
9 Nancekuke
10 Perranuthnoe
11 Roseworthy
12 St Buryan
13 Tehidy
14 Truthwall

Winnianton (W)
1 Boden
2 Bojorrow
3 Constantine
4 Cosawes
5 'Crawle'
6 Garah
7 Gear
8 Halliggye
9 Helston
10 Lizard
11 Mawgan
12 Methleigh
13 Rinsey
14 Roscarnon
15 St Keverne
16 Skewes
17 Tolgullow

18 Treal
19 Tredower
20 Tregoose
21 Trelan
22 Treliever
23 Trelowarren
24 Trembraze
25 Trenance
26 Trenance
27 Trescowe
28 Trevedor
29 Trewarnevas
30 Trewince
31 Treworder
32 Truthall
33 Tucoyse
34 Winnianton

Unidentified (Not mapped)

Hela Tregal Trelamar

The County Boundary is marked on the three Cornish maps by thick lines, broken where the 1086 boundary is conjectural; Hundred boundaries are shown by thin lines. An open circle denotes places mentioned only in Exon. (North and East Cornwall map only).

National Grid 10-kilometre squares are shown on the map border.

Each four-figure square covers one square kilometre, or 247 acres, approximately 2 hides, at 120 acres to the hide.

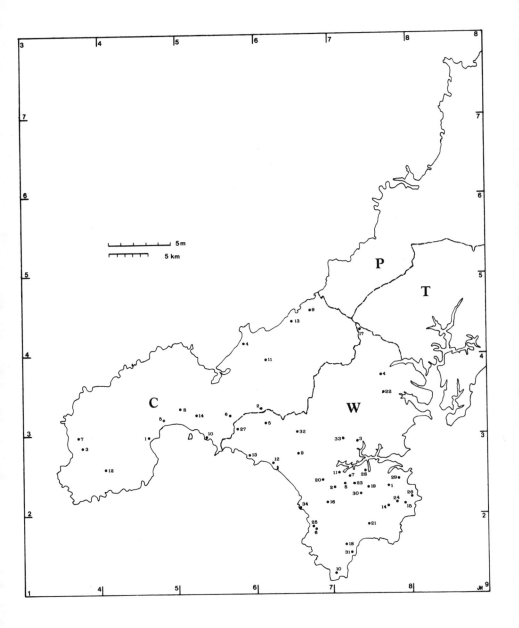

WEST CORNWALL

CENTRAL CORNWALL

Pawton (P)
1 Arrallas
2 Burthy
3 Callestick
4 Cargoll
5 Carworgie
6 Coswarth
7 Crantock
8 Ellenglaze
9 'Halwyn'
10 Lanherne
11 Padstow
12 Pawton
13 'Perranzabuloe'
14 Rialton
15 St Enoder
16 Tolcarne
17 Tregona
18 Treloy
19 Tremore
20 'Trenhale'
21 Treninnick
22 Trevornick
23 'Tywarnhayle'
24 Withiel

Tybesta (T)
1 Bodardle
2 Bodiggo
3 Bodrugan
4 Bosvisack
5 Brannel
6 Carsella
7 Carvean
8 Castle by Lantyan
9 Domellick
10 Galowras
11 Goodern
12 Gothers
13 Goviley
14 Helland
15 Idless
16 Kea
17 Lanescot
18 Lanhadron
19 Lantyan
20 Levalsa
21 Moresk
22 Penpell
23 Pentewan
24 Penventinue
25 Philleigh
26 Polsue

27 Probus
28 Towan
29 Tregaire
30 Tregavethan
31 Tregeagle
32 Tregony
33 'Trehaverne'
34 Trelowth
35 Tremoddrett
36 Trenance
37 'Trenance'
38 Trenowth
39 Trerice
40 Tretheake
41 Treverbyn
42 Treverras
43 Trevesson
44 Trevillyn
45 Trevilveth
46 Trewirgie
47 Trewoon
48 Treworrick
49 Treworyan
50 Tucoyse
51 'Tybesta'
52 Tywardreath
53 Veryan

National Grid 10-kilometre squares are shown on the map border.

Each four-figure square covers one square kilometre, or 247 acres, approximately 2 hides, at 120 acres to the hide.

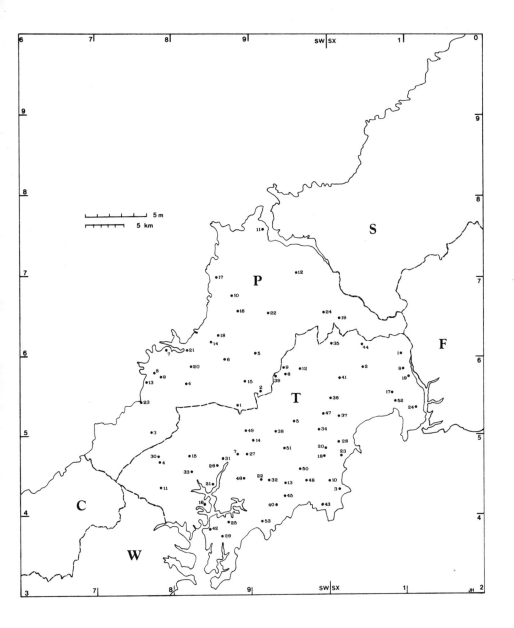

CENTRAL CORNWALL

NORTH AND EAST CORNWALL

Fawton (F)
1 Boconnoc
2 Bodbrane
3 Bodigga
4 Boduel
5 Bosent
6 Botelet
7 Braddock
8 Bucklawren
9 Cabilla
10 Clinnick
11 Dawna
12 Draynes
13 Fawton
14 Fursnewth
15 Glynn
16 Killigorrick
17 Lametton
18 Langunnett
19 Lanreath
20 Lansallos
21 'Lantivet'
22 Lanwarnick
23 Lewarne
24 Liskeard
25 Manely
26 Muchlarnick
27 Pelynt
28 Pendrim
29 Polscoe
30 Porthallow
31 Raphael
32 Rosecraddoc
33 St Neot
34 St Winnow
35 Trecan
36 Tregamellyn
37 Tregarland
38 Tregunnick
39 Trelawne
40 Trelowia
41 Tremadart
42 Trenant
43 Trenderway
44 Trenewan
45 Trethake
46 Trevelyan
47 Trevillis
48 Trewidland
49 Trezance

Rillaton (R)
1 Anthony
2 Appledore
3 Ashton
4 Bicton
5 Bonyalva
6 Callington

7 Calstock
8 Caradon
9 Cartuther
10 Climsom
11 Ellbridge
12 Halton
13 Hammett
14 Illand
15 Landreyne
16 Landulph
17 Launceston
18 Lawhitton
19 Leigh
20 Maker
21 Newton Ferrers
22 Patrieda
23 Pengelly
24 Penharget
25 Penhawger
26 Penheale
27 Penhole
28 Penpoll
29 Pillaton
30 Polyphant
31 Rame
32 Rillaton
33 St Germans
34 St Stephens
35 Sheviock
36 Tolcarne
37 Trebartha
38 Trebeigh
39 Tredinnick
40 Trefrize
41 Tregantle
42 Tregrill
43 Trehawke
44 Trelaske
45 Trematon
46 Tremoan
47 Treval
48 Trevell
49 Treveniel
50 Trewanta
51 Trewolland
52 Woolston

Stratton (S)
1 Alvacott
2 Amble
3 Balsdon
4 Barnacott
5 Blisland
6 Bodmin
7 Borough (Devon)
8 Bossiney
9 Bowithick
10 Boyton

11 Burniere
12 Buttsbear
13 Cann Orchard
14 Colquite
15 Crackington
16 Curry
17 Dannonchapel
18 Delabole
19 Delamere
20 Dizzard
21 Downinney
22 Froxton
23 'Genver'
24 Halvana
25 Hamatethy
26 Hele
27 Helstone
28 Hennett
29 Hilton
30 Hornacott
31 Kilkhampton
32 Kilmarth
33 Lamellen
34 Lancarffe
35 Landinner
36 Launcells
37 Lee
38 Lesnewth
39 Marhamchurch
40 Milton
41 Minster
42 Moreton
43 Norton
44 Otterham
45 Pencarrow
46 Pendavey
47 Penfound
48 Pengold
49 Penhallym
50 Penhalt
51 Penpont
52 Pigsdon
53 Polroad
54 Poughill
55 Poundstock
56 Roscarrock
57 Rosebenault
58 Rosecare
59 St Gennys
60 St Juliot
61 St Kew
62 *St Tudy
63 Stratton
64 Tackbear (Devon)
65 Thorne
66 Thurlibeer
67 Tinten
68 Trebarfoote

69 Tredaule
70 Tredwen
71 Trefreock
72 Tregardock
73 Treglasta
74 Tregole
75 Tregrenna
76 Trehudreth
77 Treknow
78 Treligga
79 Tremail
80 Tremb,lary
81 Trenuth
82 Treroosel
83 Treslay
84 Tresparrett
85 Trethevy
86 Trevague
87 Trevalga
88 Trevigue
89 Trevisquite
90 Trewen
91 Trewethart
92 Trewint
93 Wadfast
94 Week Orchard
95 Week St Mary
96 *Werrington (Devo
97 Westcott
98 Whalesborough
99 Whitstone
100 Widemouth
101 Willsworthy
102 Woolstone
103 Worthyvale

* Places starred are mentioned only in the Exon. book and are marked by open circles on the map.

National Grid 10-kilometre squares are shown on the map border.

Each four-figure square covers one square kilometre, or 247 acres, approximately 2 hides, at 120 acres to the hide.

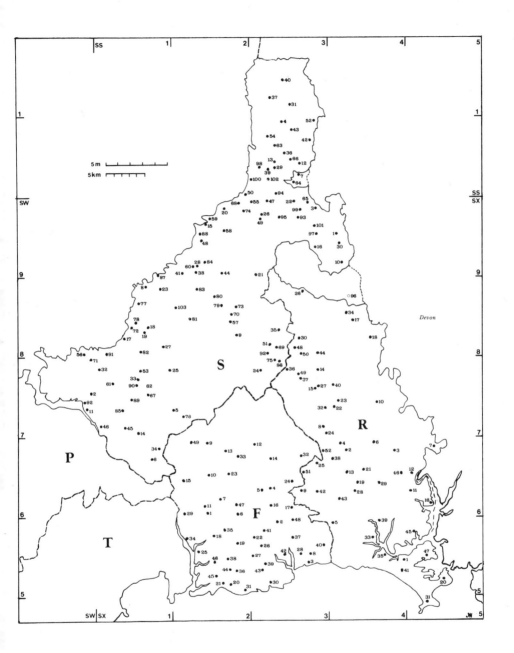

NORTH AND EAST CORNWALL

SYSTEMS OF REFERENCE TO DOMESDAY BOOK

The manuscript is divided into numbered chapters, and the chapters into sections, usually marked by large initials and red ink. Farley however did not number the sections. References have therefore been inexact, by folio numbers, which cannot be closer than an entire page or column. Moreover, half a dozen different ways of referring to the same column have been devised. In 1816 Ellis used three separate systems in his indices; (i) on pages i-cvii; 435-518; 537-570; (ii) on pages 1-144; (iii) on pages 145-433 and 519-535. Other systems have since come into use, notably that used by Vinogradoff, here followed. This edition numbers the sections, the normal practicable form of close reference; but since all discussion of Domesday for three hundred years has been obliged to refer to page or column, a comparative table will help to locate references given. The five columns below give Vinogradoff's notation, Ellis' three systems, and that employed by Welldon Finn and others. Maitland, Stenton, Darby and others have usually followed Ellis (i).

Vinogradoff	Ellis (i)	Ellis (ii)	Ellis (iii)	Finn
152 a	152	152 a	152	152ai
152 b	152	152 a	152.2	152a2
152 c	152 b	152 b	152 b	152bi
152 d	152 b	152 b	152b2	152b2

In Cornwall, the relation between the Vinogradoff column notation, here followed, and the chapters and sections is

120a	Landholders	1,1-1,3	122a	5,2,1	-	5,2,18	124a	5,9,1	-	5,12,3
b	1,4	- 1,14	b	5,2,19	-	5,3,4	b	5,13,1	-	5,14,4
c	1,14	- 2,6	c	5,3,5	-	5,3,21	c	5,14,5	-	5,21,1
d	2,7-2,15	4,1-4,6	d	5,3,21	-	5,4,10	d	5,21,1	-	5,24,12
121a	4,7	- 4,22	123a	5,4,11	-	5,5,7	125a	5,24,13	-	5,25,5
b	4,22-4,29	3,1-3,3	b	5,5,8	-	5,6,2	b	5,25,5	-	7,1
c	3,4-3,7	5,1,1-5,1,7	c	5,6,2	-	5,7,8				
d	5,1,8	- 5,1,22	d	5,7,9	-	5,8,10				

TECHNICAL TERMS

Many words meaning measurements have to be transliterated. But translation may not dodge other problems by the use of obsolete or made-up words which do not exist in modern English. The translations here used are given in italics. They cannot be exact; they aim at the nearest modern equivalent.

BORDARIUS. Cultivator of inferior status, usually with a little land. *smallholder*

CARUCA. A plough, with the oxen who pulled it, usually reckoned as 8. *plough*

DOMINIUM. The mastery or dominium of a lord (*dominus*); including ploughs, land, men, villages, etc., reserved for the lord's use; often concentrated in a *home farm* or *demesne*, a 'Manor Farm' or 'Lordship Farm'. *lordship*

GELDUM. The principal royal tax, originally levied during the Danish wars, normally at an equal number of pence on each *hide* of land. *tax*

HIDA. A unit of land measurement, reckoned at 120 acres. *hide*

HONOR. (5,6,6. 5,24,14) equivalent to *feudum*, holding. *Honour*

LEUGA. A measure of length, usually about a mile and a half. *league*

QUARENTENA. A quarter of a virgate (but see Exon. Notes for 5,2,19). *furlong*

TAINUS. Person holding land from the King by special grant; formerly used of the King's ministers and military companions. *thane*

T.R.E. *tempore regis Edwardi*, in King Edward's time. *before 1066*

VILLA. Translating Old English *tun*, town. The later distinction between a small *village* and a large *town* was not yet in use in 1066. *village* or *town*

VILLANUS. Member of a *villa*, usually with more land than a *bordarius*. *villager*

VIRGATA. A quarter of a hide, reckoned at 30 acres. *virgate*